Market Drayton's Civil War

A study of the documentary evidence from the period

1642 to 1649

GEOFF TURNER

ISBN: 9798727844410

DEDICATION

For Jo who has had to put up with me incessantly
wittering on about the Civil War

Contents

ACKNOWLEDGMENTS

I would like to thank various unnamed Record Office employees for their invaluable help with what were probably in some cases rather stupid questions. This work could not have been achieved without them.

i

Preface

Most people in Market Drayton are aware of its association with gingerbread and Clive of India, and a few will be aware of events in and near the town, such as the fire of 1651 and the Battle of Blore Heath in 1459. There has been little mention up to now though of one of the most turbulent periods in British History, the civil wars of the 1640s.

I have always been interested in local history, and several years ago I happened on a copy of "A History of Market Drayton Parish Church" by T.P. Marshall which was published in 1884. In it he states **"There was a fierce fight at Drayton in April, 1643."** I decided that I would like to find out more, but to my surprise I couldn't find much. To date, there have been few publications that even mention the English Civil War as it affected the Market Drayton area. There are previous publications which deal with the odd reference here and there, but none that put the whole story together to try to create a narrative explaining all the references and where they fit .

17th century handwriting

Marshall's publication gave me a link to a local diary, and following all the trails, I have now found over 90 primary source references to Market Drayton.

Very early on, I discovered that a Victorian transcription contained a horrendous error in terms of numbers of troops being stationed at Market Drayton, (fifteen instead of fifteen hundred!) so at that point I decided that I would re-visit all the source documents that I could find and re-transcribe them. I have not located them all, but the various record offices that I have used have been very friendly and helpful in this regard. Once I had found most of these references, it became obvious that I should not undertake all of this research without setting it down somewhere for future interested parties. However, a list of documents with no context would be very dry indeed. I therefore decided to study the history of the area using, where I could,

1

original primary source documents, in an attempt to string all of this information into some sort of narrative. Again, just taking Market Drayton references without looking at what was happening in the wider area would not give enough context, so I widened my research to include wider local and national events where I feel that they either had some bearing on Market Drayton, or where they give examples of events that would have also happened in the town, or give us a clue as to how the local residents might have been feeling.

I try hard not to express too much personal opinion, but simply record what evidence there is, to allow future interested parties to be able to find the sources and try to make sense of them in light of any further documents that come to light.

As I have now been searching libraries, archives etc. for over ten years, I feel it is time to put fingers to keyboard, in hope of prompting anyone who knows the whereabouts of any other documents to come forward, or at least to take this work as a starting point and carry on adding to it. Some events are described in multiple sources, but have wildly different descriptions depending on whether Royalist or Parliamentarian reporting is being followed. Because of the nature of conflict, sometimes an event may only be referred to by one side or the other. This does not mean that it is simply propaganda, although it may be. It may be that an outcome that one side might be very willing to shout about may not be mentioned by the other. I cannot make decisions about this except where overwhelming evidence exists to point in the right direction.

I see it as my task to produce a book that points the students of local history toward the relevant documents to make up their own mind. With this to the fore, I will list all of the sources and let them speak for themselves. (Appendix 1)

The causes of the Civil wars in the mid seventeenth century are many and various and are covered well in the thousands of histories that have been written by eminent historians. I do not pretend to be one of those, but someone living in the Market Drayton area with an interest in the past. I will attempt to provide explanations of difficult terms and concepts where necessary, but it should always be read in conjunction with the expert opinions of the many historians who have gone before and are more expert

2

in the general history of the time. I make no apology for the large amounts of narrative that do not mention Market Drayton. Leaving a gap in the narrative where no local events occur would make the Drayton events less clear and people's motives less understandable.

Dates

The period we are dealing with is before 2nd September 1752, when the country changed from using the Julian to the Gregorian calendar. Quoting from Francis Moore's "Vox Stellarum: Or a Loyal Almanack", the precursor to "Old Moore's Almanack":

> IT is neceſſary to be remembered, That by Virtue of an Act of Parliament made in the Year 1751, for Alteration of the Style, the Beginning of the Year was changed from the 25th of March to the firſt Day of January. This Change took place on the firſt of January 1752; and the Act enjoins and directs, That from and after that Time every ſucceeding firſt Day of January, in every Year to come, ſhall be the firſt Day of that Year reſpectively; and that all Deeds and Writings, of what Nature and Kind ſoever, ſhall be dated accordingly.

The effect of this was to bring the year number in line with the way it is now. Because we are before this date, it can sometimes give us difficulties in deciding which year is being referred to. As an example, a date from 26th March to 31st December will have the same year number in any year before or after the change. Documents referring to dates between 1st January and 25th March at this period can be interpreted in one of three ways:

1st January 1643	Gregorian (or new) style, so would refer to the start of the next year equating to 1643 in the current Gregorian style.
1st January 1643	Julian (or old) style, so would refer to the end of the previous year, equating to 1644 in the current Gregorian style.
1st January 1643/4	This style is used not only post-

change to ensure no ambiguity, but also by some writers in our period, recognising that on the continent the change to the Gregorian style had already taken place.

Therefore, whenever dealing with any document or previous publication dated between 1st January and 25th March that does not give the unambiguous format, a decision has to be made as to which year is being referred to. For this reason, all dates will be given in this book in the unambiguous format, and for extra clarification will give the day of the week, for example Monday 1st January 1643/4.

I would be more than happy to hear about anything that I might have missed, or whether there is new information that would throw light on events in the area at this time. I am not vain enough to suppose that I have found out everything that there is to know, and, as I have written and had this printed all on my own, any mistakes are obviously mine alone.

Geoff Turner
Moreton Say 2021
gyldageoff@hotmail.com

1 A Backgound to War

First of all, we could do with a bit of background. I cannot provide a history of the Civil War; that has already been done in thousands of books. However, knowing a little about how things came about is useful for understanding the way things went later in the story.

From 1629 King Charles I had ruled without calling Parliament. In 1639, towards the end of this **"Personal Rule"**, Charles had marched a poorly trained army north to the border of Scotland to try to enforce Episcopacy on the Scots. This was a system of church governance by Bishops, rather than the Scots-preferred Presbyterian governance without bishops. This **"First Bishop's War"** ended without any major conflict in the **"Pacification of Berwick"**.

King Charles I from a supporter's medal

This agreement ruled that all disputed points would be decided by a general assembly. This assembly reconfirmed all the previous points that had forced Charles to confront them, and the Scottish Parliament went one step further by abolishing episcopacy. Charles therefore decided to advance to Scotland again, but for this he needed more money. He called the so called **"Short Parliament"**, which met in April 1640. However, Parliament began by demanding that the previous grievances unaddressed from the eleven years of no Parliament should be addressed first and that certain unfair taxes, such as **"Ship Money"** be abolished. They further demanded a change to church governance in England, so Charles dissolved it three months later without getting his way.

The King brought the Earl of Strafford back from Ireland, where he had been Governor, and he set about furnishing Charles with money and supplies for the **"Second Bishop's War"**. Once again Charles marched north, but this time the Scots crossed into England, and with the English retreating before them captured Northumberland and County Durham. Charles signed

Thomas Wentworth, Earl of Strafford

the treaty of Ripon in October 1640, stating that he would pay the Scots for the return of the two counties. For this he once again summoned

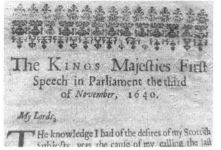

Parliament on 3rd November 1640. This was known as the **"Long Parliament"** as it would sit in one form or another until the restoration of the monarchy in 1660 without re-election. However, Parliament wanted Strafford out of the way, seeing him as a threat. They immediately moved to arrest him on a charge of High Treason related to his activities whilst governor in Ireland. After a lengthy trial this failed, but they got around this with a **"Bill of Attainder"**, a method whereby parliament could vote him guilty without the trial, and Strafford was executed in May 1641, Charles very reluctantly signing the death warrant.

Parliament went on to regulate the taxation rules, severely restricting Charles' powers to raise money without them. They also passed the Triennial Act, which meant that if Charles did not call Parliament within three years, the members could call it themselves.

One of the events that finally pushed the country towards civil war was when Charles marched into Parliament with soldiers in an attempt to arrest five of his chief opponents in early January 1641/2. He failed, as they had been pre-warned and had fled into hiding.

London was by this time becoming violent with anti-Royalist riots, and for their safety the King moved the Royal family first to Windsor and then all the way to York. Further negotiations between King and Parliament failed. Towns and cities started declaring for one side or the other. Hull, where the King had left all the arms and supplies from the Bishops War declared for Parliament, and when Charles attempted to gain control of it in April 1642, Sir John Hotham refused him entry and Charles was powerless to challenge him.

On the 1st June 1642, Parliament sent nineteen propositions, entitled the **"Grand Remonstrance"** to the King, but as these were designed to limit his power, he rejected them. Meanwhile, Charles had issued the first **"Commissions of Array"**, and on Sunday 4th July, Parliament formed the

Market Drayton's Civil War

"Committee of Safety".

Shropshire

Although heavily Royalist, the Shropshire gentry was not all for the King. Eight of its MPs, Sir Richard Lee, Sir Robert Howard, Thomas Whitmore, Edward Acton, Ralph Goodwyn, Charles Baldwyn, Francis Newport and Thomas Littleton all came down on the Royalist side, but the other four, Sir John Corbet, Richard More, William Pierrepoint and William Spurstowe were for the Parliament. Parliament appointed Lord Lieutenants, normally appointed by the King; Lord Littleton being appointed for Shropshire. They also appointed Deputy Lieutenants to form county committees. The King in opposition appointed his own Commissioners of Array for each county. The purpose of both of these sets of appointments was to try to gain control of any militias or trained-bands already in existence and the county magazines of arms and gunpowder. It was also to arm and train their own supporters, and to raise money for the same purpose.

July 1642

We need to start the narrative somewhere, so we will start on Tuesday 12th. On this day, Parliament resolved to raise an army and appointed the Earl of Essex as General-in-Chief.

On Saturday 23rd, Parliament started exerting their authority in Shropshire by appointing three of the four local MPs sympathetic to their cause, William Pierrepoint, Sir John Corbet and Richard More to take possession of the county. The two factions by this point were starting to assert themselves in the local area.

Robert Devereux, Earl of Essex

As a local example, on Monday 25th over the border in Cheshire, the Royalist High Sheriff, Hugh Calveley issued a warrant to imprison Thomas Bennet for **"opposing the execution of the Commission of Array"**. Due to Royalist attempts to take control, Parliament issued a decree on Tuesday 26th attempting to gain control of local magazines as the Royalists had been attempting to do the same thing.

On the same day, warrants were issued in Shropshire by the High Sherriff and Royalist Commissioners of Array to summon a muster to be held on the following Tuesday.

By the next day, in Cheshire, the aforementioned Thomas Bennet was being held in Chester, from where he wrote to Sir William Brereton one of the Cheshire MPs, who we shall hear a lot from in this book if not in this chapter. Brereton in turn wrote to Oliver Cromwell, enclosing Bennet's letter, to see if anything could be done. Whilst this is in Cheshire (Bennet was a Wirral constable, and only one example of those mentioned), it highlights the issues occurring at a local level, where neither party was yet in complete control.

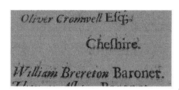

Brereton's entry in a contemporary list of MPs, next to a soon-to-be very famous name of the period

On Friday 29th, the Shropshire MPs appointed by Parliament, Pierrepoint, Corbet and Moore arrived in Shrewsbury tasked with securing the county for Parliament. They found that warrants had already been issued both there and in other parts of Shropshire three days before for a Royalist muster on the following Tuesday. As a response to this, they issued another to assemble the Parliamentarian supporters the day before.

As an example of the numbers of armed men that were being mobilised locally, we have another letter from Brereton, this time to the Speaker of the House, William Lenthall on Saturday 30th. He details a muster of Northwich Hundred (a Hundred being an administrative unit) four days before. He states that three hundred and twenty musketeers, eighty pikemen and six hundred other less well armed volunteers appeared. Once we reach August, we start to see details of how things were going in Shropshire.

August 1642

On Monday 1st the three Shropshire MPs held their muster **"in a public place"** in Shrewsbury. It did not however pass off without a certain amount of confrontation. They read out Parliament's instructions which seemed well received at first, and then the King's Commission of Array to which they stated the crowd **"gave no approbation that we could perceive"**. They then read out resolutions of Parliament and attempted to read the Declaration against the Commission of Array, but at this point the meeting was disrupted by the Royalist Shropshire Commissioners led by the Sheriff John Weld who, during the reading of the Declaration against the Commission of Array attempted to snatch the paper out of the reader's hand. Sir Paul Harris, one of the Commissioners repeatedly tried to snatch

Francis Ottley

the Declaration, but was prevented, and so he grabbed at William Pierrepoint's cloak which came off. He carried on trying to hinder the reading, and the crowd called for him to be thrown down to them. At this point, Francis Ottley, another notable Shrewsbury Royalist arrived with a party of gentlemen, with a drum beating and accompanied by a **"rabble"** carrying staves. Another of the commissioners, Edward Cressett further disrupted the reading by shouting it down. The Mayor, Richard Gibbons, ordered the Parliamentarian faction to withdraw within an hour or to be treated as rioters. Despite this, they finished reading the Declaration and retreated to an inn where they were staying accompanied by **"many hundred persons"** who they spoke to further on the matter.

The following day, both sides mustered and drilled troops in and near Shrewsbury. Captain Hunt, in charge of the Parliamentary soldiers trained his troops in Shrewsbury, while at Atcham bridge and Mountford Bridge, Sir Vincent Corbet and Richard Lloyd, two of the Royalist Commissioners trained theirs. Each of these small forces was between eighty and one hundred and fifty men. Meanwhile, Francis Ottley marched his men up and down the town. The letter from the MPs to parliament ends with **"This night there was a great uproar, but ended without hurt."**

The day after, Wednesday 3rd, undeterred, the Parliamentarian MPs sent their report to Parliament and then moved on to the read the Declaration in other parts of the county, no doubt Market Drayton included, being one of the chief market towns. I have found no specific details of this actually happening, or how this went, although the lack of information may well mean that there was less, or no trouble.

On Saturday 6th, the MP's report was read in Parliament. They immediately issued a warrant for the arrest of Richard Gibbons, John Weld, Edward Cressett, Francis Ottley and Sir Paul Harris, describing them as **"delinquents"**. Monday 8th saw a similar conflict as happened in Shrewsbury, although this time in heavily Royalist Chester. The result of this was that the Parliamentarian Sir William Brereton **"escaped his life in the tumult to Mr. Edwards house so for that time the tumult was appeased."** That day, the Grand Jury of Shropshire, following that of Worcestershire formally sided with the King, and the document has a long list of signatures.

Therefore, with most of the chief men of Shropshire, certainly in the Shrewsbury area declaring for the King, Shropshire could pretty well be considered a Royalist county. The day after, the Commons declared that all who countenance the Commission of Array were delinquents and ordered their arrest.

Near Nantwich on Friday 12th, another training of both sides almost came to blows on Beam Heath, but by negotiation it was for the time being avoided. Sir William Brereton claims that the Royalists called in men from **"Wales, Shropshire, Staffordshire and other parts"** although as he himself did not arrive until later that day, this may just have been unfounded rumour. However, it is fairly obvious that the confrontations were steadily getting bigger and more dangerous. Sir William called on Parliament for troops to be sent to the area, as he feared that the Parliamentarian faction was being heavily outnumbered.

As an example of the instructions being sent out by Parliament at that time, and how near to out-and-out war the country was at this point, we can turn to an extract from those sent to Coventry on Saturday 13th, as the wording will leave no doubt as to how dangerous things were becoming.

"You are required and authorized to exercise and train all the Trained Bands and Volunteers in the City and County of Coventry; and shall lead and conduct them against all Forces that attempt to seize upon that City, or disturb the Peace of it. And you are authorized to fight with all such Persons, to kill and slay them, and by all means to defend your City from all hostile Attempts there. You are likewise authorized to disarm all Popish Recusants, and all other dangerous and ill-affected Persons, who have opposed the Orders and

Proceedings of Parliament, or endeavoured to oppress the People by the Commission of Array, or otherwise."

On Tuesday 16th, the High Sheriff and Commissioners of Array in Shropshire declared that they would oppose any that opposed the Commissioners of Array. On the following day the King's intentions were read out in Parliament, that he would set up his standard at Nottingham on Monday 22nd, and that he required the aid of all his subjects on the North side of the River Trent and twenty miles of the South side **"for the suppression of the rebels now coming against him"**. Also in the House of Lords that day was issued a declaration to prevent disorder amongst the soldiers of the Parliamentary army and another in which they command the Lord Lieutenants of the counties to prevent plundering, looting and other outrages.

Around Thursday 18th, Parliament issued directions to various counties, the most local that survives being printed in a pamphlet entitled **"The Advice and Direction of both houses of Parliament to Sir William Brereton, and to the rest of the Deputy Lieutenants, for the county of Chester."** These new instructions start by stating that the King **"intends to make War",** and go on to give instructions on keeping the county magazines and militias under Parliamentary control, and promises exoneration from any punishment for carrying out the orders.

The next day, Thomas Fowler of Whitchurch received a letter with the Shropshire Grand Jury's **"protestation"** of the 8th from Francis Ottley. He promised to promote it, but warned Ottley that **"I fear many of my neighbours have taken infection lately."** Another local supporter of the protestation was William Pygott of Chetwynd, who wrote to Ottley about it from Edgmond on Sunday 21st promising to promote it **"with as many hands as I can."**

On Monday 22nd, King Charles formally declared war by raising his red standard with the motto **"Give to Caesar his due"** at Nottingham. Parliament ordered that a list of all the commissioners of array for each county be gathered and ordered that all of them should be arrested. Their statement begins:

"Whereas the King, seduced by traitorous and wicked Counsels, is now in actual War against his Parliament and good People…".

Meanwhile, Ottley carried on soliciting support from the Shropshire gentry. In a letter from Francis, eldest son of Sir Richard Newport, the 1st Baron Newport at High Ercall on Tuesday 23rd which again promises support, Ottley is addressed as **"Captaine Francis Oately"**.

The following day the Shropshire clergy published their support for the King. On the copy in the Ottley papers there are only seventeen names attached, but there would presumably have originally been many more. Thomas Cooke, the vicar of Market Drayton was a staunch Royalist, and it would have been odd if he failed to support it even though his name is not on it.

On Friday 26th, the House of Commons discussed the Shropshire Grand Jury's protestation, to prevent the like happening in other counties and in their words **"to prevent these and the like inconveniences arising from grand juries meddling with matters they are not concerned in"**. On the same day, they issued a command detailing punishment for unauthorised looting of Royalist property.

The following Monday, the 29th, Parliament discussed the defence of Shropshire, Herefordshire, Worcestershire, Lancashire, Cheshire, Monmouthshire and North Wales very mindful of the amount of support for the King in those counties. They added four new men to the Shropshire Parliamentary committee, Mr. Serjeant Wilde, Mr Whittacre, Mr Blakeston and Mr Wheeler. John Weld the High Sheriff of Shropshire wrote a letter to **"Captain"** Ottley promising any support that he could give, on the same day as Parliament announced Weld's impeachment. Also on this day, the King issued instructions to his Commissioners of Array.

September 1642

Perhaps one of the first indications that we have that the King was intending to head to our area is a letter written from Chester to Lord Percival on Saturday 3rd.

The House of Commons in the 1640s

It mentions amongst other things that the King had issued a warrant on the previous Tuesday (30th August) for all the Lord Lieutenant of Cheshire's horses and wagons to be sent to the King at Nottingham, and that with the Mayor of Chester and the High Sheriff's assistance they were being prepared. On Sunday 4th, Thomas Eyton, who had travelled from Shropshire to the King at Nottingham wrote to Ottley on his return stating that he had a dispatch for Ottley from the King. In his letter he mentioned that Ottley was about to travel to see the King, and provided instruction on **"how to apply yourself at Court"**.

Parliament was read the King's instructions on Monday 5th. That day, they nominated the Earl of Essex to be the Lord Lieutenant of Shropshire replacing Lord Littleton. The letter about the wagons for the King, intercepted by Parliament was also read in the House of Lords on the same day. The following day, several of the Shropshire gentry were removed from the posts of Deputy Lieutenants of Shropshire by order of the Parliament. These were Sir Richard Lee, Woollridge, Sir Vincent Corbet, Sir

Wm Whitmore, Mr Weld and Mr Eden. It was ordered that Walter Barker, Humphrey Walcot, Cap Walter Long, Sir Gilb Cornewall and Mr Hunt were to replace them. Also on this day, Sir Richard Lee and Sir Robert Howard were removed as Shropshire MPs for supporting the Commission of Array.

Sir Edward Hyde

Saturday 10th proved to be a busy day. The King's army was about to move. Sir Edward Hyde wrote to Ottley from Uttoxeter stating that the King was heading for Shrewsbury then Chester. This was in answer to concerns raised by Ottley in a letter that I have not yet found and may no longer exist. Hyde was later to become the Earl of Clarendon who wrote extensively about the civil war. He addresses Ottley as **"Sir ffrancis Ottley Kt"**, although Ottley does not appear to have been knighted at this point. The King himself addresses him as **"welbeloved ffrancis Ottley, of our County of Salop, Esqr."**, in instructions issued on the same day to Ottley to raise a company of 200 foot to guard Shrewsbury under his own command.

Monday 12th saw Richard Herbert disabled from sitting as MP for his support of the Commission of Array. Therefore, this chapter ends with the King's army about to head for Shropshire, Parliament adjusting the officers of the county to take account of loyalties, and Francis Ottley raising troops to guard Shrewsbury. Although national events had so far not mentioned Market Drayton, this was not to last.

Charles I from a 17th century woodcut

2 The Royalist Army in Shropshire

September 1642

William Villiers, Lord Grandison

When the confrontation at Nantwich mentioned in the previous chapter had occurred on Friday 12th August, the result of the mediation was that the resident parliamentary faction had agreed to refrain from increasing the magazine in the town. They went back on their word, and royalist sympathisers sent letters to the King informing him of their treachery. The King, already planning to head for the area, did not want a large Parliamentarian magazine so close by, so he resolved to remove it. On Monday 12th he appointed one of his Lieutenant Generals, Lord Grandison, to command a force to surprise the town and disarm it.

The next morning, Tuesday 13th, Richard Herbert, the second Lord Herbert of Chirbury at his castle just over the Welsh border in Montgomery received a letter from the King, stating both that the Royalist army was about to begin their march from Nottingham towards Shrewsbury or Chester and that Herbert was to march his regiment to Shrewsbury. Herbert immediately wrote to Francis Ottley at Shrewsbury with the news. The imminent movement of the army is confirmed by a letter from Sir Edward Nicholas, one of King Charles' closest advisers, to Sir Thomas Roe in London. In it he states that the army is setting off to reach Derby that night, **"and from thence by easy marches we shall go to Chester or Shrewsbury to join with five thousand foot and four hundred horse, which are raised for the King in Wales and the Borders."**

Once they had reached Cavendish Bridge after marching seven miles, they gained five hundred of the local trained bands, the rest who were not willing to march with the King being disarmed and dismissed. On the morning of Thursday 15th, the King himself wrote from Derby to the Commissioners of Array at Denbigh, ordering them to take as many troops as they could muster into Chester, **"to our Royal standard"** therefore signalling his intention to be there. His stated intention was that they should form a guard for the future Charles II, then the Prince of Wales.

Sir Edward Nicholas also wrote from Derby to Sir William Boswell, the ambassador to the Netherlands, informing him that the Royalist army so far consisted of five hundred horse, five regiments of foot and twelve pieces of artillery. He further stated that the next stop was to be Uttoxeter the following day to where the artillery had already marched, along with eight hundred dragoons and some foot. (Dragoons were not full cavalry, being mounted infantry; they rode to battle, then dismounted to fight.) At this point, Lord Essex's Parliamentarian army was in Northampton.

On Friday 16th the House of Lords resolved to write to Essex, ordering him to march his army towards the King. However, they also resolved that the formal petition and instructions should be created first. He was delayed therefore in his movements. By Saturday 17th, the King had reached Stafford, from where he wrote to Francis Ottley at Shrewsbury, giving him his official commission.

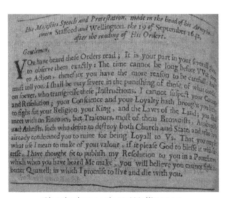

Charles' speech at Wellington

On Sunday 18th, the Royalist Earl of Leinster at his house at Cholmondeley in Cheshire wrote to the Shropshire Commissioners that he had heard that the King was on his way. He had dismissed his trained bands to their houses as it was harvest time, but was now considering calling them back in. The next day, the King crossed the county border into Shropshire. Near Wellington the King's orders were read, after which he made his famous protestation in which he promised to uphold the Protestant religion, govern by the laws of the land and maintain the privileges and freedom of Parliament.

MD Document 1

On the same day, the Royalist commissioners met at a secluded location in Delamere Forest, to discuss attacking Nantwich, which must have involved Lord Grandison, or his representative. The force for this attack consisted of a portion of the Royalist army being fifteen hundred horse and possibly a small number of dragoons, which split away from the main army whilst on the march and encamped at Market Drayton.

It might be worth a small amount of consideration as to what an army encamped at Market Drayton would entail at this period. Wherever an army camped, they generally tried to do it on unproductive land, for example heathland. We shall see later that Tyrley Heath was one of the places used for this. Any important senior officers would almost certainly have been accommodated within the town itself, so on this occasion, Lord Grandison and his closest entourage probably stayed at one of the inns. There is no evidence to suggest that Market Drayton was particularly anti-royal and some evidence to suggest it was mostly pro-royal, so the townspeople would probably have welcomed a visit from one of Charles' most senior commanders.

A letter from Sir Edward Nicholas to Sir William Boswell describes the scene of King Charles' entry into Shrewsbury on the same day. He had been met at Wellington by Sir John Weld, with a train of thirty-four livery companies. Nearer the town he was met with three companies of the trained bands and one hundred horse. The Mayor and aldermen with the livery companies processed into the town with the King. After the King there came the Banner Royal leading the Lord General's Regiment followed by the cannons, munitions and six foot regiments. This procession made its way amongst cheering crowds to the Court gates. King Charles set up his court at the Council House which still exists by the Castle.

Meanwhile in Parliament, the state of affairs in Shrewsbury was being discussed with a visit from Mr Pierrepointe, especially that Richard Owen, who had been sent for as a delinquent, having been taken by Parliament's men, was rescued by the Mayor Richard Gibbons, Edward Owen, Richard Baggott, John Davies a Constable, Richard Davies, Michael Lewis, William Dyves, Edward Morris, and Clement Owen, with about Two Hundred Persons to aid them. At this point, along with Pierrepointe, some of the main Parliamentary players in our area, Sir William Brereton, Mr. Richard Moore and Sir John Corbet were in London, being appointed to a committee to discuss the raising of a force of dragoons, which, considering the locality of the men involved were probably destined for this area.

Market Drayton's Civil War

That day, the Royalist attack on Nantwich came. The large mounted force under Lord Grandison's command set off from Market Drayton to meet with the Cheshire Commissioners of Array, and headed towards Nantwich. News of the Royalist's approach reached the town well ahead of their arrival, allowing the inhabitants time to bolster their previous attempts at fortification by erecting chains at the street ends and to send messages to all the gentry in the surrounding area that had previously promised support.

Not all of these messages received the answer they were expecting. Sir Thomas Delves told the messenger that he needed to look after himself, and abandoned his house with all the arms in it, riding off for Chester. Sir Richard Wilbraham, however, did as requested, and himself sent messengers to try and bring any Parliamentary sympathisers in the area in for the defence of the town.

At the end of Aspell Street, the representative from the Royalist force, described as the Under-Sheriff's man approached the chain, where some townsmen with muskets and other weapons were waiting. He was disarmed by a Mr Clutton and a Captain Croxon who tried to persuade the rest of the town's men that they should open fire as soon as the Royalists came within range. The rest of the town's representatives however, seeing the large force facing them, and fearing what would happen if they were successfully attacked, especially with the whole of the King's army over the border in Shropshire, entered into talks with the Commissioners and Lord Grandison to try and bring about a peaceful resolution. The Royalist leaders promised that no one would be hurt, and no goods seized if they were allowed to peacefully take the town, as long as all the arms and ammunition were laid up in the church until they had consulted with the King. At this, the town relented and let the Royalists in.

Once in possession of Nantwich however, the Royalists broke their word, disarming everyone, imprisoning anyone that resisted and plundering what they could from within the town. The only report from that day that we have of any physical violence was to a man called Radcliff at Wistaston. He was reluctant to give up his musket and was shot through the hand and into his shoulder. The following day, Thursday 22nd, the Royalist forces started to disarm and plunder the area around Nantwich. They visited all the big houses in the area, including Sir Richard Wilbraham's hall at Woodhey, Mr

Vernon's hall at Haslington and Sir Randolph Crewe's hall at Crewe. At Sir Thomas Delves' hall at Doddington, they found it empty with all the arms and armour on the hall table, where he had abandoned them. They took carts, horses, arms and other goods.

Friday 23rd the King issued a warrant for a general muster at the Gay Meadow in Shrewsbury for the following Wednesday (28th). This general muster strategy was one of the ways both sides tried to raise forces. All able-bodied men between sixteen and sixty were instructed to attend. He then left his army in Shrewsbury, and travelled with his life-guards, amounting to approximately one thousand foot and five hundred horse towards Chester, stopping at Whitchurch so that he and Prince Charles could dine. At Chester, the King was greeted in an even more splendid way than at Shrewsbury. On his procession towards the city, at Milton Green Mr Richard Edgerton of Ridley with six hundred musketeers joined him. At Hatton Heath, Lords Rivers and Cholmondeley with all their troops were waiting, and at his approach presented their colours and gave him a salute from their firearms. The King rode about the army, taking notice of the Sherriff and other gentlemen waiting for him. They then proceeded to Rowton Heath where he was joined with the same ceremony by Sir Thomas Aston and his forces.

Sir Richard Wilbraham's Effigy

They were met on the outskirts of Chester at Boughton in the late afternoon by the two sheriffs and their retinue, and the whole procession entered the city and proceeded to Thomas Parnel's house in Eastgate Street, in front of which had been erected a scaffold. The mayor and aldermen attended him there, and the mayor presented the symbols of office, the sword, mace and staff of office to the King who presented them back to him. The recorder, Mr Brerewood made a speech which was all but drowned out by the cheering of the crowd, and the King was presented with two hundred pounds and the Prince one hundred. The mayor then rode before the King accompanied by all the city officers and livery companies. The trained bands lined the street and gave a volley of fire as he passed. The King proceeded to set up his court at the Bishop's Palace with all the church bells ringing, and drums and trumpets being played.

While the King was there, Sir Richard Wilbraham and Sir Thomas Delves were brought before the King, but he refused to acknowledge them and they were taken back into custody by the sheriff. Around Nantwich the plundering carried on in earnest. In a letter sent from Nantwich, the correspondent states that the Royalists **"will have what they list, nay they will have what we have not for them, or else they will set a pistol to our throats and swear God damn them they will make us swallow a Bullet, some of them are not content to take what Arms they can find, but also Money, Plate, Linens, Clothes, Writings, Meat, Drink, and not therewith content, but steal our horses and mares"**.

The news that the local Parliamentarians were in London raising a force of dragoons had reached Nantwich, but the same correspondent writes **"there are some Dragoons coming into Cheshire for our relief, but surely they are not come, and now will come too late, for we are all plundered and undone."**

A coin minted at Shrewsbury

On the same day, one of the earliest proper battles of the civil war took place, when Prince Rupert defeated part of Essex's force at Powick Bridge.

Rupert's cavalry force was escorting plate donated by Oxford University, to be used by the King to be made into coinage at the mint being then set up in Shrewsbury. They happened upon an advance force of the Earl of Essex's army at Powick, where the engagement occurred.

The Parliamentarian cavalry was routed, largely due to them being surprised while still within their camp, and the university plate went on its way again.

Over the border in Cheshire on Saturday 24th, a Parliamentarian general muster had been called at Hatton Heath, with any arms that had not been confiscated by Lord Grandison's army. On this day, in a pamphlet, the general state of things in Shropshire was published by a Parliamentarian sympathiser.

"The Cavaliers in Shropshire, and all other places where they come, disarm all Towns and families well affected to the parliament, plundering their houses most vehemently, carrying away and spoiling all their goods, terrifying the inhabitants extremely, and driving them to fly for their lives, taking many prisoners; and they have lists of the names of all active persons whom they seize upon, and do most mischief unto; Papists' and malignants' houses generally escape their cruelty; if a running army be not raised to run as fast, the whole Kingdom is in great danger suddenly to be run over."

On the Monday, Lord Grandison, having achieved everything he set out to do in Nantwich, marched towards Shrewsbury with all the arms and supplies plundered from around the town. Prince Rupert headed the same way, reaching Haughmond that day. The King also left Chester and headed for Shrewsbury.

The inhabitants of Chester seem to have been none too pleased by the King's departure, particularly that his idea of garrisoning the city was only to put **"one hundred of the Country Soldiers… into the castle"**. He also **"commanded Sir Thomas Delves, Sir Richard Wilbraham, M. Philip Mainwaring of Badely, and M. Berkind the Pronotary, and his son, to wait upon His Majesty, and to be confined to Court…The aforesaid men which the King hath taken away with him; were the chief of those that attempted to put the militia in execution."**

On his way from Chester to Shrewsbury on Tuesday 27th, the King made a speech to the inhabitants of Denbigh and Flintshire at Wrexham. Prince Rupert arrived in Shrewsbury with the spoils of his Powick victory. Lord Falkland tells us this comprised **"fifty or sixty prisoners, but none of note, and quality, but Captaine Wingate, (a Parliament man) who is brought to Shrewsbury; The King was presented with six or seven Colours, the bearers of them either slain or taken Prisoners; Prince Maurice hath received two or three scars of Honour in his Head, but**

is abroad and merry;"

On Wednesday 28th the King made his speech at the Gay Meadow, in front of the assembled army, and anyone else who came to listen. In it, he stated that he was in the area because of the loyalty of his subjects. He promised to try and prevent all disorders by his army being billeted in the area. He then requested the support of the inhabitants, financially in this case. A large crowd was present to hear it, as is mentioned in another letter.

"… his Majesty and the Prince came in person, and made a short Speech, which the crowd being great, I could hear little of, but the substance of that he intended to speak was put in writing, and read to the people…"

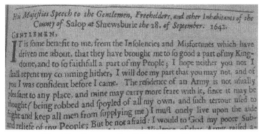

The King's speech at the Gay Meadow

While the King was at Shrewsbury the followers of his army were not unoccupied.

Taking advantage of the concentration of all the forces at the capital of the county, against the express wishes of the King, parts of his army raided the innocent inhabitants in the outlying districts.

MD Document 2

"… diverse persons have had their houses plundered by some northern persons (as is conceived that follow the camp) and especially the house of John Weever dwelling in the parish of Drayton in Hales in the County of Salop who is his Majesty's most obedient and dutiful subject …"

This is possibly the John Weever of Tern Hill who is recorded in the parish register as a gentleman, being buried on Sunday 25th May 1645. The main point here, is that a Royalist army was looting from Royalist sympathisers. The King's Gay Meadow speech was read in Parliament on Friday 30th, a remarkable two days later, and they resolved to print something to counter it.

Market Drayton's Civil War

October 1642

A letter from Shrewsbury of the day after mentions the hardships of being in an occupied town.

"Our Country is now in a woeful condition by reason of the multitude of soldiers daily billeted upon us, both of Horse and Foot. I have had of those guests all this week, and expect little better next week. We had in town on Thursday night last some twelve or fourteen captains besides other officers, and near upon two thousand soldiers belonging to them."

Several other letters were published in pamphlets detailing plundering by the Royalists in Shropshire at this time. Obviously, some of the detail could well be propaganda, as these pamphlets were produced by Parliamentary sources, but they make interesting reading when set against the personal letter from John Weever, who had no anti-royalist axe to grind.

On Monday 3rd, King Charles travelled to Wrexham once again to view the assembled trained bands of the county, who were preparing to march to Shrewsbury as Prince Charles' Life Guard. We have a good example on Tuesday 4th of a pamphlet which appears to be a spurious report of action near Shrewsbury. According to the report, a thousand foot and six hundred horse left Ludlow and headed for Shrewsbury, where they were met by six thousand Royalist horse and foot. It is further stated that the Earl of Essex arrived which caused the Royalists to flee. Not only was the Earl of Essex not near Shrewsbury on this date, but this is not confirmed anywhere else, and appears to be contradicted by other reports.

A letter from Shrewsbury of Saturday 8th (published in a Parliamentarian pamphlet), gives us a little information about the size and attitude of the King's army, which may be more or less exaggerated.

"I shall give you the best Intelligence I can of the strength of his Majesties Army: It is related amongst us, that it doth increase daily, and as I am an eye-witness myself, and have it likewise from others; It doth consist of six thousand Foote, three thousand Horse, and fifteen hundred Dragoons, which, if supplies come not speedily in, must in a few days mutiny: … …They have a saying amongst the

Soldiers, that all rich men are **Round-heads**, and therefore they may be bold with them, and certainly they make good their words, by their practice, for they have plundered many Gentlemen's houses in these parts, and those too which were not so well affected to the Parliament, whereby men see now what is to be expected from them."

It also gives us the first indication that the army was about to march away from Shropshire.

"We fear when his Majesty goes, which they say will be upon Monday or Tuesday next, we shall be ill dealt with by the common Soldiers, both in Town and Country; We have had warrants to send in Horses and Carts for his removal, which are come towards Salop, but whither his Majesty intends, is not certainly known, it is given out he intends for London."

The King gave another speech at Shrewsbury on Saturday 8th in a **"Champaine Field"** to try and persuade the people of Shropshire to donate more to his cause before his exit from the county. The following day the King himself mentions the impending march. In a letter to Prince Rupert attempting to distribute arms and armour remaining at Shrewsbury, he states that **"the more diligence is to be used, because of the sudden march of our army."**

Monday 10th saw Rupert and his forces heading towards Shifnal. The next day, they rode to Wolverhampton, and the King, still at Shrewsbury wrote to Ottley, commanding him to stay in Shrewsbury to defend it.

On Wednesday 12th, the preparations ended and the main army's march away from Shrewsbury began. Being reported as "sixteen thousand foot besides horse", they headed south for Bridgnorth on route towards London.

MD Document 3

We now come to a very interesting letter, printed in a Parliamentary pamphlet on Friday 14th. The exceedingly long title of the pamphlet is:

"A Wonderful Deliverance or God's abundant mercy in preserving

from the Cavaliers the town of DRAITON In the County of Hereford declaring how many troops of the Cavaliers came against the said Towne, with an intent to have plundered it and put the inhabitants to the Sword, Men, Women and Children. Also manifesting how they were happily discovered by a scout of our Dragoons, who gave an alarum to several troops of horse and foot, which were quartered in the adjoining villages, by whose assistance the town was preserved, and a wonderful victory obtained over the Cavaliers. Being the true Copy of a Letter sent from Mr. Tho. Kittermaster of Hereford, to Mr. William Knowles in Holborne, dated Octob. 14. 1642."

Firstly, we need to deal whether this is relevant to Market Drayton or not. We do not know what the date of the incidents dealt with in the letter is, but it would seem reasonable to assume that it was reported fairly soon after the event. According to his own journal, Prince Rupert, listed as being the chief Royalist in the action was nowhere near Herefordshire up to Friday 14th. He spent most of his time up to Monday 10th in Shrewsbury. It is interesting to note that although the letter was sent from Hereford, nowhere within the text does it state that **"Draiton"** is in Herefordshire. This has been assumed from the location of the sender by the publisher in London who was presumably not noted for his geographical knowledge of the West Midlands.

Of course, this could be pure propaganda, but certain details, such as personal names ring true. If we look into Rupert's movements at this time, we can see that on Thursday September 8th he was in Leicestershire at Market Harborough. By various stages, he made his way through the midlands, including visits to Wolverhampton on Monday 19th and Bewdley on Thursday 22nd. However, after his victory at Powick Bridge on Friday 23rd, he headed straight for Shrewsbury, via Tenbury, Ludlow and Haughmond. Therefore, the nearest we have him coming to Hereford is on his journey from Powick to Shrewsbury, but he was travelling fast, and it seems very unlikely that he would have been able to detour into Herefordshire, just to plunder a town that does not seem to exist. Therefore, if this report is to be believed, it must be at a location near where Rupert spent some time before Friday October 14th. His main location, from which it could be easily believed that he would sally out to plunder would be Shrewsbury, and it would not take long for a purely cavalry force to ride from Shrewsbury to Market Drayton. Therefore, because of this misdirection, and some personal information, it seems quite likely that this skirmish near Market Drayton did actually take place, and at some point between Wednesday 28th September and Monday 10th October.

On Saturday 15th October the King was at Wolverhampton where he was joined by the last of the Welsh levies. Parliament had not by this time heard that the King was on the march. In the House of Lords it was reported that **"By these great Violences and Oppressions, they have so exhausted those Parts, that His Majesty cannot stay long about Shrewsbury."**

By this time, both the mint and the press had been set up in Shrewsbury. A letter from Basil Waring on Tuesday 18th states that they were minting coin daily out of the plate that was being delivered from the nearby counties, as well as Wales and Cornwall. Also on this day, Prince Rupert and the King finally re-joined forces at Meriden Heath, **"where we had the first appearance of an Army."** By this time, Parliament had realised that the Royalist army had bled dry the Shropshire area and was heading towards London, planning to plunder their way there. They issued commands to various counties to be ready.

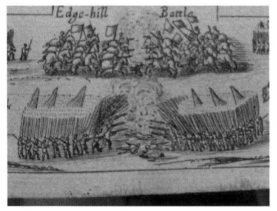

A contemporary woodcut of the Battle of Edgehill

On Sunday 23rd, the armies of the Earl of Essex and the King finally met at Edgehill, in what was the first large pitched battle of the war, and which was expected to be a one-off decisive battle to settle the issue. However, it was indecisive and war was to continue for much longer. So, part of the Royalist army had encamped in and around Market Drayton. From there they had attacked Nantwich, and there was also possibly a skirmish near Market Drayton itself. This was not to be the last time by any means that Market Drayton would see troops of one side or the other.

3 The First Battle of Nantwich

T. P. Marshall, writing in his **"History of Market Drayton Parish Church"** in 1884 tells us that **"In January, 1643, Sir Vincent Corbet and a party of Royalists were in possession of Drayton, where they had a brush with some of the troopers from Nantwich, under Sir William Brereton."** The reality is somewhat different, as we shall find out in this chapter.

To find out what was actually going on and why, we have to first examine events starting a few months earlier. After Lord Grandison had plundered Nantwich, and then joined the King at Shrewsbury for his expedition to Edgehill, it was not left garrisoned, he had simply sucked it dry of money, arms and supplies, and abandoned it. He had removed all of the chief Parliamentarian gentlemen who were now in Royalist custody, looting their estates outside the town for whatever they could find. Now that there was no large army in the area, the Parliamentarian forces settled on Nantwich as their base. They had no garrison in Shropshire at this time. The Royalists had settled on Chester and Shrewsbury as their bases.

October 1642

On Wednesday 26th, Parliament was given a report of the battle of Edgehill. Lord Wharton stated that **"on the King's Part, it is conceived, there were slain Three Thousand, and on the Parliament's Side not above Three Hundred."**

At this time, Sir William Brereton was still in London. On Friday 28th he was in Parliament being appointed to a committee for the examinations of prisoners. We also find him mentioned in the parliamentary record on the next day preparing a declaration concerning the difficulties of paying the billet monies at York.

November 1642

On Saturday 26th he was still in London being appointed to another committee. On Tuesday 29th Prince Rupert, who had been campaigning further south in Berkshire along with the King recorded in his journal that he returned to the King at Oxford, the winter quarters.

Campaigning was considered at this point to be a fair-weather occupation. Moving large armies about in the depths of winter on a poor road network was not considered worthwhile if not absolutely necessary.

December 1642

Down in London, the Parliamentarian forces of Cheshire continued

Sir William Brereton

attempting to increase their forces. Two examples of this are one from Saturday 3rd, Parliament ordering four hundred muskets and three hundred firelocks to be sent to Sir William Brereton, and another giving Brereton permission to raise three hundred horses. Perhaps considering the increasing influence of the Parliamentarians in Cheshire, the King issued a proclamation from his court at Oxford on Friday 9th, pardoning all of the inhabitants of that county with one notable exception. The King had declared Brereton a traitor.

At this point, the Shropshire Royalists were attempting to increase their own forces. A number of loyal gentlemen had, a short while before sent the King a resolution to raise a regiment of dragoons at their own expense. On this Friday he acknowledged their resolution in a letter to the High Sheriff Henry Broomley, approving the appointment of Sir Vincent Corbet as its Colonel.

Large armies were not the only issue, locally. An extract of a letter from Sir Orlando Bridgeman to Sir Francis Ottley will set the scene. It was sent from Chester on Thursday 15th. He states that more forces had arrived at Nantwich that day. The two men had arranged to meet at Whitchurch, but Bridgeman returned to Chester having been told of a plot on Chester. He mentions that Whitchurch is no longer a safe place for them to meet due to **"straggling companies abroad"**. Bridgeman was the son of the Bishop of Chester and had taken command of the city's defence.

It was around this time that the Royalists and Parliamentarians in Cheshire decided to meet to discuss a local peace. They agreed to meet at Tarporley on Monday 19th to discuss terms. The Royalist members would be Robert

Needham (Lord Kilmorey) and Master Cholmondeley, and for the Parliamentarian side were William Marbury of Marbury Hall and Mr Henry Mainwaring of Ightfield. Tarporley was chosen as a mid-way point between Parliamentarian Nantwich and Royalist Chester. The meeting began, although Orlando Bridgman replaced Cholmondeley. The Royalists arrived with full authority to discuss terms, but the Parliamentarians needed to seek further permissions, so the meeting was adjourned until the following Wednesday.

The Shropshire Royalists met at Battlefield near Shrewsbury on Tuesday 20th to fulfil their resolution to raise the regiment of dragoons. The Royalist supporters of the resolution were to bring in their horses and a monetary contribution. Sir Vincent Corbet was there to receive them.

On the same day the Parliamentarians wrote that they had not yet received consent to the Cheshire agreement, so requested a further adjournment until Thursday 22nd.

Corbet's rendezvous did not raise as many troops as hoped for. On Wednesday 21st, Sir Vincent was at Whitchurch, and was requested by the Cheshire Royalists to take the newly formed Shropshire Dragoons the following day to attend the meeting at Tarporley, but he answered that he was not up to strength and he had not had orders from his commander, Colonel Hastings.

By Wednesday 21st the King had obviously abandoned his plans to make Shrewsbury his main headquarters in favour of Oxford, because the mint was being moved, as can be seen in a letter from the King's secretary Edward Nicholas, who requested that some of his trunks should be added to the convoy.

MD Document 4

A pamphlet of the time states that the Royalists were glad of the delay at Tarporley, as they were holding a rendezvous there. They were expecting troops from Shropshire, but if these were Corbet's Dragoons they were to be disappointed. This pamphlet deals with the whole peace process, and mentions the Royalist troops heading for the area. It states that Colonel Hastings took three hundred cavalry into Cheshire, and that there were other companies at Whitchurch and Market Drayton which might be brought in.

Because the Royalist troops were present at Tarporley, the negotiators held their meeting at St. Boniface's Church at Bunbury, a couple of miles away. The following day, Friday 23rd, the meeting at Bunbury continued all that day, and in the evening the agreement was signed by both sides. There were eight points agreed to. The one that proved the most contentious was number six. This stated that neither side should bring any troops into the county except for those passing through to other areas.

At ten o'clock on the evening of Christmas Eve, Orlando Bridgeman arrived back in Chester from Tarporley. The meeting seems to have disgruntled some of the Shropshire Royalists, and they were waiting for him when he arrived. They complained that what they had agreed was a breach of the association between the counties, and that they had not been told about it.

In the meantime, despite the proposed peace in Cheshire, both sides carried on arming, and trying to gauge each other's intentions. One of the newspapers, Mercurius Aulicus, in its first issue, stated that Colonel Hastings had intercepted fifty cases of pistols sent by Brereton towards Manchester, and in a separate encounter, four carts containing one hundred and fifty muskets and firelocks, four small brass cannon, three barrels of powder and a large quantity of slow-match. It is probably worth bearing in mind that the newspapers of the day were as partisan as they are now, and as unreliable.

January 1642/3

Although Shrewsbury was officially a Royalist town, not all of its inhabitants were of the same persuasion, and for this reason, its unofficial governor, Sir Francis Ottley imposed an oath on the inhabitants of the town on Monday 2nd to try and flush out the Parliamentarian sympathisers. Refusal to take the oath was punishable by death.

By this time, Parliament had got wind of the Cheshire neutrality agreed to. On Tuesday 3rd, they ordered Sir William Brereton to bring a copy into the House of Commons. That Friday, the House of Commons voted in favour of a declaration against the agreement. They handed it to Alexander Rigby, the MP for Wigan who delivered it to the House of Lords for their assent. On Saturday 7th, The House of Lords agreed to the declaration from the Commons and Parliament ordered it to be published. On Monday 9th, the Commons discussed the Bunbury agreement further, and took into account a letter received from **"the Cheshire gentlemen"**. As a result, they compiled instructions for Sir William Brereton and the other Deputy Lieutenants to take control of the Cheshire forces and any confiscated goods. On Thursday 12th, Parliament agreed these instructions, and also issued a declaration protecting Brereton and his estate after the King had declared him a traitor.

By this time, intelligence came to the Royalist faction that Brereton was on his way north. It is not clear when he left, but it must have been after Tuesday 3rd. It was reported that he was at Heywood, near Manchester raising forces. It was not completely clear where his target was. Orlando Bridgeman in Chester, writing to Sir Francis Ottley in Shrewsbury said that it had been reported either Nantwich or Manchester, but himself thought possibly Bromfield then part of Shropshire.

On Friday 20th, Thomas Leigh, the High Sheriff of Cheshire wrote to Sir Francis Ottley, warning him that it did not look as though the Bunbury Agreement was going to be honoured by the Parliamentary side, and requested that Shropshire troops should be positioned near the Cheshire border. On the same day, Orlando Bridgeman wrote to Sir Francis Ottley giving him all the details of how the affair at Bunbury had taken place, and warning that it had started to break down, as the Parliamentary side had requested free passage through Cheshire with its forces. In accordance with article six of the agreement, this should have been allowed if there were no plans for action within the county, however, with neither side trusting the other, things were not looking good. Both Leigh and Bridgeman confirmed that another meeting was scheduled for Tuesday 24th, but it is not clear whether the two sides were still talking by that point.

On Saturday 21st, Parliament confirmed that Brereton was heading north, adding another member to a committee in his place as he had **"gone into the country"**. At about this time Sir Thomas Aston was ordered to Shropshire by the King to raise forces and defend Cheshire against

Brereton's forces.

It now looked like both parties were likely to clash. Chester, meanwhile, continued to raise troops for the Royalist cause. Bridgeman wrote to Ottley on Wednesday 25th stating that they had already brought in almost five hundred men, and that on each of the following two nights, two hundred more would be coming in, along with two troops of cavalry. John Harrington of Bishton in Shropshire also wrote to Ottley on this date confirming that Corbet had not managed to raise the expected number of dragoons. He said that every Hundred was to find ten, and that these had not been coming in as hoped.

Sir Thomas Aston

By Friday 27th, it became clear to Brereton that Sir Thomas Aston was heading to attack Nantwich. Brereton with his force was on his way from Congleton to strengthen it but he was being slowed by his baggage train. For this reason, he sent an advance force of about fifty dragoons ahead of the main army under the command of two of his officers, Captain Bromhall, and the Scottish Sergeant-Major Lothian. They marched overnight and reached Nantwich at about seven o'clock in the morning, beating Aston to the town. Aston had diverted to Stafford on the way, so his forces did not arrive until nearly five o'clock, very late on a winter's day. Aston's forces immediately started their attack in more than one place but were repulsed with minor casualties.

The local diarist Thomas Malbon states that Aston had two hundred men although Brereton puts it at three hundred. Sir William tells us that in this first attack, one of Sir Thomas' cavalry was killed along with his horse. A Parliamentary pamphleteer also tells us that in this first attack, one of the defenders was killed.

At this point, Nantwich had not constructed any permanent fortifications. With the night coming on, and having no luck gaining entry into Nantwich, Sir Thomas Aston heard that the rest of the Parliamentarian force was close by and heading for them. According to the Parliamentarian accounts, Aston withdrew from the town to a point where he could ambush Brereton's forces. Sir William also claims to have heard in advance that the ambush had been laid. It was by now very dark, and Aston formed up his men either side of the lane to await Brereton's arrival. He mentions that Sir Vincent Corbet's dragoons were part of that force. Our pamphleteer also mentions that the advantage was firmly with the Royalists. He claims that Brereton's force was only one hundred and fifty, and that Aston's was near four hundred.

However, numbers of troops in pamphlets are notoriously inaccurate, a smaller winning force always sounding good to the winning side. However, it does give some idea of the scale of troops involved in this sort of skirmish at this time. Sir William advanced towards the town, unaware of the ambush laid for him, but our pamphleteer tells us that they were told by a boy that it was there. However, by this time, they had already advanced between the two sets of Royalist forces and reportedly could hear them whispering.

Aston's recollection is somewhat different. His version has it that the fight occurred because they were retreating and Brereton was advancing, and had to pass each other. By now it was nearly six o'clock. Malbon claims that Aston's force was nearer five hundred, but confirms the ambush. However, as he claims that all of this happened at four o'clock, he may not have been an eye-witness. He does however give slightly more information as to the location of the fight. He stated that the ambush occurred between the end of Aspell Street and Cheerbrooke, and that it was so dark that they could not see each other.

Corbet's Dragoons were obviously not having a good day of it. Aston stated that the dragoons had not given fire at all, now Sir William Brereton tells us that this also happened during the retreat as well. Sir William stated that Corbet's dragoons were **"presently disordered and many of them ran away without ever giving fire."** A letter sent two days later from John Harrington to Sir Francis Ottley stated that he was sorry to see Sir Vincent Corbet so poorly furnished with raw soldiers and young commanders.

Although Aston had already retreated from the town by the time of Brereton's arrival, Brereton was of the opinion that the town was still under attack and would likely fall, so he pressed the attack even after finding himself in an ambush. After the Parliamentarians had started to pass through the Royalists who were behind the hedge on either side, Brereton's dragoons charged their Shropshire opponents, and then Sir William's cavalry charged. The hedges being an obstruction, the two forces became involved in a melee.

Sir Vincent Corbet

It was common practice, at the time, to assign a field-word, so that one could be certain that he was facing friend or foe, but in this instance, that failed. Brereton stated that the Royalists had discovered their word, which was **"Christ"**. With Brereton's force divided into three, those in the town, Brereton's own force, and those defending the baggage train, a general melee ensued, until two events decided the day.

Firstly, Brereton's baggage train had come up and they had loaded at least one of his cannons which they fired. Although completely ineffectual in terms of casualties (one would hope that they did not fire into the melee where they would have stood as much chance of killing their own men), this must have put the fear of God into the already frightened young dragoons.

Secondly, once the Parliamentarian dragoons had dismounted, either the horses were deliberately driven into the melee, or they took fright at the firing of the cannon. Brereton advanced into the town at about eight o'clock that evening, to consolidate his victory. The Royalists were defeated. It appears that they were defeated by a smaller force, and it may indeed be the case, however we are mostly reading Parliamentarian reports. Also, by the time Brereton and Aston joined battle, it was dark.

Despite Brereton's forces being split into three, the combined use of dragoons, cavalry and artillery must have convinced the Royalists that he had a much bigger force. It was now all over. Brereton started to mop up the remaining Royalists and imprison them. The Vicar of Acton tells us that Brereton took nearly one hundred prisoners, others were killed in the action. He also took horses and weapons. But what of the Royalist commanders? What has this to do with Market Drayton? Sir Thomas Aston having lost his horse headed on foot to Whitchurch. Rumour had it that he had a bullet in his buttock, but as he wrote a letter about the event from

Whitchurch at two o'clock the following morning it seems unlikely. It was reported that Sir Vincent Corbet crawled away on all fours. Whether or not that was true, he headed down what is now the A51 to Woore. From there, he would have headed through Bearstone, Norton-in-Hales and Betton to Market Drayton, where he was nursing his wounded pride at six the next morning.

MD Document 5

He must have been well aware of the number of casualties, hence writing a letter from Market Drayton to Sir Francis Ottley in Shrewsbury for surgeons to be sent to Whitchurch.

Market Drayton's Civil War

4 The Battle of Drayton

At the end of the last chapter, we left Brereton cleaning up and taking charge of Nantwich. Sir Thomas Aston was in Whitchurch, and Sir Vincent Corbet was in Market Drayton. The Royalists plan had not worked. Brereton did not come out unscathed though. He wrote that all his corporals had been killed and he had lost all of his best horses. Despite initial resistance from the people in the town, he immediately set about building fortifications and putting his instructions into action. The Bunbury peace was now firmly in the past.

January 1642/3

On Sunday 29th the day was quiet, but the following day the Parliamentarian supporters from throughout the county started to arrive in Nantwich. They continued to arrive throughout the following week, concentrating the Parliamentarian forces on what was to become the chief garrison in Cheshire. In the meantime, the Royalist forces were licking their wounds at Whitchurch.

February 1642/3

For all his apparent success at Nantwich, Sir William was an MP and not a military man. The troops that had arrived at Nantwich were privately raised, and he did not feel he had sufficient authority to control them. For that reason, he wrote to Captain Francis Rowe on Friday 10th from Nantwich to try and recruit an officer or to receive his own commission to command them. On the following day, a Royalist letter from Thomas Eyton to Sir Francis Ottley stated that the troops in Nantwich had started to sally out and plunder the area.

Sir Nicholas Byron

In Chester on Tuesday 14th, Sir Nicholas Byron arrived as the newly appointed Royalist Colonel-General of Cheshire and Governor of

Chester. In the meantime, Colonel Hastings had based himself in Stafford, from where he began to send out raiding parties. The next encounter in the immediate area between the two sides came the following Tuesday, the 14th. Our Nantwich diarist, Thomas Malbon recorded that Brereton summoned the county to Tarporley & Frodsham.

This being a general announcement, the Commissioners of Array in Chester were well aware of it, and took their troops to Brereton's route from Nantwich to Tarporley. They set themselves up near Tilston Heath with a small amount of artillery.

When Brereton arrived, there were ineffective volleys of musket fire from both sides, and artillery fire from the Royalists. However, although the artillery fire went over the Parliamentarians heads, there was some close fighting towards Beeston. The ground was so boggy that both sides were forced to retreat, and the Parliamentarians carried on fortifying Nantwich, at this point with trenches and mud walls.

On Saturday 25th, the Nantwich Parliamentarians marched from Nantwich to Knutsford. They heard that Royalist forces from Chester were plundering Norton House, and so headed that way. They drove the Royalists away, and started to fortify more places, especially Northwich. The garrison there started to plunder the local area.

March 1642/3

On St. Chad's Day, which was Thursday 2nd, Lord Brook was attacking Litchfield for the Parliament, during which he was killed, being hit by a bullet from the cathedral tower, coincidentally dedicated to St. Chad.

Litchfield surrendered on Saturday 4th, to John Gell who had replaced Lord Brook as commander. It was said that during this time, Lord Brook's forces reached Newport, but that was more than likely just a foraging party.

Sir Francis Ottley ordered that all the Dragoons in the town were to assemble under the corn-market on pain of three days imprisonment, to counter any further Parliamentary incursion. At about this time, it began to be reported that Sir William Brereton had been captured or killed, but the same sources also stated that Brereton's forces had not encountered any

Royalist forces since the attack on Nantwich, and that Norton House had not been relieved but had been saved by the defenders. The first was certainly propaganda, the second almost certainly so. These rumours were published on Wednesday 8th.

On Friday 10th, Sir Thomas Aston rode out of Chester with a force of cavalry, and headed for Middlewich, arriving the next day. They plundered many houses, sending the spoils back to Chester. The same day, Sir Francis Ottley received a letter which repeated the claims that Brereton had been killed or **"dangerously shott"**, this time mentioning that this was supposed to have happened at Delamere. Brereton at this point was at Northwich, supervising the fortification and garrisoning of the town, so he arrived outside Middlewich, fired some shot against the town, but retired back to Northwich that night.

Being better prepared, he arrived back early the next morning with all the forces he could muster having sent word to Nantwich for reinforcements. He arrived on the West side of the town to find that Aston had already formed up to receive him. The battle started, and continued until nine or ten o'clock without either side gaining the advantage. At this point, over one thousand cavalry arrived from Nantwich on the southern side of the town, which Aston had well defended, but after a while, the Parliamentarians begin to gain ground and eventually seized the cannon that the Royalists had there. Once that had happened, the Royalists started to flee, and many of note were taken prisoner. The cavalry managed to escape, but a large number of the foot soldiers were captured. Brereton and Aston both wrote accounts of the action, Brereton's praising God for the victory, and Aston's blaming everyone but himself.

The following Wednesday, the 15th, the bells rang out at Nantwich and a day of thanksgiving was held for the victory. On Friday 17th, no doubt with the severe Royalist setbacks nearby in mind, a group of Royalist officers wrote to Sir Francis Ottley from Whitchurch, to solicit the aid of a Captain Rainsford, having a shortage of field officers. Two of these officers were commanders of the Shropshire Dragoons raised at Battlefield the previous December, Sir Vincent Corbet and Thomas Piggott of Chetwynd.

Meanwhile, Brereton had headed towards Stafford, where Sir John Gell required assistance. Stafford was being held and fortified by the Royalists.

The two forces met at Salt Heath, or Hopton Heath, on Sunday 19th, where a battle ensued. At first the Royalists, under the leadership of the Earl of Northampton and Colonel Hastings, got the upper hand, forcing the Parliamentarians to retreat, and capturing the Parliamentarian artillery.

However, the Parliamentarian side was rallied by fresh attacks by Brereton and his Major Lothian, and they took back the artillery. The Royalists were driven back into Stafford, but by that time they had lost the Earl of Northampton who had died in the attack.

Orlando Bridgeman

On the morning of Tuesday 21st, Orlando Bridgman wrote from Chester to Sir Francis Ottley, that some artillery had been sent to Colonel Hastings, and urging Ottley to protect them on the way through Shropshire. The letter also provided intelligence that Aston's Regiment had marched towards Staffordshire, no doubt in the hope of relieving those troops at Stafford.

By this time, however, Brereton was on his way back to Nantwich with what spoils that he had gained from Salt-Heath, having achieved in Staffordshire what his assistance was requested for. He arrived there on Thursday 23rd.

Malbon states that he had with him a great mortar piece, many granadoes and other rich spoils. On the following day, some of Col. Hasting's Staffordshire troops were at Newport, having been sent to escort the artillery. They advanced to Wellington to attend to its progress as requested by Bridgman.

March 1643

The first day of 1643 (by the reckoning of the time, Saturday 25th), the House of Commons recommended that Brereton should receive a commission to command the forces in Cheshire. They also continued talking about associating Shropshire and Staffordshire, and as a result of hearing about the success at Salt-Heath, Brereton was added to the committee for Staffordshire. Two days later they ordered a letter of thanks be sent to the Parliamentary commanders at the battle.

About Thursday 30th, Brereton left with his forces to go to help besiege Warrington, which was being held by the Earl of Derby. On the same day, Lord Capel wrote to Ottley, informing him of twenty barrels of powder, and the appropriate amount of slow match and lead shot which were scheduled to arrive at Shrewsbury on Friday 31st, guarded by his own troop. He requested both Ottley and the mayor of Shrewsbury that it be safely laid up until his arrival. He also started to establish the chain of command. Sir Michael Woodhouse was to be Sergeant Major General of all the foot in the associated counties under Sir Nicholas Byron who was Colonel General of the same area.

April 1643

Lord Capel

By the start of April, Capel had arrived in Shrewsbury, where he held Councils of War on Saturday 1st and Monday 3rd. It had been rumoured for a couple of weeks that he was coming to take charge of the area for the Royalists, perhaps due to the disastrous encounters that Sir Thomas Aston had had. He appointed Ottley to take charge of the magazine for all the arms that were to be brought in. The next day, Capel's commission was made official by Prince Rupert, making his title **"Arthur Lord Capel, lieutenant-general to his highness the Prince of Wales, of the several counties of Worcester, Salop, Chester, the cities of Chester and Worcester, and the six counties of North Wales."**

We do not know if any Royalist (or indeed Parliamentarian) troops were stationed at Market Drayton at this point, but the Nantwich diarist mentions that there were many Royalist soldiers at Whitchurch where they did **"much hurt by plundering"**. This seemed to go against Capel's own published commands. He utilized the Shrewsbury press on Monday 3rd to print a proclamation against plundering, specifying that the taking of goods from Parliament sympathisers was only to be carried out on the express command of himself or the King.

Also on this day, a little further afield, Prince Rupert took Birmingham. The next day he travelled to Walsall.

Market Drayton's Civil War

Prince Rupert

At midnight on Wednesday 5th, the Chester governor, Byron, wrote to Capel with the rumour that Brereton had been soundly beaten at Warrington. He attempted to persuade Capel to take his forces towards Whitchurch, in order that their combined forces might fall on Nantwich. He indicated the importance of this intelligence by labelling the wrapper **"Haste post haste. Haste with speed."** Capel in turn wrote with the same effect to Prince Rupert, urging him to come with his forces, as **"all the wealth of Cheshire is brought into that town, both of those that are of their own party, and what they have plundered."**

That day, Prince Rupert advanced to Cannock, he had another target in mind. On Saturday 8th, he arrived at Litchfield. Brereton meanwhile was still in the Warrington area. Whatever the truth of his defeat, it does not seem to have been the rout that was claimed at Stockton Heath. While their leader was away, the troops left at Nantwich were not idle. The week after Easter (Easter Sunday was the 2nd), they patrolled Cheshire to prevent plundering, and at one point, probably on Saturday 8th, arrived outside Chester where there was some minor skirmishing.

Moss Hall, Audlem

Over the next two days, they marched back to Nantwich. On Sunday 9th, some of the most important prisoners being held in Nantwich (from the battle of Middlewich) were transferred to Manchester. They started out at midnight, presumably to avoid any chance of them being rescued. On Monday 10th, a force of Royalists left Whitchurch, and travelled to Audlem, nearby which is the Moss House, at that time the home of the Parliamentarian Captain Massey. They drove his cattle away, and carried off what they could of his household goods. They also took horses from other local people. Hearing of this, a small force left Nantwich to attack them, but arrived after the Royalists had left. They carried on the pursuit and encountered the rear of the Royalist force.

MD Document 6 & 7

They killed three of the royalists and recovered eleven oxen and some weapons. They also brought back to Nantwich fifteen prisoners, one of whom was a Mr Bulkeley of Buntingsdale Hall. This may be the **"alarum"** mentioned as being on that date that Lord Capel informed Prince Rupert of in a letter sent three days later. Capel had returned from Wales that morning, where he was meeting with Sir Richard Lloyd at Wrexham.

On Monday 10th, the three counties of Salop, Staffordshire and Warwick were associated by Parliament under the command of the Earl of Denbigh as Lieutenant-General, with headquarters at Coventry; and a strong committee appointed for Shropshire, with Sir John Corbet as its chairman and Colonel-General of the forces to be raised in the County. In Staffordshire on the same day, Prince Rupert started his siege of Litchfield.

The next day, Tuesday 11th, the Nantwich forces, expecting the Royalists to head back towards the Moss House to remove the rest of the goods from Massey's house, gathered as large a force as they could, reportedly approximately one thousand and headed towards Whitchurch to cut them off. The two sides met at Burleydam, where according to Parliamentary sources, the Royalists fled back towards Whitchurch, five Royalists were killed and two or three taken prisoner. Three Parliamentary soldiers were captured and taken back to Whitchurch. Presumably this put the Royalists off from carrying on the plundering. Having put the Royalists to flight, it appears that the same force headed towards Cholmondeley House to attempt to take it, but they were repulsed by the Royalist garrison of four hundred men who were ready for them. It was reported that they returned with a booty of sixty horses, but with fifty-two men less.

That night some of the prisoners that were being held at Nantwich were removed and distributed among the other local garrisoned houses, as it was suspected that they were passing out intelligence, including the attack on Cholmondeley. On the same day, Sir Thomas Aston was finally relieved of his command by Lord Capel, who took over command of the Royalist war effort in Cheshire.

One of his first actions the next day (Wednesday 12th) was to write to Sir Francis Ottley, to investigate why the troop of dragoons raised there was short of men and money, both of which had been promised. He gave Ottley permission to imprison any who had promised men and/or money, who did not send them in.

He claimed in a letter to Prince Rupert that he gave the Parliamentarians an **"alarum"** on this day, but we appear to have no other record of it. Capel wrote from Whitchurch to Ottley on Thursday 13th, for our purposes merely recording where he was. Rupert had commanded Capel to supply him with ten barrels of gunpowder and twenty bundles of slow-match. He sent five barrels and the appropriate amount of match, claiming it was all he could spare, the local alarums and requests from others for powder having depleted his supply, and also that he was expecting more engagements as Brereton had returned to Nantwich. He further stated that if he had to send the rest that he would be forced to disband his forces.

On the same date, he also wrote to Ottley, requesting that he make a catalogue of those people in the town capable of donating money to the Royalist cause, and to make a **"thousand weight of Musquett Bullet"**. (Twenty hundredweight makes an imperial ton, so a thousand weight, or ten hundredweight is half an imperial ton). To give some idea of the number of skirmishes going on between the two sides at this particular time, we have a letter from Sir Vincent Corbet, now quartered at Malpas with the Shropshire dragoons, stating that they were on continual service, and that they were in need of a surgeon as their men were being hurt on a daily basis.

That Sunday, the 16th, Prince Rupert's forces made an attempt to capture the Cathedral close at Litchfield, but on this occasion were repulsed.

One of the Parliamentarian newspapers summed up the local situation quite well, when it stated on Tuesday 18th that Lord Capel had assembled an army of approximately two thousand Salopians and Welshmen and was sitting with them at Whitchurch, and also that Brereton had been forced to abandon his attempt on Warrington to strengthen his forces at Nantwich which he had done to the tune of approximately three thousand including some reinforcements from Manchester. The numbers were probably guesswork, but the net effect was that Royalist Whitchurch was facing Parliamentary Nantwich across the Shropshire/Cheshire border.

On Thursday 20th, at Litchfield, Prince Rupert's forces, who had been digging a tunnel up to the walls of the close, packed it with gunpowder, and then blew it up, making a huge hole in the Parliamentarian's defences.

On this date, most of Brereton's forces seem to have been away from Nantwich, as Capel with a force from Whitchurch and Cholmondeley came within sight of the Nantwich defences and plundered everything they could from the surrounding villages, the defenders of Nantwich being unable to do anything about it.

The next day, Friday 21st, Prince Rupert attacked through the hole in the defences at Litchfield, capturing the garrison. They were allowed to leave with **"colours flying, trumpets sounding and matches lighted"**. Rupert congratulated them on their courage. Having left a decent sized garrison, he marched away towards Warwickshire the next day. The following Tuesday and Wednesday (24th and 25th), more alarums were raised at Nantwich by Royalist troops plundering in the area.

May 1643

Colonel Hastings

MD Documents 8, 9, 10, 11, 12, 13, 14 & 15

At some point around the end of April, Capel decided to fortify Market Drayton. On Wednesday 3rd May, he wrote a letter to Colonel Hastings to try and persuade him that they should join forces to drive Brereton's forces out of the area. He requested that Hastings should come to Market Drayton, where **"I shall by such time as I can receive your resolution be ready there."**

This suggests that by this time that any fortifications at Drayton were at a very early stage. Indeed, Malbon, our Nantwich diarist stated that at this date Sir Vincent Corbet and about three hundred horse and foot soldiers were **"beginning to make some works (for their safety) about the town."** Brereton must have got wind of the changes; secrets were very difficult to keep at this period. At about midnight, some Parliamentary infantry and cavalry marched out of Nantwich and headed towards the town. Malbon described what followed on Thursday 4th as **"Drayton Battle"**, in reality it was more of a skirmish.

Market Drayton's Civil War

The Royalists, whether through inexperience, or for some other reason, did not post guards overnight. Therefore, when the Parliament troops arrived just after sunrise, they were all still in their beds. With very little in the way of fortification and no warning, it was a foregone conclusion. There was some resistance, nine of the defenders being killed, and there must have been just enough warning for Sir Vincent Corbet to escape in his shirt and waistcoat. He had left the rest of his clothing behind, and several letters were taken from his coat pocket, no doubt providing some useful intelligence. The haul was considerable, and must have been quite a blow to the Royalist cause. Many of the Royalists were taken prisoner. All the arms, supplies and horses were taken back to Nantwich, most of the infantry riding captured horses. Two of the Shropshire Dragoon's captains had been killed, Captains Kynaston and Sandford.

The Parliamentary sources we are following at this point took pains to point out that Brereton's men did no harm to the town, only dismantling the fortifications that had been started. A handful of Parliament's soldiers were wounded from shots from out of windows. The pamphlets claimed that six troops of Sir Vincent's horse had been taken or routed.

Colonel Hastings the same day received instructions from the King stating that he should be ready to assist the general of Lincoln, Rutland, Huntingdon, Cambridge and Norfolk, so Capel's idea of joining forces was not going to happen in any case. By Sunday 7th, Hastings had been ordered towards Newark. On Monday 15th, Brereton, having joined with the Staffordshire troops stationed at Newcastle-under-Lyme and Leek under the command of Colonel Ridgley, using the same night-time tactics as at Market Drayton entered Stafford with the minimum of resistance. They arrived at about three o'clock, when as at Market Drayton, everyone was in bed.

On Tuesday 16th, Capel, still at Whitchurch wrote to Ottley, concerning rumours of troop movements, which had been informed to him by Mennes. On the next day he rode from Whitchurch to Nantwich with his forces, including some cannon. They exchanged shots with the town, but left early the next morning to return to Whitchurch.

On Friday 19th, Capel still at Whitchurch, wrote to Ottley, informing him that his trip to Nantwich had brought Brereton's troops back from

Stafford. During the day, some Parliamentary troops marched from Nantwich towards Whitchurch, possibly planning an attack. Near Whitchurch they took some Royalist prisoners, and brought them back to Nantwich with about sixty head of cattle. According to Malbon, Brereton arrived back at Nantwich that night.

On Saturday 20th, the Royalist newspaper, **"Mercurius Aulicus"** refuted the attack on Drayton, stating that **"there is not one word true; Sir William Brereton being so cooped up in Nantwich by the Lord Capel's forces, that he dare not stir."** However, the attack on Market Drayton is mentioned in several places including local diaries and letters, so there is little doubt that it actually happened.

This must have been terrifying for the ordinary people of the town. They had, for a few days Royalist dragoons setting up primitive defences, possibly disrupting the market, followed by an early morning alarm call consisting of gunfire and troops of both sides being shot and wounded outside their houses. The parish register only records two burials at this period and they appear to have been locals. John Hopp of Drayton and George Colley son of Walter Colley do not sound like invading or defending soldiers so they were probably not as a result of the attack, being recorded on Friday 12th and Saturday 13th respectively. This is not the last time that Market Drayton would see conflict during this war.

5 Parliament Moves into Shropshire

May 1643

From Saturday 20th to the following Saturday 27th, when it was surrendered, the Parliamentarian troops besieged Warrington. Warrington was a relatively small town, but strategically important because of the bridge. Various modern writers have stated that Brereton was there, but I have not yet found contemporary references to it. Cheshire forces under his command, along with those of Manchester were certainly involved.

Mercurius Civicus printed on Wednesday 24th that Brereton had taken Wolverhampton, but this appears to have happened in March, so was old news.

Sir John Mennes

During that week, on Friday 26th, Capel wrote to Ottley, Mennes and Sir Thomas Scrivener the governor of Whitchurch, ordering the three of them to oversee the repair to Shrewsbury's fortifications. Sir Francis Ottley was under great pressure, which would explain the association with the two others, especially as there were apparently quite a number of Parliamentary sympathisers still within the town.

On Saturday 27th, the food running out, Warrington surrendered. The Royalist defenders marched out, leaving all their arms behind them. The next day, Sir George Booth was installed as governor.

On the evening of Sunday 28th, Lord Capel, having heard of the siege of Warrington, but not how it was progressing, took troops out of Whitchurch and Chester to attempt its relief. By two o'clock on the following afternoon while he was resupplying Halton Castle near Runcorn, he received intelligence that it had already fallen. By the time he wrote to Ottley later on that day, he had obviously realized his mistake, as he writes **"Haste Haste Post Haste Haste for life"**.

Capel also wrote to Ottley on Monday 29th, to try to get Ottley to arrest any known Parliamentary sympathisers in Shrewsbury, and to bring in any friendly troops. He wrote that he was trying to find out where all his troops were, so was still at Chester at this point.

While he was still marching his forces back that night, Brereton took all the forces he could out of Nantwich, and headed for Capel's headquarters at Whitchurch. This is one of the reasons that I do not believe that Brereton was aiding with his troops at the Warrington siege. He would have had a great deal of trouble getting his troops back to attack Whitchurch. However, Capel must surely have believed that he was there, else he would not have left Whitchurch so exposed, having very insubstantial fortifications.

Brereton's troops arrived outside Whitchurch at about three o'clock on the morning of Tuesday 30th. The figures that we have suggest that the attackers were about eight hundred horse and foot, and the defenders about six to seven hundred. After about two hours of a fierce firefight, Brereton's troops managed to drive the defenders away from the defences near the Clay Pits, and entered the town at that point. The Royalist defenders fled, leaving everything behind them. Brereton's men, having taken several prisoners, plundered everything that they could but had to leave a large amount behind them, not having enough carts to transport it. As with Market Drayton, it was stressed that they did the town itself no harm, returning to Nantwich by three o'clock in the afternoon.

The Whitchurch parish register records burials of fifteen soldiers on that date. Burghall states that they returned the next day to take the rest, although Malbon states that they returned on Friday 2nd June with fourteen carts. Burghall would have been reading Malbon, and may have simply disbelieved that they would have waited three days before going back. I have found references in later writings that the booty contained Capel's war-chest, containing two thousand pounds for paying all the soldiers under his command.

June 1643

At about this time, rumours started reaching Parliament that troops no longer needed in Ireland were to head to Chester to boost the Royalists there. This may have been the reason why on Thursday 1st they commissioned Sir Thomas Middleton to be Sergeant-Major-General for the six counties of North Wales.

Brereton himself at this time was in Liverpool, unloading ammunition from shipping there. The following week, on Tuesday 9th, Mercurius Civicus reported that the possibility of admitting the Irish into Chester had forced many previously loyal Royalists to leave the city, not wanting to admit the Irish into their houses. This may well simply be propaganda, but it is obvious that the possibility of the arrival of the troops from Ireland was concentrating the mind.

Earl of Denbigh

It should be noted that although Civicus calls them Irish, these would be in fact mostly English troops that had been fighting the Irish in Ireland. On the same date, Parliament started the process to make the Earl of Denbigh Commander in Chief of all the Forces in Warwickshire, Worcestershire, Shropshire, and Staffordshire.

On Wednesday 10th, Nantwich troops carried on their plundering of Royalist houses by heading for Carden, and attacking Mr. Leech's house, killing a serving maid as they did so.

On Friday 12th they continued, a force of dragoons travelling over to the Welsh border at Holt during their fair. From the area, they returned to Nantwich that night with a large number of cattle and horses. The same day, Brereton's taking of Whitchurch was detailed in the Parliamentarian press, in the shape of the newspaper **"Certaine Information"**, but the details are slightly different. The newspaper stated that he also marched to Prees and Wem, seizing **"Armes, Horses, Plate and Moneys"**. It also mentioned that the sum of money recovered in the Whitchurch attack was only five hundred pounds. This could well be the more likely amount, because their own press would be unlikely to have underestimated it. It also raised doubts about the loyalty of the Shrewsbury populace, and stated that the people of Shropshire were getting fed up of the amount of money that Capel was collecting by **"unreasonable Taxes and Impositions"**. This is of course a Parliamentarian publication, but it has the ring of truth, not apparently wanting to exaggerate the money taken at Whitchurch, and the Shrewsbury loyalty was certainly in question.

Meanwhile, Brereton had returned to Nantwich from Liverpool, with six loads of ammunition on Saturday 13th.

On Monday 15th, Parliament started to discuss some letters that were taken in the capture of Whitchurch which had been sent to the Speaker, William Lenthall. One dated Wednesday April 5th, stated that the Royalists were expecting supplies from Ireland. His letter mentions that there are Irish already landed and in Chester, and more ships of **"Irish rebels"** currently in Chester Water. The captured letters talked about here, amongst many others were sent from Chester's

William Lenthall

governor Sir Nicholas Byron to Capel, and he states that Shrewsbury and Chester must be the Royalists last refuge if things go badly, and therefore must be provided with as many supplies as possible.

At this point, Capel was stuck in Wrexham, complaining about the unseasonableness of the weather, and how he could not travel.

MD Document 16

On Friday 19th, a certain William Young at Caynton House near Shifnal complained to Ottley that he had already complied with Capel's request for

men and horses. He already had **"horse and arms now in Sir Vincent Corbet's troop"** and he had another in Captain Thomas Piggot's troop which **"were taken away at Drayton when their commander was in bed"**.

MD Document 17

Saturday 20th saw the Parliamentarians from Nantwich march past Whitchurch to Hanmer,

Sir Richard Willys

where for once they did not get things their own way. A force of horse under Captain Sankey (Captain of Brereton's own troop) and a Lieutenant-Colonel were attacked by Capel's forces. Capel's force was the greater and he routed the Nantwich troops, killing some, wounding others and taking more prisoner. Malbon quoted it as the worst day's work that **"ever Nantwich forces had from the beginning"**. Sankey and the Lieutenant-Colonel were amongst the prisoners. In Mercurius Aulicus it is mentioned that Capel's forces that were victorious at Hanmer were originally intended to march towards Market Drayton and Newport, to make incursions into Cheshire and Staffordshire. They were under the command of Sir Richard Willys, Capel's Serjeant Major General and were on their way from Wrexham when they encountered Sankey's troops.

On about this date, a Royalist force rode out from Cholmondeley to Bunbury church, where one of our diarists, Edward Burghall, was conducting a funeral. He recorded that **"They aimed to take some Roundheads, & especially me; but through God's Mercy I escaped."**

July 1643

Our information about July starts on Monday 3rd with a disagreement between the Shropshire Parliamentary representatives who were all in London, trying to get started on their attempt to capture Shropshire. Sir John Corbet had been given the command, but he had been unable to leave Parliament, his presence being constantly requested.

Because of this, on the next day, the arms assigned for that purpose were given over to Colonel Thomas Mytton, so that they could begin. At this point, it is not recorded what Brereton was up to, but two letters he sent, one on Tuesday 4th, and another on Wednesday 5th, were sent from Stafford. Capel on the 5th was at Wolverhampton with about two thousand troops from Shrewsbury, where he was aiming to link up with the Queen, whose troops from Yorkshire were making their way to the King at Oxford. The letter that gives us this information also tells us that Eccleshall Castle is **"yet besieged"** by the Parliamentarians, indicating that this had been occurring for a while.

On Friday 7th, Capel was still at Wolverhampton, but now "**attending the Queen's commands**". A letter from Secretary Nicholas to Prince Rupert on Saturday 8th records that **"My Lord Capel is before this joined with the Queen."**

By the 7th, Capel tells us that **"Brereton is run from Stafford to his old burrow Nantwich, and hath left Stafford very slenderly guarded, and hath withdrawn his forces from Eccleshall castle."**

On Tuesday 12th, Capel was at Bidford in Warwickshire where he wrote to Prince Rupert informing him that his troops were very distracted, as a rumour was circulating amongst them that the Parliamentarians had invaded Shropshire.

Five days later, Monday 17th, Brereton took forces from Nantwich and travelled to Chester, to attack the defences. However, as happened quite often at this time, news of their coming reached Chester before they did, and so the defenders were ready. He stayed in position for three days, but news arrived that Capel had got as far as Orton Maddock, heading to relieve the city.

On Thursday 20th Brereton returned to Nantwich having left two of his men dead. Capel didn't arrive with his cavalry (he couldn't get the foot to leave their own county) until after the Parliamentarians had retreated, and so missed an opportunity to attack.

The following Tuesday, the 25th, Mercurius Civicus reported a letter from Brereton, in which he gave the intelligence that two barques of Irish had landed in the Wirral and gone into Chester. Prince Rupert took Bristol on Wednesday 26th.

On Friday 28th, Stafford Castle, which being a little outside the town had not capitulated when the town did, fell to the Parliamentarians. Burghall's report stated that Col Hastings had relieved the castle with four hundred horse from Lichfield, but shortly after a force of Brereton's had arrived with about one thousand from Stone, and the Royalists fled, leaving the Castle unattended with all its arms and supplies intact. Neither Burghall or Malbon were there of course, so must have heard the story later.

August 1643

At about this time, the Shropshire Parliamentarians had decided to make a move, and had settled on Wem as being a good place to make their headquarters in the county. The religious writer Richard Baxter, being a Shropshire man, and wanting to get out of Coventry where the local committee were having a heated dispute with the Earl of Denbigh, had been persuaded to go with them.

In the meantime, on Thursday 3rd, Capel travelled to confront Nantwich again, his third attack on the town, arriving in the afternoon. Brereton was away in Stafford at this time, but the garrison of Nantwich were more than capable. At first, part of Capel's force appeared at Ravensmoor, and there was a skirmish, which was inconclusive. Only seeing part of Capel's force, the defenders came out to meet them, but Capel's force being bigger than expected, they retreated back into the town. Capel set up his positions for the following day.

The next day, which started out extremely foggy, Capel's forces attempted a dawn assault of the southern defences. At six o'clock in the morning, they opened up with their artillery and then attacked the defences. The to-ing and fro-ing of men and musket balls carried on until mid-morning, when the fog cleared, at which point Capel realized that he had set his positions much too near the defences, so they retreated away. Once they had left, the Parliamentary defenders then burnt down a number of buildings outside the walls so that if Capel returned his troops would have no shelter to attack from.

Sir Thomas Middleton

On Thursday 10th, Brereton was still based in Stafford, where he left to attack Chillington Hall near Wolverhampton. The next day it yielded, so Brereton headed back towards Nantwich. Shortly after he arrived, so did Sir Thomas Middleton with a large number of troops, artillery and ammunition. Middleton that week headed to besiege Eccleshall Castle.

On Thursday 17th, Capel at Wrexham wrote to Sir Francis Ottley to try and ascertain the numbers of dragoons that had been raised in Shrewsbury, as he needed them to relieve Eccleshall Castle. On Tuesday 29th, Capel joined with Staffordshire troops under Colonel Hastings, and they set out to relieve it. This they managed to achieve, and they took a large amount of supplies in with them, but the Parliamentarian troops from the town kept them pinned down with musket fire from the church until Brereton's forces from Stafford were almost upon them. At this point Capel's men were attempting to remove the castle's wealth and to escort the ladies and gentlemen out of the area using seven carts that they pressed into action. They were also carrying the body of the Bishop of Litchfield who had just died there. Hearing that Brereton's forces were nearly upon them, Capel's men fled, leaving behind them most of the plate etc., and also leaving the Bishop's body on the drawbridge. The rest in the castle itself surrendered when Brereton's men managed to breech the walls on the following day. Brereton emptied the castle, taking it all back to Nantwich, to join with Middleton who had been holding the fort there.

September 1643

Sir Thomas Mytton

Brereton was in charge in Cheshire, Middleton in North Wales, and Mytton had been appointed to take charge in Shropshire. However, at this point there were no Parliamentarian garrisons in Shropshire, so there was nowhere that Mytton could use as a base. With the large amount of money and supplies raised from the attack on Eccleshall, they could now afford to enlist and supply more troops, so the trio spent the next fortnight planning the move into Shropshire. They gathered all the troops that they could afford to remove from Nantwich, leaving the garrisons there and at Cholmondeley, and the Trained Bands of Nantwich Hundred, and formed up on Thursday 14th outside the town.

MD Documents 18 & 19

The following day they marched to Market Drayton with the intention of holding a muster of Shropshire Parliamentary sympathisers. They arrived on Friday 15th, and camped around the town. The muster was announced for Tuesday 19th, to give enough time for people to gather. Mytton had with him Mackworth and Hunt, along with Richard Baxter. Despite the efforts of Brereton, Mytton and Middleton, overall control of Shropshire, along with Warwickshire, Worcestershire and Staffordshire was given to Basil Fielding, the second Earl of Denbigh on Saturday 16th.

Fortunately, Fielding has left a large number of documents and letters which still exist in the Warwickshire Archives. The muster was held the following Tuesday, and it seems that the local Parliament supporters responded well.

Having raised more troops, they marched to Wem on Friday 22nd. The small town did not put up any resistance, not having been garrisoned or fortified. They immediately set about fortifying it. At first this would have taken the form of ditches, the earth that was dug out being made into a bank on the inside. These would be supplemented with wooden palisades, gates and artillery sconces. Any buildings outside the line of the defences would have been demolished to prohibit attackers from using them as shelter as had recently happened at Nantwich.

As an initial defence against the Shrewsbury Royalists, a force of dragoons was stationed in Loppington church under Captain Bromhall. The church was surrounded by ditches as a defence.

MD Documents 20, 21, 22 & 23

A second small force encamped at Market Drayton on Friday 29th. This was the trained bands of Nantwich who were accompanying a case of drakes (artillery) to Wem. They camped at Market Drayton that night and the following morning marched to Wem.

At some point in this period there appears to have been another encounter between the two sides. We only have a Parliamentary pamphlet as the source for it, but something about it rings true, even though the date of Wednesday 27th in it seems unlikely as the force had moved on to Wem on the 22nd. No more troops are recorded as being at Market Drayton until the Nantwich Trained Bands a couple of days later. According to the pamphlet, a thousand cavalry came from Shrewsbury to attack the force encamped around Market Drayton. The numbers may be exaggerated for both sides, as it is reported that these thousand were beaten off by thirty or forty cavalry and dragoons commanded by Captain Monk. It is possible that these thirty or forty were another small troop on the way to assist at Wem, or it could have been the troops that arrived later that week, but the next statement suggests that it was part of the original force as it is stated **"That we were not interrupted in our march to Wem the next day, nor**

disquieted or disturbed there during six or seven dayes untill we had made some works of defence though they were then but slight and weak, yet of some encouragement and advantage to our men." The pamphlet, **"Shropshire's Misery and Mercy"**, was not published until Wednesday 8th November, so the details being sketchy may just be separation of place and time.

The next day, Thursday 28th, Capel's forces, heading for Wem, encountered the force at Loppington. The Parliamentarian defenders managed to keep the Royalists at bay for a while, but being heavily outnumbered they retreated into the church. Brereton's troops in Wem, hearing the battle occurring, assembled a force and left the town to relieve Captain Bromhall.

However, before they arrived, the Royalists had set fire to the church and the defenders were forced to surrender. During their retreat towards Shrewsbury, the force from Wem caught them up and the two sides exchanged fire for a couple of hours, but by this time night was coming on and the Royalists managed to escape.

The following day, Friday 29th, the Trained Bands from Nantwich, which had previously been left in the town started to march towards Wem, possibly to try and bolster the forces with the Royalist army being nearby. That day, making slow progress as they were marching with a small amount of artillery, they got as far as Market Drayton, where they spent that night. They left for the remainder of their journey to Wem the next day.

October 1643

Farrow, in his **"Great Civil War in Shropshire"** tells us that in response to Parliament fortifying Wem, Capel gathered over four thousand men from different Royal garrisons, with considerable artillery on Prees Heath on Sunday 1st. Unfortunately, he does not tell us where this information comes from, and I have so far not found the original source documents to support it. At Wem, so close to the enemy, Sir Thomas Middleton was feeling out on a limb. On Friday 6th he wrote to Parliament about his situation, although it would not be read in Parliament until Thursday 17th. He complained that there was no money or any horses left in the area after the Royalists had been in charge.

Market Drayton's Civil War

We don't know for certain, but it seems likely that Brereton's main force had returned to Nantwich by this time. Middleton complains that he has few forces, and that those he has from Cheshire are likely to desert for want of pay.

The following Tuesday, the 10th, Capel assembled an army at Colemere, about a quarter of the way from Ellesmere to Wem. According to the Earl of Denbigh, he had not been able to raise as many forces as he would have wished which delayed his march by a day. Whether that was true or not, their obvious target was the still weakly fortified town of Wem. They did not, however, head in that direction. Brereton estimated their force at nearly five thousand, including six artillery pieces including a mortar that fired a thirty-pound shot. They were also well prepared for the march, having about one hundred and twenty wagons filled with provisions.

The next day, in Market Drayton, there were two burials. The first was of Mary Naginton, the surname still recognizable in the town to this day. The second is of more interest historically. The parish register reads **"Eodem die Sepultus fuit Willm Gooddian soldier"**. Translated, this means **"The same day [as Mary Naginton] was buried William Gooddian, Soldier"**. We have no particular action we can ascribe this death to. It may even have been disease or accident rather than military action. There is a slight possibility that he died as a result of the attack recorded on Wednesday 27th September 1643. Of course, there may well have been regular unrecorded skirmishes, and this may be the result of one, or even of a previous action.

In the meantime, Middleton and Brereton were watching Capel's movements. The Royalists on Saturday 14th were still in the same area. Brereton tells us that they were at Welshampton, and made to march over Blackhorse Ford towards Wem, but a party of the Parliamentary cavalry encountered them there, and faced him. Capel stood his army in the field, and stayed there all night.

Meanwhile, Nantwich had heard that Capel was heading for them. They mounted a strong guard all that night but the Royalists did not appear. The day after, which was Sunday 15th, to the consternation of the watchers at Wem, Capel marched nine miles north-east across Maelor, that part of Wales that juts into Shropshire, as far as Whitchurch instead of the expected south-east towards them.

From there Capel sent a letter to Abraham Shipman that seemed to indicate that at that point he had not decided whether to attack Wem or Nantwich. He stated that it depended upon intelligence, but as he asked Shipman to put the word out that the Chester forces were about to march for Nantwich, it seemed as though he was trying to confuse the enemy. The people of Whitchurch seemed glad to have Capel in their town again, Brereton stated that they rung the bells and added more soldiers to his army. Whether Capel knew where he was heading at that point or not, the Parliamentarians were definitely unsure. Brereton himself stated that it was either Nantwich, as most of the troops were with him near Wem, or to double back and attack Wem. The Nantwich garrison was still hearing reports of the approach of Capel's army and that morning and again on that night they stood a strong guard.

Deciding that the Royalists were not heading for Wem, at midnight that night the Parliamentarian army marched eight miles towards Capel arriving at Prees Heath about dawn on Monday 16th, about two miles from Capel's army. However, instead of the expected battle occurring, early in the morning, Capel and his army left and headed towards Nantwich.

MD Document 24, 25 and 26

The Parliamentary army initially decided to directly follow Capel's army either to catch him up, or to overtake him and get between the Royalists and Nantwich. They could not move as fast as Capel, and fearing that ambushes may be set for them, Brereton decided to march to Nantwich the long way round. His fear of ambushes may be down to the fact that he had captured some of Capel's Welsh scouts and had interrogated them. He therefore changed direction and headed southeast towards Market Drayton passing the two villages of Ash Magna and Ash Parva on his left, therefore seemingly travelling down what is now the A41.

The Earl of Denbigh, when he wrote about this action criticized Brereton for this decision, and it certainly seems strange, as it is such a long diversion. Because the Royalists had headed for Nantwich by the direct route, they marched the eleven miles towards Nantwich very quickly, arriving at Acton early in the afternoon. As the front of the Royalists army arrived, the rest forming up further back out of sight of the town, two companies of infantry and some dragoons came out of Nantwich to meet them. The Royalists being fired upon took refuge in Acton church. They also took up positions in the churchyard and Deerfold House from which they could fire upon any approaching Parliamentarians. The Parliamentarians, realizing that they would not be able to achieve anything, retreated back into Nantwich.

The main problem for the defenders in Nantwich was that most of their forces were not there, being with Brereton, by this time at Market Drayton where they stopped to eat before continuing their long march.

Drayton mentioned in a pamphlet on the Wem attack.

Description of the Wem ditch from Garbet's History of Wem.

The Royalists tried another assault on the other side of town. The defenders again sallied out to meet them, and initially were doing very well, but a party of horse arrived and they retreated back behind their defences. The garrison decided to stay inside the town, and fire upon anyone who came near. This meant that there was a stand-off, the two sides shooting at each other for the rest of the daylight. While all this was going on, Capel's army plundered what they could from around the town.

All that night the defenders stood guard at the defences. Overnight, Brereton's force marched another thirteen miles to Nantwich. According to their own press, they did not march the quick way north through Audlem, but went via Norton-in-Hales, and Bearstone to

61

Woore, presumably to come upon the town on the other side. Because of this, they did not arrive until dawn on Tuesday 17th.

Unfortunately, having marched well over twenty miles, they discovered that Capel and his Royalists had heard of his approach and already marched the eleven miles back to Whitchurch arriving at about the same time as Brereton's relieving force arrived from Market Drayton. There seemed to be no doubt now what Capel's actual target was. Whether by luck or sound military judgement, he had found himself in the fortunate position of being able to march back the way he came with no opposition, so after his army stopped to eat and rest for three or four hours, later that morning they marched the ten miles to Wem arriving early in the afternoon. It would be worth considering the state of Wem at this time. Brereton and Middleton had drawn out almost all the troops, leaving about three hundred in the garrison. The Reverend Richard Baxter states that the defences were still quite slight. He stated that that the ditch was **"little bigger than such as husbandmen enclose their grounds with, and this not finished."** He also stated that the gates had not yet been attached to the posts, having no hinges. The defenders were made up of Colonel Mytton and some of his regiment including some small artillery, along with about eighty of the townspeople that they had persuaded to take arms, but without ever having shot a musket.

The Birmingham archaeology evaluation (Project number PN1578) which was carried out when the **"Saxon Fields"** development was being considered at Wem in 2007 found ditches in the approximate location expected, and these are considered to be evidence of the 1643 fortifications. They are considerably wider than Baxter suggests. This may well be because when he was there, the fortifications were at an early stage, but they would have had a rampart and a palisade on the inside. No evidence for either of these was found, but the ditch was still visible in the fields around Wem until comparatively recently, and the line of parts of it can be seen on Victorian maps of the town.

Brereton now realized what Capel was up to, whether by design or not. He immediately ordered a march towards Wem, but his forces, having arrived at Nantwich after marching a total of about thirty miles, all during the evening or night since midnight on Saturday refused to move any further asking for a day of rest, which he was forced to grant. Wem was given up as lost. The Royalists started their attack on Wem that afternoon. They approached the walls holding improvised shields made of wood and straw. They could only attack on one side, because the rest of the low-lying fields were waterlogged.

The defenders managed to repulse this first attack. Denbigh in his report praised the local townspeople for sticking to the walls while being attacked by an army of nearly four thousand. Many Royalists had been killed by the time that Capel's men ceased their attack at about seven o'clock in the evening.

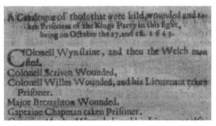

The published casualty list from the attack on Wem

One notable casualty was Colonel William Wyn of Llanvar in Denbighshire, commanding a regiment of about seven hundred Welsh infantry. According to which report is read, the Welsh either fled, or could not be urged to attack any more once their commander had been killed. That was the end of the attack for that day.

Overnight, the defenders could see the camp fires of the Royalists in the surrounding fields. Very early the next morning, Wednesday 18th, having had their rest, the Parliamentarian army set off from Nantwich to march the twenty miles to relieve the siege of Wem. They went back by a quicker route, as they were at Prees Heath by the time that they received news from Wem.

Meanwhile, on this second day of the siege, the Royalist forces were having trouble with their artillery. They started their bombardment at about eight o'clock in the morning, but things were not going their way. Their large mortar fired once, but the shot failed to explode. On the second it broke its carriage which effectively put it out of action. They attacked several times up to about mid-day.

At that point, intelligence came to Capel, who, it was said, was commanding from the Soulton Road where he sat on his horse smoking his pipe. He heard that Brereton and Middleton's force was approaching, so he ordered that the attackers should withdraw and head back towards Shrewsbury. There is a suggestion contained in a few histories of the attack on Wem, that the women in the town helped in its defence, and as there were so few soldiers this seems entirely possible, despite Denbigh calling the extra defenders **"Townsmen"**. The following rhyme is often quoted, but I have not been able to find out any contemporary source for it, the earliest mention I have found being in Garbet's history of Wem published in 1818 as an **"old rhyme"**. I may, of course, simply be missing a contemporary reference.

> The women of Wem, and a few musketteers
> Beat the lord Capel, and all his cavaliers.

Quote from Garbet's History of Wem

One Parliamentarian pamphlet states that a single cannon shot from the defenders killed fifty of the Royalists. If that was true, then the defenders must have been using **"grape shot"**, loading the cannon with musket balls or similar small pieces of metal that would have splayed out. Another casualty was Sir Thomas Scriven, who had been the governor of Whitchurch before it had fallen in May, who was mortally wounded.

Brereton and Middleton's account praised both sides, calling the Royalists **"Courageous"**. Having marched from Wem, the Royalists needed to get all their troops and equipment, apparently involving over one hundred carts back to Shrewsbury. Needing to protect their very large baggage train while it headed for the town, they left a force at the best defensible point, the bridge over the River Roden near Lee Brockhurst, to delay the enemies' pursuit. The two sides exchanged fire for a while, but the night approaching, at around midnight, the Royalists left the bridge, either because the force of Parliamentarians coming against them had overwhelmed them, or because it had left enough time for the rest of the army to get back to Shrewsbury.

Some of Brereton and Middleton's force followed them for a while, but gave up fearing ambush in the dark. The Parliamentarians gathered everything of use from the area where the fight had taken place and retreated into Wem. The result had been an overwhelming defeat for the Royalists. Wem had withstood an attack by a fair-sized army. The death toll was relatively small for the Parliamentarian side, in total less than ten including Colonel Marrow. On the other hand, the Royalist toll was heavier; three Colonels, a Major, five Captains, six carts of dead taken away and thirty more left on the ground.

Leaving a strengthened garrison at Wem the next day, Brereton's forces, on the way back to Nantwich stopped at Whitchurch. It was said that they demanded three hundred pounds to prevent the army from plundering it.

Two footnotes come out of this, both contained in the Wem Parish Register. On Friday 27th Colonel Wynne was buried, and on Saturday 4th November one John Rosseter, a **"cannoneer"** who was wounded at Wem was also buried.

Although the town of Market Drayton was not directly attacked at this point it would be worth considering all the troop movements that had occurred at this time. Friday 15th September, Brereton's troops arrived and camped around the town, including the surrounding villages. They stay, attempting to recruit more troops for a week. Possibly while they were there, they were attacked by a force from Shrewsbury. A week after they left, the Nantwich Trained Bands arrived for the night with some artillery. Also, on the night of Thursday 16th October, Brereton's force stopped to eat. Most of this would probably have not had much effect on the town itself, as the troops were outside it, but after it was attacked previously it must have been a worrying time for the inhabitants.

6 The Second Battle of Nantwich

September 1643

The Duke of Ormonde

In September a cessation of arms in Ireland was agreed. This left a large number of unnecessary troops. The commander in Ireland, The Duke of Ormonde, being firmly on the side of the King, began negotiations to start shipping them towards North Wales or Chester to join with his Majesty's forces. The Council of Ireland had long since been requesting victuals, money, clothing and armaments, but they had not been forthcoming. This meant that the troops that were to be sent home were ill-equipped, poorly paid and under-supplied.

October 1643

Ormonde wrote to the Archbishop of York in North Wales and Orlando Bridgeman in Chester to try and ensure that there would be clothing, arms and money waiting for the returning English troops when they arrived. The fear was that because these troops had never been tested as to whether they supported King or Parliament, that Parliament would make them a better offer.

November 1643

However, before any troops embarked, Brereton moved into North Wales. On Tuesday 7th the Cheshire forces joined with some from Lancashire and marched across the border. This force consisted of five infantry companies, three or four troops of cavalry and three or four companies of dragoons from Cheshire, along with five infantry companies, one or two cavalry troops and one or two companies of dragoons from Lancashire, and about two hundred infantry and one cavalry troop belonging to Sir Thomas Middleton.

Market Drayton's Civil War

On the following day they took the bridge at Holt, and then the town, but not at this point the Castle, which was garrisoned for the King. Leaving a good force in the town to besiege the castle, the main body of troops then marched on to Wrexham where they spent that night.

Brereton now had troops at Tarvin, North Wales and on the Wirral, effectively surrounding Chester. By this time, the ships had arrived in Ireland, and preparations were well underway to transport the first part of the force. On Friday 11th, they were waiting for good weather to transport this first part, which consisted of three thousand infantry. The officers all took an oath of loyalty, but it was sensibly decided to leave the troops' oaths until they had embarked. On the same day, Parliamentary forces consisting of nine troops of horse and two small foot companies under Brereton's command marched from Wrexham and faced Hawarden Castle. It was so under-supplied, that upon Brereton's summons it was surrendered.

Brereton stayed to supervise the repair and re-supply of the castle, while Sir Thomas Middleton returned to Wrexham, a muster having previously being called for the following Monday.

Sir Edward Nicholas

The following day, Sunday 12th, Royalists forces issued out of Chester and attacked the garrison at Tarvin. The action was fairly inconclusive, reinforcements coming from the garrison at Cholmondeley forced the Royalists back into the city.

Having been informed of Brereton's incursions, Sir Edward Nicholas wrote to Prince Rupert to hasten the dispatch of Lord Byron to the area. The following day, Monday 13th, the King himself wrote to Rupert to reinforce the issue. Middleton held his muster at Wrexham that day, to raise forces to fight against **"four thousand bloody Irish rebels"** and given their first opportunity, the men of Wales loyal to the Parliament started to arrive to increase the Parliament's forces. Brereton had received intelligence at some point in the previous few days that eleven Bristol ships and fifteen Wexford barques had arrived at Dublin on Tuesday

7th to transport the Royalist troops over, and he wrote to the Speaker of the House, Sir William Lenthall on Wednesday 15th to request that Essex's army be looking in his direction.

Sir Michael Earnley

Meanwhile, the convoy of ships containing the Royalist army from Dublin was finally under sail. They arrived at Mostyn in Flintshire on Saturday 18th, and started to disembark. The troops were made up of the regiments of Sir Michael Earnley, Sir Fulk Hunckes, Colonel Richard Gibson, part of Colonel Robert Byron's regiment (under Sir Francis Butler), and two hundred firelocks under Captain Thomas Sandford. These were from the army in Leinster. At this point, Brereton was still at Hawarden with the main Parliamentary force at Wrexham, and Holt Castle was still holding out. At some point around this time, Brereton left Hawarden, leaving a garrison of one hundred and twenty men in the castle.

On Monday 20th, a part of the force that had landed at Mostyn arrived and surrounded Hawarden. The following day, Lord Byron left Oxford to head for Chester with a thousand cavalry and three hundred infantry. On Wednesday 22nd, the commanders of the Parliamentary garrison of Wem wrote to the Earl of Denbigh, as they had started to panic because of the two different Royalist forces heading for the area. The auxiliary troops that

Lord Byron

they had from Cheshire had now left, leaving a very small garrison. By this time, Lord Byron was at Evesham, and by the following day was near Chipping Norton.

Brereton and Middleton, who were still recruiting in North Wales, now started making preparations to leave the area. They fell back on Holt. Friday 24th saw the artillery train leaving to travel back to Nantwich. On Sunday, the rest of Brereton's forces started the march back home, the Lancashire forces heading for their own county. The combination of the large force from Ireland, and the presence of the Earl of Newcastle near

Cheshire's eastern border had persuaded him that he would be better off in Nantwich, having raised all the men he could at that point from North Wales.

That same day, once again the commanders at Wem wrote desperately, this time to the Earl of Essex to try to get relief. On Monday 29th, Lord Byron arrived with his thirteen hundred men at Shrewsbury and was commissioned as Field Marshall General of Cheshire, Shropshire, and North Wales.

December 1643

The following Sunday, the 3rd, Hawarden Castle was surrendered by the Parliamentarian defenders. They were allowed to leave and promised safe passage back to Wem and Nantwich, but the Welsh defenders who headed home towards Wrexham were attacked by Welsh Royalists who killed and injured many of them. On Monday 4th, a further fifteen hundred troops from Ireland landed at Neston on the Wirral, which were Henry Warren's regiment and Robert Byron with the remaining part of his. They immediately marched to Chester.

Tuesday 5th saw the first part of Brereton's troops arrive back at Nantwich with the commander of Hawarden's garrison, a Mr. Ince. Parliament noted at this time that Sir William Brereton was in need of recruits, and money to pay and supply them. They granted him an excise on salt produced in Cheshire to not exceed a halfpenny a gallon.

Wednesday 6th, Lord Byron arrived in Chester. Mytton and the Wem forces, short of supplies continued to try and extract anything they could from that part of Shropshire around their garrison. A letter from Mrs. Susannah Dicken dated Thursday 7th in the State Papers records that the Parliamentarians under Mytton, Mackworth, Lloyd and Hunt plundered everything from a house in Hodnet. Mytton's letter to Parliament requesting arms in order to raise more troops was read in Parliament on Monday 11th. Lord Byron's army, which the Parliamentarian propagandists were now calling the **"Irish"** army prepared to march from Chester for the Nantwich campaign on Tuesday 12th. According to reports, it consisted of four thousand infantry and a thousand cavalry.

Market Drayton's Civil War

The first port of call was Beeston Castle the next day. A small force of Captain Sandford's firelocks surprised the castle by getting unseen into the inner ward just before dawn. It was surrendered without a fight. The castle contained large amounts of booty that local Parliamentarian sympathisers had sent in for safety along with half a year's supplies for the castle. The garrison commander, Captain Steele marched with his arms and colours back towards Nantwich, but was thrown into prison the moment he arrived for surrendering.

The Royalists now definitely had the upper hand. The Parliamentarian forces had all retreated back into their garrisons, Beeston had fallen, and the large Royalist force swelled with the troops returned from Ireland was heading towards Nantwich, which was immediately placed on alert. The following Sunday, the 17th, hearing that Royalist troops were at Burford, one of Nantwich's commanders, the Scottish Major Lothian, who had performed so gallantly at the first battle of Nantwich, took some cavalry and infantry towards the village. The cavalry arrived first, and immediately encountered some Royalist cavalry. Before the infantry arrived, they had charged into a melee. Once the infantry arrived, the Royalists fled, but not before capturing Lothian, leaving the Parliamentarians without one of their best professional soldiers.

From this time forward, Royalists gave continual alarms to Nantwich. They spread their army into all the villages on the west side of the Cheshire town, plundering everything they could from the area as they went. The following Friday, they crossed the River Weaver and started to plunder villages to the south of Nantwich, around Audlem, Hankelow and Bruerton.

That Saturday, the 23rd, occurred a shocking event, that nowadays we would certainly call a war-crime. It was considered thus in the seventeenth century as well, and was amongst the evidence prepared for King Charles' trial, although in the end it was not needed as he refused to plead. East of Nantwich, the Royalist troops faced Crewe Hall, and perceiving it garrisoned, they passed onto Barthomley. About twenty local men took to the church for safety. When the door was forced and the Royalists gained access to the church, the defenders retreated up into the steeple. The attackers piled rush matting and benches below them and set light to it, in order to smoke them out. Having nowhere to go, the local men surrendered.

Once down from the steeple, twelve of them had their throats cut, several more being wounded. A letter from Sir John Byron to the Marquess of Newcastle stated **"The rebels had possessed themselves of a church, at Barthomley, but we presently beat them forth of it, and I put them all to the sword: Which I find to be the best way to proceed with these kind of people, for, mercy to them is cruelty."** I have only seen this letter, which was apparently intercepted by Brereton, quoted in a Parliamentary source.

On Christmas Day, a Monday, The Royalists continued encircling Nantwich, plundering as they went. They sacked Sandbach, but encountered a force of Parliamentarians. It was reported that these were Lancashire troops under Brereton. The Parliamentarian forces were forced to withdraw, being heavily outnumbered, and some sources say that it was a remnant of those that took refuge in Barthomley Church. However, as one of the church defenders had been the son of the vicar, and several others shared the surname Steele it seems unlikely. Having fallen back to Middlewich, on St. Stephen's Day the Royalists encountered them again and defeated them in the second battle of Middlewich.

The Lancashire Parliamentary forces headed back towards Manchester. The garrison at Northwich was now abandoned by Brereton. The Royalists now had Brereton's forces cooped up in Nantwich, Wem, and a few small houses. Things were looking bad for the Parliamentarians.

On Thursday 28th, the Royalists again faced Crewe Hall. They attacked, and there was a fair amount of bloodshed, but in the end the defenders surrendered through lack of ammunition, and no hope of being relieved. Having mopped up the pockets of resistance around the town, the besieging forces started to close in, and on Saturday 30th the siege began in earnest.

January 1643/4

On the first couple of days of the month, the Royalists strengthened their siege by taking in the last few Parliamentarian houses that had small garrisons, finishing up with Acton Church. The garrison were allowed to leave in the clothes they stood up in, with no other equipment, and told to go to Wem, not Nantwich. By the end of the first week, they had started to dig siege works, and had planted their cannons on all sides. Before they started their attack, a letter was sent into the town requesting their surrender. However, it was answered verbally at the gates in a very loud voice so that the defending soldiers could hear. The answer was that they would not at which a great cheer rose up from the defenders.

On Friday 6th, Prince Rupert was made Captain-General of the forces in Cheshire, Lancashire, Worcester, Shropshire and North Wales. He was not in the area at this time, arriving in mid-February, so he was not a part of the Nantwich campaign. By this time, of course, the garrison at Wem were feeling very vulnerable. An anonymous letter to Sir Francis Ottley on the next day detailed that there were less than seven hundred troops there, but that a Captain Ward had ridden for Manchester to try and persuade the troops there to come to their aid.

On Tuesday 10th, late in the evening, the besiegers finished placing a very large cannon near Deerfold House. They started firing. The first shots were not greatly effective, setting fire to a rick, but this was quenched by the quick work of the women of the town. At this point was recorded the first casualty, John Davenport's daughter. Supplying the besiegers with weapons and gunpowder would have been a top priority in this situation. A ship had been sent to the Chester Royalists from Bristol, but the Master and officers of the ship took it to Liverpool instead, which was being held for Parliament.

Therefore, the besiegers were left short of supplies. For this reason, a convoy of carts from Chester was sent to Shrewsbury, to take on supplies there. The Royalists must have felt very secure with their large presence in the area, as, when they were camped near Ellesmere on the way back on Thursday 12th, they were successfully surprised by a force from Wem led by Colonel Mytton. The commanders were all taken, including the governor of Chester, who was Lord Byron's uncle, Sir Nicholas Byron. Along with him were captured the Sergeant-Major General of the horse, Sir Richard Willis and one major, four captains and a hundred inferior officers and troops. In one fell swoop, Mytton had simultaneously solved his supply problem, and cut the Nantwich besiegers off from their arms and ammunition, which were now on their way to Wem instead.

Sir Thomas Fairfax

Thursday and Friday, the 12th and 13th saw the defenders sally out from Nantwich, stealing some carriages containing supplies, and also to burn down buildings outside the defences that were being used by the besiegers. At this point, word came to Lord Byron that Sir Thomas Fairfax was on his way with a force to relieve the town. Byron wrote to Prince Rupert on Saturday 14th that he had sent some troops to Newcastle-under-Lyme where they had encountered a part of his force.

Monday 15th, Captain Thomas Sandford, the commander of the firelocks, and the man who took Beeston Castle, took it upon himself to start sending letters into Nantwich. He claimed that this was because he had friends in the town that he was trying to convince to persuade the commanders to surrender. Whatever the reason, these letters are full of threats to **"batter, burn and storm"** the town. Tuesday 16th saw another attack on the besieger's trenches from the town. They killed some of the besiegers, and brought some clothes, arms and ammunition back into the town.

Also on this day, Ormonde in Dublin wrote to Byron to let him know that another thousand infantry and one hundred and sixty cavalry were almost ready to embark. Also on the same day, Byron himself wrote into the town, stating that he had heard that a former summons had been suppressed and not communicated to the town. George Booth sent the answer that Byron's claims were untrue, and that they would not give up the town. On Wednesday 17th, the artillery barrage started in earnest. On that day, over one hundred cannonballs were sent into the town. Orders were issued for an attack to be mounted at several places the next day. The attack on Wickstede's sconce was to be led by Sandford's firelocks with scaling ladders. Thursday 18th just before dawn the attack began. A barrage of artillery was followed by the ordered attacks. This did not have the desired effect, however, and there were various reports of casualties amongst the attackers, but they all agree that Captain Thomas Sandford was among the dead. Those inside the town were by this time getting short of food.

Market Drayton's Civil War

Sir George Booth

The snow, which had been on the ground had now started melting, and the Royalists, fearing that the river rising would cut part of their army off, on Tuesday 24th, started moving their forces back across the river towards Acton. As they retreated, some forces from the town attacked their rear, and took some cannons. By this time, Brereton had met with Fairfax in Manchester, and their force of eight thousand infantry and cavalry, mostly from Derbyshire, were heading towards Nantwich.

On Thursday 25th, the Parliamentarians arrived and faced the Royalists near Acton. I will leave the description of the battle up to the victor Sir Thomas Fairfax who seems to describe it as a close run thing. **"I marched from Manchester towards Nantwich, to relieve that town with 2500 foot, and twenty eight troops of horse. The enemies forces were above 3000 foot, and 1800 horse. The first encounter we had was with a party of theirs upon the Forest of Delamere, where about thirty were taken prisoners. About six miles further they maintained a passage against us with about 200 men. I caused some foot and dragoons to be drawn out to force it, which by God's assistance they did in half an hours space, and there took a major and some prisoners. Having advanced some two miles further, we found a good body of them planted around Acton Church a mile from Nantwich; we drew up within cannon shot which some-times played upon us, but without hurt God be thanked. We there understood that the Lord Byron who had besieged the town on both sides of the River, was prevented by overflowing of the water from joining with that part at Acton Church, but heard that he was taking a compass to get over the river to join with it. We resolved to fall upon that party at the Church before he should get up to it, but staying to bring up our rear and carriages, we gave him time to obtain that he sought for. Then we resolved to make way with pioneers through the hedges, and then to march to the town to relieve it, and to add some more force to ourselves to enable better to fight with them; but being a little advanced on our march, they told me the enemy was close upon the rear, so facing about two regiments being Colonel Holland's, and Colonel Booth's, I marched not far before we came to be engaged with the greatest part of their army.**

Then the other part presently after assaulted our front; there Sir William Brereton and Colonel Ashton did very good service, and so did Colonel Lambert and Major Copley with the horse. They were once in great danger, but that they being next to the Town were assisted by forces which came to their succor in due time. We in the other wing were in as great distress, but that the horse commanded by Sir William Fairfax did expose themselves to great dangers to encourage the foot, though capable of little service in those narrow Lanes. Yet it pleased God after two hours fight they were forced by both Wings to retreat to the Church, where they were caught in a Trap."

Thus it was that the Royalist army, bolstered with the forces returned from Ireland were defeated. Lord Byron roughly agrees with how the battle went, blaming the fact that it happened at all on the Earl of Newcastle, who he had previously written to in an attempt to get him to attack Fairfax on his march. On the same day as the battle, Prince Rupert announced his intention to take up his command and make his headquarters in Shrewsbury. If he had arrived earlier, the outcome may have been somewhat different.

On Saturday 27th, Nantwich market started up again, and Burghall records that there were **"Plenty of all necessaries at reasonable rates."** Two days later, Thomas Steel, who surrendered Beeston Castle to Captain Sandford and his firelocks was executed for the event. Two days after that, a thanksgiving service was held, although this was not in the church, as they had been holding some prisoners there and "it was not yet cleansed".

7 Prince Rupert's Cavalry Charge!

February 1643/4

Thursday 1st saw the Parliamentarians begin to mop up the Royalist garrisons that had been left from Byron's activities around Nantwich. They surrounded Crewe Hall.

During the previous month, Prince Rupert had been given command of our area. However, at that point he was in the south of the country. He now started his preparations to take up his command, intending to use Shrewsbury as his base. On 25th January he had written to Sir Francis Ottley requesting that the castle be supplied for his arrival, and that rooms were prepared for a magazine, having already sent fifty barrels of gunpowder to the town. One of the chief Royalist concerns in Shrewsbury at the time was that there was still a strong Parliamentary faction in the town. A plot had recently been uncovered, and a man hanged, with more awaiting judgement.

After Nantwich, seven hundred of the Anglo-Irish army had already deserted and joined Brereton. Therefore, although a large party had escaped after the battle, the Royalists were very insecure. On Friday 2nd, Sir John Mennes, Rupert's man in Shrewsbury, wrote to him detailing the state of the town. He complained that the council were not telling him anything and that all the troops were ready to desert due to lack of pay and victuals. Mennes himself was planning to quit the town due to the obstinacy of the townsfolk and lack of money.

On the same day, Sir Richard Newport also wrote to Rupert from the town, confirming much of what Mennes stated. He requested that a suitable officer be sent to re-supply the castle before Rupert or the gunpowder arrived. Again, on the same day, Sir Francis Ottley wrote to the prince, but in more positive terms stating that a fit place had been found for the ammunition until such time as the castle could be repaired, which was currently underway. He also mentioned the execution and imprisonment of the plotters.

Three days later, Monday 5th, the Nantwich Parliamentarians finally attacked Crewe Hall, and it quickly surrendered on condition that the defenders could march away without their weapons. Some of them arrived at Nantwich and changed sides.

The next day, Tuesday 6th, Rupert's forces left Oxford to head towards Shrewsbury, getting as far as Chipping Norton on that day. Rupert's journal describes this as **"The Shrewsbury March"**. Rupert joined them there the next day, and they marched on.

Colonel Robert Clive's signature

On Wednesday 7th, Francis Billingsley wrote from Bridgnorth to Ottley, mentioning a quarrel that had taken place between a Captain Bennet and Colonel Clive, during which Bennet was seriously wounded. This is interesting to us for no other reason than that this is Robert Clive of Styche, who later became a member of the Shropshire committee for Parliament. It was the heavy Parliamentary presence in the area, and the dreadful reputation of Clive which reputedly gave rise to the following rhyme, although I have not found a contemporary reference for it:

A contemporary woodcut of Prince Rupert

"From Wem and from Wych and from Clive of the Styche, good Lord deliver us."

This same day, Doddington Hall near Nantwich was surrendered by the Royalists, and again many of the defenders headed into Nantwich. While this was going on, the next wave of Royalist troops arrived from Ireland, some landing at Beaumaris and the rest nearer Chester. These were the troops of Colonel Broughton, Colonel Tillier, Sir Fulk Hunckes and five other troops of horse.

Thursday 8th saw Rupert arrive at Worcester. On Friday 9th, Sir Michael Woodhouse wrote from Shrewsbury that the town Marshall had let one of the Parliamentary plotters escape, and he should have been sentenced to death in the escapee's place. However, they were waiting until the prince arrived, as there was too much ill-feeling in the town.

On Saturday 10th, Sir John Mennes at Shrewsbury wrote to inform Rupert that the seventeen hundred newly landed men were on their way to Shrewsbury, and that the prince needed to order Shrewsbury to provide for them, as Chester could not afford to keep them.

Ottley wrote to the prince on Monday 12th, warning him that Mytton and the Stafford garrison had marched to Longford (near Newport) to group together to try and head him off. Rupert was only accompanied by six hundred horse at this point. Meanwhile, Brereton was in London on Tuesday 13th being given great thanks for his services by the House of Commons.

On Wednesday 14th, King Charles wrote to Sir Francis Ottley, requesting a loan of thirty pounds. It was in the form of a printed letter with the **"thirty pounds"** written in by hand. On Thursday 15th, Mytton, contrary to Ottley's expectations was at Bangor-on-dee where he took the bridge. He then went on to plunder around Oswestry. The same day, Brereton was in Parliament, informing them of the cruel practices of the **"Irish"** army with Lord Byron.

They formed a committee to consider the security of the counties of Cheshire, Lancashire, Staffordshire, Shropshire and how to prevent the arrival of more troops from Ireland and how to prevent any devastation or spoil from the arrival of Prince Rupert. Prince Rupert arrived at Bridgnorth on Friday 15th.

On Friday 16th, the Nantwich forces carried on their process of mopping up small pockets of Royalist resistance and took Adlington House near Congleton. Rupert finally arrived in Shrewsbury on Monday 19th.

Meanwhile, in Parliament on the following day, Brereton and Middleton were requested to write down what men, arms, ammunition and money they needed, and also for their intelligence of the whereabouts of the Lancashire, and Sir Thomas Fairfax's troops. On that same day, Lord Byron informed Prince Rupert that the newly-landed troops were on their way to Shrewsbury, and that Rupert should send someone to Oswestry to take charge of them in Shropshire from the cavalry that were convoying them through Cheshire. Byron pointed out that there were no resources to keep them in Chester. He also mentioned that Lord Brereton and his family (not to be confused with Sir William), were being besieged in Biddulph Hall in

Staffordshire, offering to cause a diversion of the Parliamentarian troops if the prince wished to stage a relief. However, Biddulph fell the next day, mainly due to the lack of water and the entire garrison was carried as prisoners to Stafford increasing the Parliamentarian control of the area.

The same day Wednesday 21st, Byron again wrote from Chester to Rupert at Shrewsbury, having not yet heard of the surrender. He again suggested the diversionary tactics from the previous letter. He also gave a report of the progression of the latest recruits from Ireland, who at this point had got as far as Ruthin. He requested that they be given new uniforms, shoes and stockings, along with regular pay, to prevent them from mutinying.

An interesting aside at this point is a note from the King's court at Oxford, where the King is commanding the paying of Francis Walker of Shropshire for the casting of cannons and cannonballs. Ironworking in the county did not start with the 18th century Iron Bridge!

Regardless of the arrival of the troops from Ireland, or perhaps unaware of it, on Thursday 22nd Mytton and the troops from Wem crossed their path. They passed Buildwas bridge by pretending that they were the King's forces, took Sir Thomas Eyton's house at Eyton, and then attacked and defeated the guards at Buildwas on the way back.

The following day, detailed in an anonymous letter out of Shrewsbury, Major Legge was ordered by Prince Rupert to take six troops of horse and one hundred foot to have a look at Wem. Mytton, being away, the defenders did not send out any troops to face them, and the Royalists managed to take twenty to thirty loads of hay. It is not clear when, but Rupert is reported to have said about Wem, **"It was a crow's nest that would not afford each of his men a piece of bread."** I have not found an original source for this, but it does seem to have been his impression, not bothering about it while attacking forces in other places. There is an interesting detail given in a letter at this point, that demonstrates how information sometimes passed from one side to the other. After the battle at Nantwich, many of the troops from Ireland had defected to the Parliamentarians at Wem. Three of them had re-defected and returned to the Royalists at Shrewsbury, giving intelligence of the disposition of the town. The build-up of the Royalist army was continuing, and the letter goes on to state how this was going. Rupert was still waiting for the arrival of his infantry from Oxford, with two hundred barrels of gunpowder.

That day, the troops from Ireland had arrived in Shrewsbury, adding fifteen hundred. Lord Byron was also said to have arrived with his troops. The upshot of this was that Rupert could count seven to eight thousand men, plus three thousand loyal to the prince stationed in Lancashire.

On Saturday 24th, Sir Thomas Fairfax wrote to the Earl of Essex mentioning all the Royalist houses that were taken while he was in Cheshire, but stating that he was now to march towards Yorkshire.

On Monday 26th, Parliament recorded the wants of the Parliament commanders in our area. Sir William Brereton listed fifteen hundred muskets, swords, bandoliers and head pieces, and thirty barrels of gunpowder and five thousand pounds. Middleton listed forty barrels of gunpowder, three hundred-weight of match-cord, two hundred carbines, eight drakes, and two petards. It was also recorded that twenty barrels of gunpowder and one ton of match be sent to Col. Mytton, along with one thousand pounds.

MD Document 27

On Wednesday 28th, Mytton left Wem with forty horse and travelled to Nantwich. The next day, Sir Vincent Corbet wrote from Moreton Corbet to Sir Thomas Dallison serving with the prince. He was writing to inform the prince of the Parliamentarians movements, and stated that his spy in Wem had reported that Mytton was away and that only one hundred horse were left there, and that the foot were fearful that they could not defend it if attacked. Others of the Wem horse, three broken troops of Mytton, Captain Lloyd and Captain Mackworth were quartered in Ightfield, where they had barricaded the street ends with upturned carts. In the moated Ightfield Hall itself were quartered eighty dragoons. Corbet also reported that there were five troops of Sir Thomas Fairfax's horse due to quarter that night at Market Drayton.

A general muster had been issued for the area around Prees for all eligible men to come in to join up. Rupert's build-up of forces did not escape the attentions of the Parliamentarians. That same Thursday, the Earl of Denbigh, at Coventry, wrote to the Earl of Essex warning him of the fact and that the prince would raise even greater forces if he was not allowed to oppose them. That day also saw an event that would later take Rupert and his army away from Shropshire for a while even though it was many miles away. Sir John Meldrum for the Parliament, started to besiege Newark in Nottinghamshire.

March 1643/4

For the moment though, Rupert was concentrating on our area. Possibly

Sir William Fairfax

taking Corbet's intelligence into account, on Friday 1st he took some cavalry to have a close look at Wem, before returning to Shrewsbury. The London-based newspaper, Mercurius Civicus reported that Rupert summoned the town to surrender but that Mytton replied **"That he would keep the Town for the King and Parliament: but if Prince Rupert would please to stay, he would come forth and discourse with him about it"**. However, it must be borne in mind that this is Parliament propaganda; it also stated that Mytton attacked and took sixteen of Rupert's troopers prisoner, and that Rupert was forced to retreat. In Parliament, it seemed that Mytton's requests for arms, powder and money was being dealt with. They ordered twenty barrels of powder and a ton of match to be sent, and set about ways of providing one thousand pounds including selling off confiscated Royalist goods.

MD Documents 28, 29, 30, 31, 32 & 33

On the evening of Monday 4th, Rupert dispatched five to six hundred foot from Shrewsbury towards Market Drayton, where he had heard that seven hundred Parliamentary cavalry were quartered under the command of Sir William Fairfax. John Lewis, the editor of Captain Francis Sandford's memoranda states that these Royalist infantry were most probably equally split between the regiments of Henry Tillier and Robert Broughton, and therefore from the part of the army in Ireland who had landed in early February. The Parliamentarian force seems to have been some of Sir Thomas Fairfax's cavalry, Sir William Fairfax's own and Colonel Mytton's. One original source states that Denbigh was there with his, but this is unconfirmed by others and seems unlikely. The fact that Sir William Fairfax, a cousin of his more famous namesake was in charge has confused some writers, the name Fairfax leading them to claim that Sir Thomas was there, but this does not seem to be true, Sir Thomas being either in Lancashire or on his way to Yorkshire at this point. Prince Rupert, in his journal also states that it was only Mytton and Fairfax who were present.

Later that night Rupert himself set out with approximately eight hundred cavalry. Lewis has it that the probable make-up of this force was as follows: one hundred and forty of these were Rupert's Lifeguard under Sir Richard Crane, five hundred were Rupert's Regiment under Major William Legge, and one hundred and fifty troopers of Sir John Urry's Regiment. Early on the morning of Shrove Tuesday, the 5th, Rupert's cavalry overtook the infantry and they arrived at Market Drayton at about eight o'clock.

The view from Tyrley ridge towards Market Drayton

His sudden march was intended to surprise Fairfax's force, but a rider from Shrewsbury must have been sent out by the Parliamentary sympathisers there, as when he arrived, he found that Parliament's men were ready for his arrival, with Sir William Fairfax's cavalry formed up on Tyrley Heath, and the rest, Sir Thomas Fairfax's and Col. Mytton's, near Shifford's Bridge. Mercurius Aulicus stated that Sir William Fairfax advanced through Market Drayton to meet the prince but that they were beaten back through the town. It also mentions that there were only two Royalist troops in the initial attack, and Sandford confirms this by stating three hundred horse.

Therefore, it seems that Rupert's regiment was at this point a few miles behind with the infantry, and that this attack was probably carried out by the Prince with his Lifeguard and Sir John Urry's horse.

Having broken Fairfax's cavalry, Prince Rupert now chased the fleeing roundheads back towards the rest of their force, and if we accept all the sources that state that they charged **"through the town"**, the only sensible route either takes them up Great Hales Street or along the Newport Road, then along the High Street, turning right down Stafford Street towards Shifford's Bridge, where the rest of the roundheads were.

The 18th century replacement for the original Shifford's Bridge over which now runs the A53.

Seeing Rupert's approach, Fairfax's entire force retreated into the grounds of Tunstall Hall, and they drew a chain across the gate to prevent the cavalry charging straight in. Thus, a stalemate occurred until the rest of Rupert's force arrived, at which point, being heavily outnumbered and faced with infantry, the roundheads were forced to flee.

Rupert's cavalry chased them through Betton, Norton-in-Hales and Bearstone, back towards Nantwich. Although Mercurius Aulicus states that the escape route was towards Eccleshall, the others all agree that they headed back to Nantwich and the former route seems correct. As is usual with this sort of event, there are as many estimates of the casualties as there are sources. The estimate of Parliamentarians killed is between twenty two and one hundred and twenty. The numbers of prisoners taken varies between twelve and one hundred and forty.

The Crown, one of the few buildings to have survived from this period

Malbon's diary reported that a Captain Shipley was recorded as being taken prisoner by the Royalists, and he also stated that the rest of the Parliamentary soldiers returned safely to Nantwich. Fairfax had lost one hundred horses; he also lost one of his colours, which had 'For Reformation' as its motto. This battle must have been a terrifying sight for the people of Market Drayton. Having two forces of cavalry fighting through the town, the townsfolk must have barricaded themselves into their houses or hidden in doorways to avoid being trampled underfoot. Our original sources, only dealing with the military side of things do not report any civilian casualties as a result of this action. However, there are no burials recorded in the Parish Register between the 3rd and the 11th, so it seems unlikely that any of the people of the town were killed.

At least it wasn't market day when the town would have been full of people and traders. The Royalists, having spent the previous night marching, and the daytime fighting, set up camp at Market Drayton that night, Prince Rupert himself probably staying in one of the town inns, which he did in other places.

On the morning of Wednesday 6th, Prince Rupert's forces left Market

Drayton and marched back to Shrewsbury. He left after dinner, arriving back later in the day. It now being a week since the siege of Newark began, news had travelled fast, and the King wrote to Prince Rupert to move as fast as possible towards Newark with his army to relieve the town. At this point both Sir William Brereton and Thomas Middleton were in London about Parliament's business.

On Thursday 7th, it was recommended to the House of Commons by Sir Arthur Haselrigg that they both be sent **"into the country"** as the view was that their service there was necessary. Parliament also discussed the position of Wem, and whether to send relief. While all this was going on, Parliament were attempting to put a force together to counter the prince.

Sir John Gell

They ordered that two infantry regiments from Lancashire, five hundred of Sir John Gell's foot troops, six hundred from Cheshire, three hundred and fifty from Staffordshire and three hundred from Warwickshire should head for Shropshire to join with the three hundred already in Wem. They also ordered that two hundred Warwickshire cavalry, one hundred and fifty from Staffordshire, one hundred and fifty of Lord Grey's, three hundred from Lancashire besides those of Cheshire and all Lord Willoughby's to join with the two hundred in Wem.

All of these forces were to be commanded by the Earl of Denbigh. They obviously did not know of the defeat at Market Drayton, and that Col. Mytton's cavalry had been routed, presumably the two hundred they thought were at Wem. They wrote to Denbigh and all the other commanders involved, detailing these forces and included letters to all the other commanders involved. Therefore, Denbigh was ordered to relieve Wem.

As far as Parliament knew, Mytton was pinned down in a heavily royalist area, with the forces from Shrewsbury plundering right up to the town gates. Wem had very few forces and they felt that they could do nothing about it. Denbigh's only get-out clause was the statement that if any of the forces should fail to arrive, they desired him to go with the rest if he conceived the resulting force able to oppose the enemy.

On Sunday 10th, Prince Rupert travelled to Chirk Castle in Denbighshire on his way to Chester. He was now gathering forces for the Newark expedition. The following day, Rupert made a grand entrance into Chester. All the civic dignitaries were present in their official robes. The Mayor, Randle Holmes gave a speech in which he welcomed the prince. The prince, on the next day, Tuesday 11th, inspected the fortifications, but while he was there, an urgent message came from the King to urge him quickly to Newark. Newark was on the direct line of communication from the King at Oxford to York, and it was vital that it was held for the King. He dispatched Major Legge immediately to Shrewsbury to assemble the troops. He followed very shortly after.

Rupert immediately sent Broughton and Tillier's musketeers, totalling about a thousand men to Bridgnorth along with one humdred and twenty of Sir Fulke Hunke's men. In London, Parliament were still trying to get Brereton sent back to Cheshire. Prince Rupert rode back to Chirk trying to gather as many forces as he could for the Newark march.

The following day Denbigh wrote to Parliament that he had not managed to gather all the forces to relieve Wem yet and that it would probably be a fortnight before he could. Prince Rupert returned to Shrewsbury that day but the following day he rode to Bridgnorth to join his forces for the march east. Rupert's small army moved rapidly. On Saturday 16th he was at Wolverhampton, on Sunday at Lichfield. Monday 18th they got as far as Ashby de-la-Zouch.

On this day, Colonel Marrow gave an alarum to Nantwich and drove off many cattle. Brereton was sorely needed back in the area. That same day, Denbigh wrote with his latest excuse for not relieving Wem. He had received reports of the prince's army near Tamworth, and would not move into Shropshire for fear of being attacked. The following day, Parliament re-ordered Lord Willoughby's troops to join with Denbigh, but they diverted the Lancashire regiments that were meant for that expedition to Yorkshire.

By this time, Rupert had reached Remson in Leicestershire, the following day at Bingham. The day after that, much to the surprise of the Parliamentarian besiegers, who did not believe that Rupert could travel so fast, Sir John Meldrum's men were attacked and pushed back onto an island, Rupert capturing the bridges. He was therefore forced to surrender and the siege was raised. Rupert captured three thousand muskets, eleven brass cannons and two mortars. The Prince immediately marched west again.

8 Oswestry Falls

March 1643/4

On Saturday 23rd, Lord Denbigh was at Coventry, where he wrote to Fairfax that he could not relieve Wem as ordered by Parliament, as Newark was occupying his attentions. Wem was not being fully besieged, but Lord Byron was ensuring that the occupying Parliamentarians were keeping their heads down. In reality, Denbigh was having his own issues, mutinies amongst his army, and arguments with the Coventry Committee were the chief things keeping him stuck at Coventry.

The next day, sixteen miles south of Market Drayton near Wellington, Apley House, which had been garrisoned earlier in the month by the Parliamentarian Robert Charlton, was taken by the Royalists Colonel Ellis and Sir William Vaughan. Ten of the defending officers were taken prisoner, to be swapped for imprisoned Royalists later, the rest being allowed to march to Wem, with the exception that they allowed any of the soldiers that had served in Ireland to change sides.

March 1644

On Monday 25th, having heard the news of the Royalist attack, Colonel Mytton headed with a small force of five hundred from Wem to attempt to relieve the castle. However, by the time they reached the small Parliamentarian garrison at Longford House near Newport, Ellis and Vaughan had arrived. The two sides met, and Mytton was routed. The Royalists surrounded Longford House, and settled down to besiege it.

Denbigh marched from Coventry to Leicester, hoping to give some relief at Newark, not having heard that it had already fallen. Sir John Mennes at Shrewsbury wrote to inform Prince Rupert about this the following day. By this time, Rupert was on his journey back from Newark.

At this point also, Sir William Brereton was fulfilling his Parliamentary duties in London. Byron at Chester was taking advantage of his absence to start mopping up some of the smaller Parliamentary garrisons around him. Emrall fell on Wednesday 27th. Over the following couple of days, Hanmer, Fens and Betchfield suffered the same fate.

Parliament were keen to get Brereton back to Cheshire, and on Saturday 30th, they ordered that he presented a list of what was stopping his return. On the same day, Wem wrote to Denbigh that they were being besieged by Byron, and that they were getting desperate for his aid.

April 1644

Rupert arrived back in the county at Newport on Wednesday 3rd. Maybe due to this or maybe not, Longford House surrendered on the same day. He had brought with him a large amount of arms and artillery with powder and match in plentiful supply, and he arrived back at his base in Shrewsbury on the next day.

MD Document 34

On Sunday 7th, Byron sent out a raiding party to Audlem, where he took fourteen Parliamentary cavalry, but narrowly missed a convoy of ammunition heading towards Nantwich. On the same day, he wrote to the prince, urging him to now look towards Lancashire. In his letter, he advised Rupert that the best route from Shrewsbury would be via Whitchurch and then Market Drayton, presumably to avoid Brereton's garrison at Nantwich.

On Friday 12th, Parliament decided that the relief of Wem should be uppermost in their minds. They wrote letters to Lancashire, Cheshire, Warwickshire and Staffordshire for troops to join up with Denbigh to go for the relief of the Shropshire town. By this time, Denbigh was back from Leicester and on the following day he wrote to Parliament giving details of Rupert's movements and requesting orders and a commander to lead his forces. He wrote again on Monday 15th, stating that he needed cavalry before relieving Wem. In response to his requests, on Wednesday 17th they ordered four troops of horse from Lancashire to head for Shropshire, and also wrote to Denbigh stating that he could use Col. Barker's troop for the Wem trip.

The following day, Parliament awarded Mytton one hundred pounds and sent thanks for all the good work he was doing at Wem. On Good Friday, the 19th, they left Denbigh in no doubt as to what his main priority should be. They wrote, telling him that they would consider no other issues than the relief of Wem.

On Easter Monday 22nd, Rupert left with just his bodyguard to travel down to Oxford, arriving at Ludlow that day. Moving fast, he arrived in Evesham on Tuesday. That day, the committee at Nantwich wrote to Parliament requesting that Brereton be speeded north.

The following Sunday, the 28th, Denbigh wrote to Parliament, stating that he could not use Barker's cavalry, as against orders they had gone with Purefoy towards Gloucester. He asked Parliament to order Purefoy and Barker to follow him to Stafford, where he expected to be able to increase the size of his force.

On Tuesday 30th, Mytton wrote to Parliament in a last desperate letter. He stated that they now had no money or supplies and that Byron was aware of this. He stated that Parliament no longer needed to provide a governor, as Prince Rupert would take Wem very soon.

May 1644

On Wednesday 1st, Parliament wrote to Denbigh stating that they should not wait for Purefoy and Barker, and that they should immediately head for Wem.

That Sunday, Rupert left Oxford to head back towards Shrewsbury. By this time, Parliament had realised that Rupert's sights were set on leading a large army north. By the following day, Parliament had received Mytton's plea, and re-iterated their troop requests made earlier in a series of letters to the county committees.

On Tuesday 7th, Parliament finally received the Nantwich committee's letter that had been sent on April 23rd. They were, by this point, already preparing for this, and granting money, arms and armour for that purpose. Rupert had now reached Ludlow on his way back from Oxford.

A small force left Nantwich on Wednesday 8th for the Royalist garrison at Cholmondeley, near which they took five cavalrymen prisoner, having killed another. They took them back to Nantwich. On the same day, Rupert arrived back at Shrewsbury.

The next day, another Nantwich force headed for Cholmondeley, where they attempted to persuade the house to surrender. In this they failed, but they took back with them a flock of a hundred sheep and lambs, and some goods from an outhouse.

Denbigh finally prepared to leave Coventry on Friday 10th with a force of two thousand. The Lancashire committee had written telling him that they could not spare any troops because of the siege at Lathom. As an interesting aside, on the following day, no doubt by request, Prince Rupert wrote a letter to William Cotton of Bellaport, exempting him from any Royalist plundering. Although this is not a Market Drayton document, Bellaport is near Norton-in-Hales, so very close.

Denbigh wrote to Parliament on Tuesday 14th stating that their journey north had been delayed due to having to wait for some horses to lead the artillery, and because of a mutiny amongst Thomas Middleton's troops but that he had finally now marched towards Stafford. Parliament, having now realised that Prince Rupert was planning to travel with his army in Lancashire, changed their priorities. Instead of relieving Wem, they decided to abandon Shropshire's only Parliamentary garrison and ordered Denbigh to follow him.

Rupert left Shrewsbury on Thursday 16th having appointed a rendezvous at Knutsford, Byron leaving Chester with his forces on the same day to join with him. Meanwhile, at some point around this time, Colonel Mytton travelled to London to plead his case for Wem.

MD Documents 35, 36 & 37

On Saturday 18th, Prince Rupert followed Byron's advice and left Shrewsbury. According to the local diarists, they marched to Whitchurch and then to Market Drayton on the same day, but Rupert's recollections were different, stating that they marched to Whitchurch on the 18th, moving on to Market Drayton the next day. His army at this point is estimated at about eight thousand. The Lancashire committee wrote again to Denbigh on Sunday 19th, re-iterating that they could not send any troops.

On Monday 20th, one thousand troops from Nantwich marched towards Rupert's forces, but they did not meet and therefore the Parliamentarian troops retreated. By the end of the next day, the prince's army had reached Betley in Staffordshire and over the following two days they marched to

Market Drayton's Civil War

Knutsford and away from our area.

Moreton Corbet

Colonel Mytton returned from London on Friday 24th having failed in his efforts to gain relief for Wem. That night, he took some troops to Morton Corbet near Shrewsbury, capturing some iron, and killing ten royalists.

Denbigh meanwhile, had decided that not having enough forces to attack Rupert, he would ignore Parliament's orders and attack Rushall in Staffordshire.

The next day, Mytton had decided that he would have to sort out the Wem issue himself. He marched out of Wem and headed towards Oswestry. Before he reached it, however, he came across a convoy of goods which was heading from Ireland to the Royalist Colonel Hunckes. The convoy of six carts was guarded by four troops of horse and some infantry, but they were beaten off and the Parliamentarians returned to Wem with their booty.

Denbigh headed south from Stafford towards Rushall on Saturday 25th. He marched to Bloxwich, sending his cavalry to surround Rushall and by Sunday he had marched the rest of his force to surround the Royalist garrison. Denbigh himself quartered in Walsall. On the following day, Parliament once again wrote to Denbigh ordering him to attend to the movements of Prince Rupert although he would not have received this order for a few days. They also wrote to Lancashire, reiterating the importance of sending the previously ordered forces to meet with him.

Prince Rupert with his army by this time had reached Eccles near Manchester. On Tuesday 28th, he took Bolton in a particularly brutal attack. By now, Parliament had decided that Rupert was most likely heading for York. They sent out a flurry of orders to all their forces to attempt to form an army to oppose him by joining them together. Again, that included writing to Denbigh ordering him to follow Rupert, but he was still besieging Rushall. They also ordered the Earl of Manchester to pass any intelligence to the Scottish army, just in case Rupert headed that way. Denbigh took

93

Rushall, and captured a large amount of goods that had been plundered by the Royalists. He also took a Colonel and two hundred other prisoners. He ascribes his victory to the fact that Sir Thomas Middleton's infantry had arrived the night before.

Parliament were still preparing to send Sir William Brereton north on Thursday 30th.

June 1644

Denbigh wrote from Wednesbury on Sunday 2nd claiming that he had received no orders about pursuing Rupert, and that his last orders had been about relieving Wem, which he could not do because the Lancashire forces would not join him. He was now besieging Dudley Castle and seemed to have no intention of leaving to aid the Shropshire Parliamentarians or pursuing Parliament's agenda. In any case, the urgency of Wem's situation had reduced by the Royalist army heading into Lancashire, where it was by now besieging Liverpool. Mytton had gone from Wem to aid in the siege of Dudley.

So, for the moment, with all the main players away, the area around Market Drayton had gone quiet. This situation was not to last very long. At some point in early June, Brereton was finally heading north. By Saturday 15th he was at Stourbridge with Denbigh and others including Mytton. Mytton returned to Wem on Tuesday 18th, but as soon as he had retired to bed, he was informed that a convoy of carriages had been summoned to be in Royalist Oswestry by the morning of the following day. This convoy was to carry forty barrels of gunpowder to Prince Rupert's army. He did not meet with the convoy that day, but he did learn of a group of musketeers being commanded by a Lieutenant, and he routed them, taking some prisoners. In the same letter in which news of this was sent, he signalled his intention to attack Oswestry once he had received troops from Denbigh.

MD Documents 39 & 40

His message obviously persuaded Denbigh to pause in his march north to help, because in an anonymous letter from a member of Denbigh's army, it is stated that both the cavalry and infantry left Stafford on Thursday 20th to intercept the convoy. They did not get as far as they would have liked that day due to heavy rain, but the next morning, Denbigh left his main force of infantry at Market Drayton, and took his cavalry to Ellesmere where they joined with a small force of two hundred infantry commanded by Mytton.

Denbigh's orders from Parliament were still to follow Rupert, but this small diversion proved very successful. This small force of Denbigh's cavalry and Mytton's two hundred infantry marched to Oswestry, and they attacked at about two o'clock in the afternoon of Saturday 22nd. They entered the town before five. They at first took the church, the castle falling the next morning.

Denbigh immediately appointed Mytton Oswestry's governor, leaving Wem to the command of the Shropshire Committee. The rest of Denbigh's army which were encamped around Market Drayton were forced to wait until Wednesday 26th before Denbigh returned with his cavalry. In the meantime, Sir William Brereton finally returned from his long stay at the Parliament on midsummer's day, Monday 24th.

MD Document 41

The next day Sir Thomas Middleton, now also at Nantwich wrote to Denbigh to urge him to take his army from its encampment to Newcastle-Under-Lyme via Woore to meet up with more Staffordshire forces. He did also warn, however, that Colonel Marrow was planning to retake Oswestry.

Denbigh, always a law unto himself, entered Nantwich on Thursday 27th with a single troop of horse, having ordered his forces to encamp between Whitchurch and Nantwich. The following day, the army assembled and marched north towards Prince Rupert's army.

On Saturday 29th, Colonel Marrow as expected began to surround Oswestry with fifteen hundred cavalry and three and a half thousand infantry.

The same day, Denbigh's forces arrived at Knutsford, joining with the forces of Lord Gray and Sir John Gell, giving them a force of twelve thousand compared with Rupert's fourteen thousand, which had by this time advanced into Yorkshire. However, whilst Denbigh was at Knutsford, he was told on Sunday 30th of Mytton's plight and dispatched a force from Knutsford, Wem and Nantwich under Sir Thomas Middleton to help.

July 1644

Middleton's force got as far as Fens Hall in Flintshire on Monday 1st, on their way to Oswestry. Meanwhile, Prince Rupert had managed to raise the siege of York.

Denbigh, following a council of war had also left Knutsford with his own regiment and some Staffordshire troops to aid Oswestry. The next day, Colonel Marrow's men managed to make a breach in the defences and took the church, but were fought off. Sir Thomas Middleton, not having received the news that Denbigh was on his way, decided to attack immediately, and managed to raise the siege, the Royalist besiegers being driven back in disarray towards Shrewsbury.

Over in Yorkshire on the same day, Prince Rupert and the Marquess of Newcastle were defeated at the battle of Marston Moor by the combined forces of Lord Fairfax, the Earl of Manchester and the Scots under the Earl of Leven.

Following up their routing of the Royalist troops at Oswestry, on Thursday 4th Denbigh marched a forward force of his troops to Montford Bridge near Shrewsbury, which was guarded by Parliamentarian musketeers. They drove the defenders from the bridge, aided by some cavalry who managed to ford the river nearby, then marched their men and carriages across to within three miles of Shrewsbury. There they waited for the rest of the army to arrive. Once they had arrived, Denbigh moved forward to attack the town, hoping that the Parliamentarian sympathisers inside the town would help.

However, the outworks at Frankwell were so well defended and a force of cavalry issuing out to attack them, Denbigh retired across Montford Bridge and burnt it down before retreating to Wem.

The next day, he returned his attention to the conflict in Yorkshire, not having had reliable intelligence of what had been occurring there. Sir Thomas Middleton wanted to take his troops into Wales, but was persuaded by Denbigh not to.

On Saturday 6th, they decamped and marched to Prees Heath, quartering there and around Whitchurch that night. That day, Parliament having heard of the Yorkshire victory, wrote to Denbigh, ordering him to keep in contact with those armies, but giving him a free hand to do whatever he felt necessary to suppress the Royalists, especially in those counties he controlled. Perhaps they had finally realised that it was pointless telling him what to do…

Market Drayton's Civil War

9 Events Leading to the Fall of Shrewsbury

July 1644

The Committee of Both Kingdoms wrote to the Committee at Coventry on Tuesday 16th stating that while they were willing to keep some of their forces in Shropshire, they should do so, confirming this in another to the Committee at Wem. They also wrote to Denbigh, telling him that Sir Thomas Middleton should now prosecute their design in North Wales, but should still give support to Shropshire if needed, along with a request that the Warwickshire troops currently in the Shropshire garrisons should be left there if he and the Warwickshire Committee could spare them.

On Thursday 25th, Prince Rupert, having been travelling around Lancashire reportedly with eight or nine thousand dragoons arrived in Chester. The Committee of Both Kingdoms, not knowing this yet, wrote to the Committee in the North and Generals Fairfax, Manchester and Leven, to send some troops to Lancashire.

They also wrote to Sir William Brereton to gather his forces together to try and stop Rupert marching southward, copying this information to Middleton and the Lancashire Committee. The northern generals, having received Parliament's request wrote to them on Tuesday 30th that Rupert was now in Cheshire, and that they were sending a thousand of Sir Thomas Fairfax's cavalry to Lancashire with the aim of joining up with Brereton's forces.

August 1644

Brereton and Middleton wrote from Nantwich to Parliament on Friday 2nd stating that none of the promised extra troops had yet arrived. He confirmed that Rupert was in Chester, and that he was recruiting foot soldiers to replace those lost at Marston Moor. His five thousand cavalry were quartered just over the border in Wales, and Colonel Marrow's eight hundred were quartered near Tarvin. Rupert was keeping quiet, partly due to his recruiting efforts, but also because he was low on powder and shot, for which he was expecting a resupply out of Dublin.

Brereton wrote again the day after, reiterating his previous letter, and notifying Parliament that Prince Rupert was fortifying Chester. Sir Thomas Dallison was quartered at Welshpool with Rupert's own horse on Sunday 4th, from where he wrote to the prince giving him a status update. He told him that they were very weak in horse, having lost many from the great march they had undertaken after their lost battle in Yorkshire. He requested supplies, pointing out that they were having to turn out the horses to grass during the day and fetch them in at night. At this point he was totally unaware that a force of cavalry and dragoons led by Middleton and Mytton were heading towards him. They were not spotted until they were within a quarter of a mile from Dallison on Monday morning while it was still dark. Not knowing the town, the attackers missed capturing Dallison himself, and many of Dallison's troops escaped, but the Parliamentary force captured between two hundred and three hundred and fifty horses and fifty or sixty prisoners, depending on which source is used, along with some arms and equipment. They retreated to Oswestry with the spoils, as they were fearful that those Royalist troops that had escaped would launch a counter-attack.

By Tuesday 6th, Parliament were becoming increasingly worried about Rupert's presence in Cheshire. They wrote to the Earl of Manchester desiring him to join his forces with those of Nottinghamshire, Derbyshire, and Lancashire, and the forces of Brereton and Middleton. This army was then desired to march towards Rupert and **"attend his movements"**. There was no order for a straightforward attack, they would not be large enough a force for an out and out battle, but they were to **"secure any advantages that may be offered"**.

They sent letters to all the other parties involved to the same purpose the following day. On Friday 9th, Parliament sent intelligence to Lord Essex.

"Prince Rupert has divided his forces which were in Lancashire, and with the best of his horse passed over into Cheshire at Hale ford upon Wednesday the 24th July. His foot and dragoons were conveyed over in boats in several days from Liverpool into Cheshire. The rest of his horse under Goring, Clavering, and Montrose are gone into Westmorland and Cumberland. The armies in the north have thereupon divided themselves, the Scottish marching northward for the security of those counties against the forces with Goring and that company, and to intend the taking in of Newcastle, and the Earl of

Manchester southward, to whom we have given order with all his forces and those here named to follow Prince Rupert wherever he shall go, in order to hinder his recruiting and to watch all advantages against him."

Having received the instructions from Parliament, the Earl of Manchester replied from Lincoln on Saturday 10th with a set of reasons why he would not be complying. Middleton and Mytton's raid on Rupert's cavalry at Welshpool was reported in Parliament on Monday 12th.

Wednesday 14th saw a reply from Parliament to Lord Manchester's reasons for not sending his forces to aid Brereton. They included a reduced requirement, requesting **"a party of your forces"**. On the following day, they confirmed this in letters to Brereton and Middleton. Also on Thursday 15th, Parliament wrote to the Wem Committee, as Denbigh had complained that his troops left there were not being given the same pay and provisions as others.

Because Rupert had divided his forces between Cheshire and Cumberland and Westmoreland, Parliament requested the Lord Admiral to send some shipping to the coast nearby so that fresh supplies may not be landed from Ireland.

On Tuesday 20th, Sir John Meldrum wrote to Parliament, informing them that he was having difficulty stopping a part of the prince's forces under Sir Marmaduke Langdale returning from the north through Lancashire to Cheshire. Prince Rupert, meanwhile had left Chester and travelled as far as Ruthin.

The following day, Manchester again wrote to parliament, stating that he would send a party towards Cheshire, but that he needed to consult with the committees of Derby and Nottingham

Sir Marmadule Langdale

first. Meanwhile, Meldrum was still trying to stop Rupert's forces getting through Lancashire. They encountered them a mile from Ormskirk where they managed to kill many of the enemy.

Prince Rupert by this time had reached Bala. On Wednesday 21st, Parliamentary troops from Northwich with the aid of Brereton's horse and some troops from Halton Castle, set upon the Royalists in their quarters at Tarvin. They reportedly killed fifteen, took forty-five prisoners and two to three hundred horse. They retreated quickly with their spoils because, being so close to Chester, a force was sent from the city towards them. Rupert reached Newtown in Montgomeryshire.

On Friday 23rd in the morning, news reached Nantwich that a thousand of the enemy's horse had been taken in Lancashire with over four hundred men being taken prisoner, with many killed. Langdale had now reached Malpas.

On Saturday 24th, news came to Brereton of Langdale's army's approach. One source states that this was from a trumpeter who defected from Prince Rupert's force, although whether this is true or not is unknown. Brereton himself said that 'intelligence came to Nantwich'. One source states they were about a thousand, but the rest state two to three thousand.

Some of Brereton's cavalry had not returned from Tarvin, but on the next day he prepared what forces he could muster, eight troops of cavalry and seven foot companies. So that they could move quickly, each infantryman was mounted behind a cavalryman on the same horse. reportedly numbering eight to nine hundred, and they marched out in the early evening towards the Royalists.

At daybreak on Monday 26th they arrived at Oldcastle Heath near Malpas, where the infantry dismounted and formed up. They marched towards the enemy, cavalry in front of the infantry. The Royalists sent out a forlorn hope, but it was ineffective.

There were several charges, and the Parliamentarian forces ended up chasing the Royalists through Malpas. By this time, the Parliamentary cavalry had lost contact with their infantry, and Brereton, fearing a regrouping by the Royalists decided that the cavalry should stand until the foot came up to them. By this time, having faced several attacks, they were growing tired but they stood firm. Once the foot had come up, the attack was renewed, and Brereton ascribed his victory to the fact that so many of the Royalist officers were killed that their troops faltered and retreated.

Brereton did not follow, his troops now being tired, and being still heavily outnumbered. His estimate was that there were still about two thousand men in Langdale's force. He stated that they fled back towards Chester.

He assessed that they were on their way to join with the King's army, and realised that they would still be able to once regrouped, so he wrote to London to try and speed any forces that were already on their way to join him.

On Tuesday 27th, Parliament wrote to both Brereton and the Earl of Manchester in order to speed more forces to Cheshire. On the next day they wrote to Manchester about intelligence that Rupert with his forces was marching south, having joined with Langdale. They requested that he send troops towards them.

The next day, confirming that Rupert was nowhere near the area, (his journal says he had arrived in Bristol) Lord Byron wrote with intelligence of the Malpas skirmish. Interestingly, Byron says that the enemy was two hundred horse and two hundred foot. He stated that Langdale's forces were now marching through Wales, not being ready to fight another enemy.

On Friday 30th, Parliament wrote to Brereton to request him (this was not an order, as they knew he was busy about Chester), to spare five hundred foot to help maintain the garrisons of Wem and Oswestry, as Sir Thomas Middleton was about to withdraw his troops from the two garrisons. They also requested that he let the Shropshire Committee know what he was doing.

On the same day they read a letter from Brereton at Northwich, detailing the latest success over Langdale and the Royalist forces near Malpas. Locally, all available forces marched out of Nantwich, to start garrisoning and fortifying Tarvin, Hixley Hall and Oulton Hall.

September 1644

On Monday 2nd, The Earl of Manchester wrote to Parliament from Lincoln confirming that he had recalled the troops that were on their way to Brereton, but that he would march with his force to Abingdon, following Prince Rupert.

Parliament reported another letter from Brereton, stating Rupert was advancing to join with the King. The next day they ordered that Brereton was sent thanks for Malpas. Meanwhile, Sir Thomas Middleton marched out of Oswestry, having received orders from Parliament to march towards Montgomery. At Newtown, they encountered a party of the King's forces which he took by surprise. This yielded four wagons containing powder and ammunition which had been heading to re-supply Chester.

The next day, Wednesday 4th, Middleton marched on to Montgomery, where Lord Herbert allowed them to enter the castle. In response to this, the Royalists drew together what forces they could, some of Langdale's scattered forces from Malpas, and some from their garrisons in the area. This created a force of about two thousand cavalry and two thousand infantry under the command of Lord Byron.

On Sunday 8th, this Royalist force attacked Middleton's army. His infantry retreated into the castle, and the cavalry fled back towards Oswestry. The Royalists then started to lay siege to the castle.

On this same day over the border in Shropshire, Moreton Corbet fell to forces from Wem. The governor and some officers along with about seventy other soldiers were taken, along with some very useful booty including six barrels of gunpowder.

On Monday 9th Brereton wrote to Parliament, stating that he had already supplied extra troops to Wem, but that he would supply more if they were needed. These extra forces and their commanders were the very same troops that had just taken Moreton Corbet. He also explained his plans at Tarvin, how he was attempting to block up Chester.

News of the Montgomery siege came to Brereton's attention later that day, at which point he started assembling an army to relieve it.

On Friday 13th, Parliament was read news of the taking of Moreton Corbet. They also discussed what could be done to aid Middleton, which resulted in a letter being sent to Wem, Lancashire and Brereton to try and gain aid for the besieged forces at Montgomery. However, by this time, Brereton was already assembling the required force, and on Tuesday 17th we find that force approaching Montgomery. It was made up of over three thousand men from Cheshire, Staffordshire and Lancashire under Brereton, Meldrum and Sir William Fairfax. As they approached, Lord Byron withdrew his men from the siege to a little distance away.

The next morning, Meldrum, who led the Parliamentary force, decided not to attack Byron's Royalists, but to send in provisions to the castle. Byron, seeing this, marched from his position to attack the Parliamentarians. Initially the Royalists did well, the cavalry forcing their opposing cavalry to retreat several times, and the infantry, having more pikemen also did well. However, after about an hour, Parliament's men began to push Byron's army back, after which they soon broke and ran, pursued by Meldrum's men.

Sir William Fairfax was wounded in the battle and died the next day. Brereton and his forces arrived safely back in Nantwich on Monday 23rd. This same day, Parliament were read the news of Montgomery's relief. They sent letters of thanks to all the commanders concerned. Middleton then started asking for money to consolidate his success.

On Sunday 29th, Sir John Meldrum wrote to Parliament that he wanted to attack Shrewsbury on his way back, using dissenters in the town to open a passage for them. However, the dissenters were reluctant, and Meldrum was carrying with him many prisoners, so this did not happen. Instead, he headed back to Lancashire.

On Monday 30th, Middleton marched with a small force from Montgomery to Welshpool, where he quartered.

October 1644

On Wednesday 2nd, very early in the morning, Sir Thomas Middleton, with a very small force, marched from Welshpool to Powis Castle. He only attacked it with three hundred foot and fifty horse claiming that apart from another hundred men left to guard the baggage train, these were all the troops he had left, the rest having deserted for want of pay. While firing was going on between the attackers and defenders, Middleton's gunner had attached a bomb to the gate, which exploded, blowing the gates in. Middleton's troops stormed in and captured it. This meant that Middleton now had command of the strongest castles in that part of North Wales.

Saturday 5th saw Brereton in Stanney in Wirral, where he quartered until Tuesday 8th, having taken in Brimstage Tower where the enemy kept a small garrison. They had hurriedly left on news of Brereton's approach, leaving behind in it the provisions intended for the relief of Liverpool. Liverpool was now the only place that stood in the way of Chester being completely encircled, and that the want there was so desperate that it could not hold out much longer. From there he marched to Tranmore near Liverpool, staying there for seven days, expecting Liverpool to be given up.

On Wednesday 16th, Nantwich forces surrounded and started to besiege Beeston Castle.

Saturday 19th, Middleton, having received intelligence of the enemy's fortifying the town and castle of Ruthin, decided to gather what forces he could out of his garrisons of Montgomery and Powis Castle, with the aid of some from Colonel Mytton in Oswestry, and to attack Ruthin. There were one hundred and twenty cavalry and two hundred infantry in the town, behind well prepared barricades. Middleton's infantry broke through the barricades, allowing the cavalry to charge in. The Royalist foot fled into the castle, and the horse were pursued towards Denbigh. They broke down all the defences in the town, but a couple of days later, they left without attacking the castle as they were not strong enough a force, especially as Mytton's men had returned to Oswestry, claiming the enemy were near there.

On Thursday 24th, Parliament wrote to Brereton. The main letter stated that they desired him to join with Sir John Gell and to take some forces from Eccleshall and Stafford, for a design that was mentioned in the enclosed letter which was in code. They also wrote to Gell and the Stafford committee, requesting those troops but not mentioning what they were for. The purpose of this (unknown to anyone) was to take those troops into Stafford, to weed out some dissenters there. Brereton received the letter from Parliament containing the other in code, but had no key to unlock the code, so was unaware that they wanted him to go to Stafford. The letter also took a day longer to receive than it should, Brereton having returned to Nantwich to meet with Middleton. He informed them that Meldrum wanted to storm Liverpool, but that he believed they were so close to being starved out, that they should delay.

On Wednesday 30th, the Archbishop of York wrote to Ormonde in Ireland, stating that Prince Rupert was discouraged by defeats at Marston Moor and Montgomery. News from Chester was that he would be coming with three thousand men, joining with Gerard with five thousand. The same day, Brereton and Middleton wrote from Nantwich to Parliament requesting Scots troops to help reduce Chester, now that Newcastle had fallen. They stated that the enemy was being encouraged by news that the prince may be coming. Also, Middleton wrote to Parliament asking for weapons and money, as he had received nothing since his first arrival.

November 1644

On Friday 1st, at about noon, Liverpool finally surrendered. Conditions had become so bad in the city, that the soldiers mutinied against their commanders, and let the Parliamentarians in. Some goods were being carried away in boats, but Meldrum captured these also. The same day, Beeston castle troops left the castle to gather supplies, and they were set upon by troops from Nantwich and Tarvin. Also, about this time, Parliament troops raided cattle from the area around the castle.

On Saturday 2nd, Brereton again wrote to Parliament, listing what had happened at Liverpool, and again asking for three to four thousand Scots to help with Chester. He again told them that he could not read the previous letter as he had no key to the code. Meldrum wrote to Parliament stating that he had placed Colonel John Moore in charge in Liverpool. He also wrote stating that he needed to leave a very strong garrison there.

On Monday 4th, Sir John Meldrum wrote from Liverpool to Parliament. He agreed with Brereton, suggesting that now was the appropriate time for all the forces that could be spared to attack Chester, before the prince arrived. The following Monday, the 11th, Parliament wrote to Brereton thanking him for his good services, and asking that he send Middleton five hundred infantry, which would help block up Chester on the Welsh side.

On Tuesday 12th, Parliament's forces began to besiege Beeston Castle. Three days later, Middleton wrote from Powis Castle, again requesting aid to help stem the flow of his deserting troops, and to send some Scots to help reduce Chester. Brereton wrote to Parliament again, on Monday 18th, requesting the three to four thousand Scots to help reduce Chester.

Market Drayton's Civil War

December 1644

On Tuesday 3rd Brereton wrote to Parliament from Stafford, having finally deciphered their coded letter. He entered Stafford with two hundred horse and a hundred foot. He removed some of the commanders and sent them as prisoners to Eccleshall Castle. He put things in place to support Stone, the commander and removed those with designs against him.

On the same day, Parliament ordered that four hundred muskets and three hundred firelocks to be sent to Brereton for his Chester campaign. They also ordered that Brereton should have liberty to raise three hundred horse.

On Wednesday 4th, the Royalists burnt several large houses in the eastern part of North Wales, to stop Parliament fortifying them, which would be detrimental to Salop and Chester. That Saturday, the soldiers defending Beeston Castle sallied out and killed twenty-six soldiers dining at a Mr. Owen's house near the castle.

On Saturday 21st, Parliament wrote to Stone confirming him as being in command at Stafford on Brereton's recommendation, and another confirming this to Brereton, also asking that he sent to London the arrested Col. Chadwick, Lieut.-Col. Chadwick, and Capt.-Lieut. Hughes. Also on 21st, Middleton attempted to take his own castle at Chirk, but did not want to use artillery, so as to not damage his own house. They arrived on 21st, and besieged it until Christmas day, Wednesday the 25th. He failed. On Saturday 28th, Parliament wrote to Brereton, Stafford and Gell. They had Col Ridgeley in custody in London, but didn't have anything particular to charge him with. They needed it within twenty days or they would have to release him.

January 1644/5

The start of January saw Prince Maurice, a man of far less ability than Rupert being sent to accomplish the task in which his brother had failed. He was appointed Major-General of Worcester, Salop, Hereford and Monmouth, and made Worcester his headquarters.

On Thursday 9th, a troop of Parliamentary soldiers were set upon by troops from Chester, and many of them taken.

The next day, Brereton wrote to Parliament from Nantwich that he did not have the resources to send to London the arrested officers. He had not received the letters until now, as the messenger had to take a detour to avoid Royalist forces.

Brereton had decided to release Hughes, as his regiment was now not in Stafford. He told Parliament that the information against Ridgeley needed to come from Gell.

The next day, Brereton wrote to Parliament that intelligence was that Prince Maurice was heading from Oxford to Worcester. He was worried that if Maurice came his way, he would have to abandon his siege of Beeston and his attempt to block up Chester and retreat into his garrisons. Ten thousand more troops from Ireland were rumoured to be on the way and he was short of foot and dragoons.

On Tuesday 14th, Mytton beat up some troops of horse near Chirk.

On Thursday 16th, Brereton wrote to Parliament from Nantwich stating that the two Chadwicks had been sent to London, with as much information as he had, but that Stafford had the evidence. Hughes had not been sent, as he was needed with the troop he was in, but he would send him up if commanded. Beeston Castle was still holding out, but they were in distress, having requested to send out their sick, which had been refused. Chester garrison had issued out several times, attacking his forces.

The following day, two captured Irish were hanged at Nantwich for the crime of being Irish. On the same day, Brereton wrote from Nantwich to Parliament as he was worried that the Royalist army under Prince Maurice was about to head in his direction. He wrote a second letter on the same day, stating that they needed to keep a better eye on Chester, and therefore had advanced nearer to it. He had placed troops at Christleton, only about a mile from Chester's defences, under Lt Col Jones and Major Lothian with his regiments of horse and foot. Beeston Castle was suffering even more, and Brereton informed that it should shortly be delivered, and hoped to make short work of Chester. They just needed to be uninterrupted by a Royalist army.

The following day, a large force of Royalists issued forth from Chester, to attempt to relieve Beeston and laid an ambush for the approaching Parliamentarians, probably fearing that once Brereton had settled, they would get no more chances.

Brereton wrote from Nantwich that at about two o'clock in the afternoon, eight hundred foot and three hundred horse left the city. Brereton's cavalry charged through the ambush and harassed the Royalist cavalry right up to the city gates, while the Parliamentarian foot harassed their opposite numbers and attacked them almost up to the artillery. This was the force from Christleton, as the foot were led by Lothian, and the horse were led by Jones.

Whilst this was going on, Parliament were discussing a request from the Shropshire committee for aid to take Shrawardine and Tong. They resolved to write to Brereton to request that he aid them. They also determined to ask Denbigh why he had reduced the Wem garrison to three companies.

On Thursday 23rd, Parliament stated that they wanted Col Ashton's regiment in Lancashire to aid Brereton, but that fifteen hundred pounds was needed to achieve it. The same day, there were services of thanksgiving held in Nantwich, marking the anniversary of the battle of Nantwich. That night, rumour had it that Royalist troops were at Whitchurch, so Nantwich was put on an overnight guard. The following day, Friday 24th, Parliament wrote the letter they discussed on 22nd, asking Brereton to aid Shropshire with some forces. The same day, another captured Irishman was shot at Nantwich for being Irish, and two more were hanged that week at Christleton for the same offence.

Sunday 26th, a force of Cheshire and Lancashire parliamentarian soldiers headed to Cheshire, arriving at five o'clock in the morning. Word had been sent in advance of them, and therefore Chester was ready for them. This could be seen by the light of their slow-matches, so the roundheads retreated. Two days later, Cheshire forces crossed from the Wirral into North Wales overnight. The following morning, Wednesday 29th, they marched via Hawarden to Holt. The defenders of the bridge at Holt fled into the Castle, so Parliament took the bridge, allowing free passage for their forces from Wales to England. They brought back sixty to eighty cattle ready for slaughter.

On Friday 31st, the Shropshire Committee at Wem wrote to Brereton. The forces they had lent to him had returned. Wem was in a sad condition, having about one hundred and thirty more foot than they could pay as they had been planning something that would need them. They stated that they had to give up two small garrisons at Moreton Corbet and Stoke-upon-Tern, but also indicated that they had an opportunity to undertake something momentous, and requested that Brereton lent them one hundred and fifty foot. They indicated that they would not get any help from Mytton who they were now at odds with. They were planning to take Atcham. Amongst others, this was signed by Colonel Clive.

February 1644/5

On Monday 3rd, Brereton wrote to Parliament. He told them that Prince Maurice was on his way, with a design to relieve Chester. He stated that if Maurice approached, it would ruin his design on Chester and Beeston and that they would have to abandon Wales and retreat into their garrisons. He requested a force to attend Maurice's movements.

On Wednesday 5th Parliament decided that they would discuss the 'business of Prince Maurice and Shropshire' on Friday afternoon. The Earls of Essex and Manchester were present. On the same day, Col. Ashton's regiment were ordered to move from Lancashire into Cheshire. That day, Maurice with his army reached Shrewsbury. On Friday 7th, Parliament discussed the issue, and decided to order two hundred foot and a hundred horse from Staffordshire, one hundred and fifty horse from Warwickshire, two hundred foot and one hundred horse from Shropshire, three hundred horse from Derbyshire and a hundred horse from Leicestershire to proceed towards Sir William Brereton to try and stop Chester being relieved. Also, to request five hundred or more horse from Lord Fairfax and Col Ashton's regiment of foot and two troops of horse.

The next day they wrote to Brereton informing him of the forces sent. Brereton was at Wrexham on Monday 10th from where he wrote to Parliament that he was still besieging Chester and Beeston, and that he still had his quarters at Christleton and Wrexham. He informed them that he was expecting to hear of Maurice's army very soon, some of them being about Wellington having come from Evesham. These, he informed them, were about a thousand horse and foot well-armed and furnished with powder and that the rest of his army were on the other side of the River Severn. He had already received four hundred Warwickshire and three hundred Staffordshire horse with two hundred Staffordshire foot. Sir John Gell had promised some horse and Lancashire some foot and he was also expecting expect five hundred Yorkshire horse. He stated that he had divided his forces between Wrexham, Christleton, Farne Holt and Beeston.

He also let them know that Maurice's army was within ten or twelve hours, and that once they approach they would have to consolidate their forces. He requested a force of Scots, basically indicating that if they didn't send more troops then the two sieges of Beeston and Chester would have to be given up.

The same day, Ferdinando Lord Fairfax wrote from York to Parliament. He had heard of Maurice's approach towards Chester so ordered a thousand horse to go that way. The forces heading by order of Parliament to aid Brereton started arriving on Tuesday 11th and Wednesday 12th. They rendezvoused on Prees Heath. Maurice's army, about two thousand, moved towards Chirk Castle. The Welsh Parliamentarian forces attempted to follow but couldn't catch him.

Parliament wrote to Brereton confirming that they had ordered forces to him, and that they should all be paid equally. Brereton replied to them from Whitchurch. On Wednesday 12th, forces continued arriving at Prees Heath.

On Friday 14th, the Shropshire committee at Wem issued orders for the taking of Shrewsbury. They made it very clear that Lieutenant Reinking was in command, and that Mytton, Lloyd, Hunt and Clive were subordinate. The Shropshire committee promised good pay if successful, with special payments for special valour. They also stated that anyone looting would be tried for their life. Reinking stated that he had been in consultation with the Shropshire committee for many months over this design.

Their first attempt was that night, but day arrived before they did, so they retreated. On Monday 17th, the parliamentary forces in Wales that had failed to catch Prince Maurice came back to Cheshire fearing his approach. On Tuesday 18th, Parliament wrote to the committees of Shropshire, Staffordshire, Warwickshire and Sir John Gell, requesting that they continue their forces with Brereton. They also wrote the same to Lord Fairfax,

Lancashire, and the forces already with Brereton.

Sir William having been informed of the design against Shrewsbury, and having been asked for a party of horse and foot to join with Col. Mytton, he made no delay. Col. Bowyer, an able soldier was assigned the task, under whose command Brereton put four hundred Cheshire and Staffordshire horse, three hundred Staffordshire foot, and a company of his own regiment, and sent them on Wednesday to Wem. They were well armed and he also sent other necessaries for the storming of Shrewsbury, including petards to break open the gates, or for the like service.

On Thursday 20th Maurice arrived in Chester, but retreated to Holt, where he made a bridge of boats under the castle allowing Royalist troops to come over. On Thursday 20th, Col. Mytton with five hundred of the Shropshire forces met Colonel Bowyer with the aforesaid forces at Wem, their number in all being about twelve hundred, and there they received instructions from the Committee for carrying on the business against Shrewsbury, Reinking receiving his orders from the Shropshire Committee to undertake the Shrewsbury attack. Early evening, Friday 21st, he took the foot he had at Wem and marched to Hadnall Heath along with the Committee men, where he rendezvoused with forces from several garrisons and Colonel Bowyer's Staffordshire horse, in all amounting to about twelve hundred men. He appointed Bowyer to take charge of the horse while he commanded the foot himself.

Reinking then read out the orders about payment and plundering to the officers so that they would communicate these to the common soldiers. He assigned the field token, distributed ammunition, and then assigned a forlorn hope of thirty firelocks. He ordered that each company should only keep two slow matches alight, so that they should not be seen in the march up to the town. Reinking selected thirty more men from the Shropshire dragoons under Colonel Benbow, which he joined with the Forlorn Hope. Along with them he added thirty pioneers with boat, ladders, picks, crow axes, and other tools.

The Attack on Shrewsbury

There are several different accounts of the taking of Shrewsbury on Saturday 22nd. I have tried to piece them all together to create a narrative, but it should be borne in mind that different people have different recollections. One thing is certain though. Col Mytton was not wanted there by the Shropshire Committee, and had no command, turning up unannounced. He later attempted to take credit for the whole operation.

Brereton was very clear to state this to Parliament after the event. At three o'clock in the morning, the Parliamentary forces arrived about half a mile from Shrewsbury, so far undetected. Reinking sent Lord Colvill with sixty foot into the suburbs, so that he could create a diversion if it proved necessary. He was also aware that a party from the town had left to gather hay, so he assigned another eighty foot to ensure that they weren't surprised from behind.

Reinking was aware of a low point in the walls, possibly due to the fact that it was near to Sir William Owen's house, Sir William having for a long while been sending information to Wem. This low point was however behind some wooden palisades, and so Reinking sent boats up the river, the first containing eight pioneers with axes, the rest containing firelocks and dismounted cavalry armed with pistols. They also took ladders with them.

The pioneers set about chopping down the palisades, and a short while after, sentries on the walls, hearing this started shooting at them. The troops in the rest of the boats had by this time landed and lit their slow matches. It took about fifteen minutes to remove enough of the palisade to get the troops through.

In the meantime, Lord Colvill, now near the town gates, hearing the shooting, created a diversion to attempt to draw the defenders towards him, and away from the Forlorn Hope heading through the palisades. The firelocks headed through the palisade with their ladders to the low section of wall which was only about eight feet high. The initial force to gain entry were the firelocks and dismounted cavalry, who were being led by a minister, Mr. Huson, Captain Willers and Benbow. Once this initial force was in, Reinking himself led another three hundred and fifty foot into the town. Reinking ordered Major Fenwick to take men to open the gates, and he led the rest into the market place where after an exchange of shot, they overpowered the main guard by taking their officers at which point the rest retreated.

Market Drayton's Civil War

One version of events states that on their way they encountered the Governor with a Captain Cressy. He wounded a musketeer before being overpowered and wounded himself. Another version gives that he was surprised in bed.

In the meantime, before Fenwick could get to the gates, the officers that were with him during the palisade cutting had reached them and opened them. The cavalry and the Committee men entered through the gates, and, on encountering Reinking, who was by now getting very tired, Colonel Lloyd gave him his horse. Reinking, along with a party of twelve musketeers headed for a party of defenders who were attempting to put up some resistance, and managed to subdue them, but not before Reinking's horse was killed beneath him.

By this time, dawn had arrived. Having taken the town without much effort, Reinking now turned his attention to the castle, opening negotiations for its surrender. In the meantime, despite having been promised money not to plunder the town, and having been threatened with the death penalty for doing so, some of the troops started to plunder the town. Reinking therefore sent some troops to guard Sir John Weld and his son, and their property.

Shortly after this, and with the castle negotiations ongoing, the Shropshire committee immediately wrote to Brereton with the good news, stating that they had captured the Governor Sir Michael Earnley, and Sir John Weld and his son. At nine o'clock, the Shropshire Committee in Shrewsbury sent Brereton another message requesting the loan of some foot to help keep Shrewsbury. Frankwell fort had not capitulated at this point. Sir William Brereton, at this point in Tarvin, and so unaware of the successful taking of Shrewsbury, wrote to Parliament, giving them the intelligence that Maurice was in Chester, with his army of five to six thousand quartered on the Welsh side of the River Dee.

Because of this, Brereton had pulled his forces back out of Wales, and dug trenches at Christleton to prevent a cavalry attack. He requested two thousand foot and provisions, to make a good account of Chester, Shrewsbury and Wales. Shrewsbury castle held out until midday, at which point it surrendered, having agreed that the officers and soldiers in the castle would be allowed to leave with their arms, but leaving all the ammunition behind. This did not include the officers and soldiers who had been captured in the town. The agreement for the castle also did not include any Irish troops, who were held back for summary hanging. On receipt of the first letter from the Shropshire Committee, Brereton immediately wrote to Parliament from Tarvin to tell them the good news.

He promised that he would march some forces towards Shropshire's other garrisons to ensure their safety, being much weakened by the removal of forces for the Shrewsbury attack. Meanwhile the fort at Frankwell had requested quarter, which was granted. Therefore, the Shropshire committee had their greatest achievement, and they immediately decided to transfer their committee to the town, leaving Wem in the capable hands of Major William Brayne.

A couple of things that may have contributed to the easy taking of the town may well have been that the garrison had been much reduced by Prince Maurice, and that the Governor had been unwell, but it seems likely that the main reason was that the Parliamentary faction in the town, who had long been a thorn in the side of the Royalist governors had given enough intelligence to Wem that could ensure an easy victory.

Only two of Reinking's men had apparently died, along with a captain and five royalist soldiers. However, the haul of both important Royalist prisoners, and the town magazine, along with all the prince's possessions in the town and all the valuables entrusted to the town by Shropshire Royalists, made this an incredible victory for the Shropshire Committee.

On Sunday 23rd February, the Shropshire Committee wrote to Brereton requesting foot both to help secure Shrewsbury, but also to strengthen the now much weakened Wem. They informed him that they had decided to slight and abandon their garrisons at Moreton Corbet and Stoke on Tern, moving the few troops that were still in them back to Wem. On Monday 24th, the Shropshire Committee wrote to Brereton that despite their promise of money to prevent plundering it had happened on a large scale.

They requested his presence, as the troops still wanted the money they were promised for not plundering. By Tuesday 25th, Brereton had not yet arrived. The Shropshire committee again wrote to him requesting his presence, as they were fearful of being set upon by Prince Maurice. The letters from

Brereton and the Shropshire Committee were read in Parliament on Wednesday 26th. They were so delighted with the news that they gave twenty pounds to the messengers that brought the news. Brereton wrote from where he was now, in Shrewsbury, to William Ashurst in Lancashire hoping that more forces could be sent. But he also stated that he had so many forces that he was having difficulty commanding them, and that if some Scots could be sent, he would happily fall under their command.

He was to return to Cheshire from Shrewsbury either that evening or the following morning. Brereton also wrote to Parliament giving a further account of the condition of Shrewsbury, and intelligence of the Royalist forces in the area. He also requested some Scots forces to help.

On Thursday 27th, Parliament ordered that the most important prisoners be sent to London. On Friday 28th, Parliament wrote to the Shropshire Committee thanking them for the taking of Shrewsbury. They promised to do what they could to supply their needs and stated that they were requesting that Brereton and the Stafford Committee do what they could to support them. The nominating of a governor they left to the Shropshire Committee.

March 1644/5

On Saturday 1st March, Parliament wrote to Brereton desiring him to give the Shropshire Committee all assistance he could, in case the forces with the princes should attempt to retake it. The next day, the most important prisoners taken at Shrewsbury were transferred to Nantwich, on the start of their journey to London. That Monday, Parliament wrote to Sir John Gell and to Yorkshire, to keep their forces currently with Brereton with him.

Market Drayton's Civil War

10 The Two Princes

February 1644/5

Woodcut of Prince Maurice

On Friday 28th, the governor of Gloucester, Col Edward Massey wrote to Brereton to let him know that Prince Rupert was on his march north towards him. He stated that Rupert's army had split into two. Two thousand horse and foot commanded by Rupert himself had the previous day forded the Avon just north of Evesham; the other group, approximately fifteen hundred horse and foot under the command of Sir Marmaduke Langdale and Lord Northampton had marched past Banbury. However, Massey's information was either incorrect or hopelessly out of date, as Langdale was at this point in Yorkshire where he was successfully raising the siege of Pontefract Castle.

March 1644/5

With Prince Maurice already in the area, the possibility of a conjunction of Rupert's, Maurice's and Langdale's forces helped to concentrate Parliament's mind. By Wednesday 5th, they were aware of the issue and set aside some time on the following day to discuss what to do to support Sir William Brereton. When they met, they discussed how they were going to get troops to Shropshire and Cheshire, and how to pay for them. The decision was made to gather what troops they could at Coventry and ordered Major-General Crawford to head there to take command of them. They requested large numbers of troops from the Earl of Essex and the Earl of Manchester along with other troops from Worcestershire and Lancashire.

MD Document 52

At this point, one of our main sources, Prince Rupert's journal, unfortunately becomes very unclear. His secretary, who was compiling it later to help Clarendon write his 'History of the Rebellion', stated that the notes of this period had been lost and that he was compiling it from 'Mercury', i.e., newspapers. It records:

> **My notes of the marche to relieve Beeston Castle are lost: these following I tooke out of Mercurye.**
>
> ~~**April 1645**~~
>
> **9 Wednesday, to Bridgnorth. Sir Marmaduke Langdale came.**
>
> **10 Thursday, to Wenlock**
>
> - **To Draiton**
> - **To Whitchurch**
> - **To a little village**

Although the journal is also confused about a number of other dates later in the month, the dates of those can be confirmed from other sources. Therefore, in light of this being an entry that mentions Market Drayton, we need to try and consider what was going on. Firstly, as the secretary initially thought that he was dealing with April which he struck out once he realised his mistake, the days of the week are incorrect. March 9th was a Sunday, and 10th was a Monday. The next definite entry we have is Saturday 19th, when Maurice and Rupert joined forces, so this trip to Market Drayton must have occurred between these dates. Therefore, the narrative below is an estimate of what I consider could have reasonably happened, bearing in mind other sources, and distances travelled etc.

Unfortunately, a lot of the sources disagree on some of the dates. I have therefore used the following priority. First, anyone who was there, second other local diarists, thirdly other less local sources. I am prepared to be proved wrong by any further discoveries. What is not at issue is whether these events occurred.

By Saturday 8th, Rupert was at Ludlow, announcing his intention to somehow join with the forces of his brother, Prince Maurice, although at this point stated that he did not see how they could, but that they would try. The next day, Rupert travelled to Bridgnorth, and Sir Marmaduke Langdale arrived there on the same day. Monday 10th saw Rupert travel to Wenlock and back. Lord Leven wrote to Brereton in response to an earlier request that he could not immediately send Scottish troops to his aid. In the House of Commons, three thousand pounds was allotted to pay troops with Brereton which was approved by the Lords the day after. They also sent word to Brereton detailing the troops that were on their way to him and also granted the garrison at Shrewsbury two thousand pounds for its defence. At this point, there are far too many letters flying back and forth trying to enlist aid for Brereton to list the content of them but suffice it to say that aid was being sought from all the county committees in the Midlands as well as attempting to coax the Scots to come South. Brereton's position on his **"posture of defence"** was also clarified by the Lords, stating that he should not risk his army, but he should be allowed to take the advantage if it arose.

On Tuesday 11th it was decided that Rupert and Langdale should join their forces at Wellington on Thursday 13th and this large force should then combine with Maurice's at Ellesmere the following day. The Scots had also been persuaded to send some troops, although they did not march immediately, as they were waiting for some of their foot troops to come up. Things did not turn out quite as expected, as at that point Maurice was on the other side of the river Dee heading towards Chirk.

On Saturday 15th, Rupert marched to Market Drayton. Langdale was at Apley, with his forces still around Bridgnorth, whilst Maurice was at Chirk. Brereton started to prepare for their approach by sending some of the Royalist prisoners captured at Shrewsbury from Nantwich to Manchester. Sunday 16th saw Rupert continue his march from Market Drayton to Whitchurch. Brereton continued his preparations, removing more Shrewsbury prisoners to Eccleshall, and removing troops from Christleton to shore up his garrison at Tarporley. By the end of the day, Rupert's forces were at 'a little village' probably Cockshutt. The next day Rupert and Maurice headed for Fenn's Moss, where they were to rendezvous. Rupert's rear-guard encountered a force belonging to Mytton near Oately Hall. Mytton only just escaped with his life, most of his small force being captured by Rupert's men. The rendezvous having occurred, the combined force did not dally, they headed straight towards Beeston Castle which was relieved, and Christleton which they burned to the ground. Tuesday 18th saw the Royalists start plundering the area in earnest. Bunbury was especially hard-hit. Meanwhile all of Brereton's troops were in garrison, Sir William being at Middlewich himself. Major Braine at Wem offered a thousand troops to Brereton and offered to send them to Whitchurch, but Brereton wrote back suggesting that Whitchurch was too dangerous, and that Market Drayton would be the better option.

MD Documents 49 & 57

By Wednesday 19th, Brereton was still in his posture of defence. The Scots had not yet arrived, being now around Urmston and Flixton. The promised force from Coventry had not even assembled yet, Crawford himself not having arrived in the city, let alone the troops that were needed. Meanwhile, in reprisal for the Parliamentary order to hang any Irish captured from the Royalist army, Rupert hanged a number of the men taken from Mytton near Oatley Hall. He then proceeded to visit Holt Castle, whilst his army marched to Whitchurch. On Thursday 20th, Rupert's army marched from Whitchurch to Market Drayton where he re-joined them. A little too late, the Scots finally arrived in Cheshire, Brereton rendezvousing with them on Knutsford Heath. The following day, Rupert's army continued to march away towards Newport with Rupert himself visiting Lord Newport's house at High Ercall. At a Council of War in Middlewich, the Parliamentarians resolved to march to Market Drayton to prevent the Royalists from plundering the area, as they stated, **"that part hasn't been [plundered] yet"**.

MD Documents 44, 45, & 46

However, the Scots were reluctant to march any further south despite Brereton trying to get them to Market Drayton. A compromise was reached, and they later marched as far as Whitchurch, arriving on Wednesday 26th. It is not certain whether Rupert had yet abandoned his plans to retake Shrewsbury, but whilst at Newport he heard of a rising at Hereford, and if anything, it was this that saved the town from attack. Rupert's army stayed around Newport until 24th, while Brereton was still trying to ascertain what had happened to his relief force, urging them to hurry as Rupert had paused in his march. The Scots would not march any further south unless Crawford arrived, but as he was still at Bedford waiting for troops to arrive, this was not going to happen. It seemed that Rupert was going to fortify Newport, perhaps as a base for taking Shrewsbury, as the report was that he sent out warrants to bring in great quantities of provisions, pickaxes and spades. Monday 24th saw Rupert finally march away towards Shifnal. Possibly his pause about Newport was to decide whether to head for Shrewsbury or Hereford, but as he was renowned for impulsive decision making, it is more likely that his army just needed rest and to consolidate for a few days. In any case, Shrewsbury could now breathe a sigh of relief.

March 1645

On Tuesday 25th, (New Year's Day) Parliament wrote to Brereton ordering him to follow Rupert's army south with his English forces, but Brereton later claimed that he never received it. Brereton requested that Parliament should order that the Scots remain with him to advance his cause of the taking of Chester. By Wednesday 26th, Brereton had started to re-assert his control on the area, moving to once again block up Chester. The Royalists had plundered the area but had not attacked any of the garrisons with the exception of burning the abandoned ones.

MD Document 47

Brereton wrote again to Crawford at seven o'clock in the morning, requesting that he still come to aid in the capture of Chester. This was probably as a result of receiving a letter from Crawford that stated he was not yet up to full strength and could therefore not yet march. Brereton also received intelligence that Rupert was now as far south as Bromsgrove. The following day, Brereton wrote to Lord Leven requesting that he continue his army with Brereton for another three weeks. Chester had not received any aid at all from the princes' visit to the area and was now in as poor a state as previously. He confirmed in another letter that he could not follow Rupert south, as the Scots would not follow him past the Cheshire/Shropshire border. That same day, Parliament wrote to Brereton to inform him that they had ordered Crawford to aim at the Royalists instead of heading to Sir William's aid. Rupert's army marched further away, reaching Tenbury. On Friday 28th Brereton was still trying to get permission to keep the Scots with him although his opinion was that he had little hope of them remaining. The forces that had managed to arrive from other counties had already been sent back. He heard a rumour that the princes were returning with ordinance, but he obviously doubted its veracity, adding to his letter, **"with no certainty"**.

In a letter he sent to the Committee of Both Kingdoms, he listed his strength as now being **"only one thousand foot and the seventeen companies in [Shrewsbury]"**. He also stated that he had sent a party of three horse regiments and the Cheshire and Staffordshire foot from Shrewsbury against High Ercall.

MD Document 48

He wrote another letter which is mostly interesting in that it states that Fairafx's troops sent under Colonel Bethell had quartered at Market Drayton. Lesley wrote to Brereton that his forces were rendezvousing at Woodhouses, along the Nantwich road at 7 the next morning. The compilers of the Tanner MS catalogue in the Bodleian Library created a curious entry. They list a document as **"Extract of a letter from Lieut-gen. D. Lesley to the Scotch Commissioners; Sambrook, Saturday March 29th"**. If this was written from Sambrook, it would be very interesting, putting Lesley South of Market Drayton. However. On examination of the contents, the location is not clear, being written as **"Sambuk"** or **"Sambich"**, and on consideration of the route of the Scots army's intended march, it should be read as **"Sandbach"**. One of the first sentences contained in the body of the text is **"As I was marching out of Shropshire back again to Yorkshire"**, a phrase which can only lead to the Sandbach interpretation. I only include it here to save confusion for any future scholar. On Sunday 30th, Rupert arrived at Hereford.

April 1645

MD Document 50

On Tuesday 1st, Brereton was still hearing that the princes were likely to return, so he once again requested that the Scots could be sent back to him. However, Brereton's previous statement that the Scots would not engage the enemy until Crawford had come up had angered the Scots. Brereton had stated that the enemy was then about Newport and that he would have attacked them with the Scots' support and that he had much desired that the entire force should have advanced to Market Drayton.

Thursday 3rd April would prove to be a momentous day. Not because Parliament were discussing how to complain about Rupert's hanging of the prisoners, but because it also marked the passage of the **"Self-Denying Ordinance"** through Parliament. This was designed to exclude politicians from being in charge of troops once a period of forty days had passed. This would have stripped Brereton of his command, but this being very prejudicial to their aims, they managed to continually gain an extension of the forty-day grace period in his case. To mark his importance to the Parliamentary cause it should be noted that there were very few exceptions, one being for Oliver Cromwell. One of the reasons for this act to be passed was the desire to remove the ineffectual nobles from leadership of the army, especially Essex and Manchester, and it paved the way for Cromwell's New Model Army.

On Friday 4th, Parliament wrote to Prince Rupert with their explanation why they had ordered the hanging of Irish amongst the Royalist army, but Rupert's retaliation had won the day, and this policy was not followed thereafter. Therefore, the arrival of the princes' army in the area had achieved very little except by way of plundering. Chester was still besieged. Beeston was under siege again, and Market Drayton had seen a lot of troops both Royalist and Parliamentarian passing through and quartering there.

11 Will the Princes Return?

April 1645

MD Documents 51 & 53

On Tuesday 8th, Sir William Brereton wrote to let the Committee of Both Kingdoms know that he had once again blocked up Chester, stopping any provisions from entering the city. He was aware that the princes and their army may return, as he had been questioning prisoners, and concluded from what he heard that his area was likely to be the seat of that summer's war. He requested that the forces originally assigned to assist him be kept prepared, and that on any sign of the princes returning Northwards towards him, that the Scots be ordered to head for Market Drayton or Whitchurch. The King wanted Chester relieved and Shrewsbury re-captured.

Money was still an important issue. The Derbyshire and Yorkshire Horse were close to mutinying, and Sir William promised them that he would get them some money from Parliament, Wales or the taking of Chester, to try and keep them from deserting. Parliament, realising the importance of holding onto Shrewsbury and not letting Chester be relieved, requested five thousand pounds to be sent to Brereton for this purpose. The Scots meanwhile had received intelligence that the princes were intending to head for Newark, but Brereton answered Lord Leven that their intelligence was false and that he needed them to return to him at the first Royalist movement in his direction, intending to meet the enemy in battle at Market Drayton or Newport. Parliament agreed with Brereton, also writing to the Scots requesting their presence. At this point, the Shropshire Committee were besieging High Ercall.

On Sunday 13th, the Coventry Committee told Brereton that Prince Maurice was at Bromsgrove and Rupert was marching towards Bridgnorth. The following day, Parliament wrote to the Committees of Derbyshire, Staffordshire, Lancashire, Nottinghamshire and Shropshire to send supplies to Cheshire, also to Fairfax to send his best horse troops. The Derbyshire Horse were ordered to return to Derby to recruit and refresh, their forces now dwindled by desertion through lack of pay, but the Yorkshire Horse still remained, despite making threats to cut Sir William into small pieces, stealing from and threatening the people around Wybunbury where they were now quartered.

MD Document 54

By the following Tuesday, Parliament had also received intelligence that the princes would be heading back to Shropshire/Cheshire and they assured him that the five thousand pounds would be forthcoming, as would supplies from the surrounding counties and the Scots troops. By the next day, Wednesday 16th, the Shropshire committee hearing that there were a number of enemy troops nearby, abandoned the High Ercall siege. They had heard that there were two thousand Royalist troops at Wellington. This proved false, but they still believed that there were numerous troops in the area.

On the Friday, Brereton wrote that the princes were still around Hereford, but their preparations seemed to be more for heading towards Bristol. He still believed that there was a force in Shropshire, and that because most of the forces that had been with him had now returned to their respective counties, he was very vulnerable. The amount of intelligence that was coming in at this point was very contradictory.

The best information seemed to be that Prince Maurice had headed towards Oxford, to escort the King to Worcester and that Rupert was still at Hereford. This still indicated that the Royalists were heading north, and Shrewsbury/Chester would be the most likely target. In the meanwhile, Brereton moved the Yorkshire Horse to Mold, perhaps hoping that a move to a fresh area would persuade them to cause less trouble.

MD Document 56

By Friday 25th, the five thousand pounds finally cleared the Parliamentary red tape needed before it could be sent. Brereton received a note from Parliament telling him to take care in his dealings with the Scots, as a letter he had sent previously stating that they had been less than keen to pursue the enemy south had given them offence. They also told him that once he had the money, he needed to stay and finish the job at Chester, and not to travel to London until the period specified by the Self-Denying Ordinance had passed. The Royalists of Chester and North Wales had, by this time, realised that the Self-Denying Ordinance meant that Brereton and Middleton would have to vacate their command shortly. Brereton was starting to consider what was to happen once he had to leave his post.

He once again wrote to the Scots requesting them to march towards Market Drayton. The Shropshire committee were still receiving intelligence that the Royalists were preparing to march to recapture Shrewsbury, or at the least, relieve Chester. The following Wednesday, 30th April, Brereton had decided what to do about his end of command. He wrote to the Parliament that if the Royalists arrived first, that he would leave Lothian and Jones in charge, but if the Scots arrived first, he would let the commander of them have charge.

The next day, the Yorkshire horse requested to be sent home, but Brereton stated that until he knew the princes' motions, that they could not be released. He asked them to move their quarters to near Whitchurch, suggesting Ightfield, Ash, Combermere, Marbury or Norbury. However, their Lieutenant-Colonel declined stating that it would just exasperate them further to move until definite news of the princes' motions had been received. Part of their force under Major Goodricke did move to Ightfield but suggested that no further movements would take place until they got paid.

May 1645

On Saturday 3rd May, the Cheshire gentry petitioned Parliament over the removal of Brereton, and what would happen as a consequence. The next day, however, definitive information was received over the princes' movements. They had all marched to Oxford, and so it seemed that, for the moment, at least the danger was over, and that Shrewsbury and the siege of Chester were safe.

Market Drayton's Civil War

12 The Royalists' Summer Campaign

May 1645

On Sunday 4th, the two Princes arrived at Oxford to urge the King to march Northwards to encounter the Scots in Yorkshire, and that on the way, Chester could be relieved. Three days later, the King ordered the march out of Oxford. They started out at daybreak, and the army consisted of horse and foot totalling five to six thousand, mostly horse. They also had with them eighty carriages and thirteen pieces of ordinance. This first day they marched to Woodstock. The next day, near Stow on the Wold, the King and Prince Rupert's armies joined together. The King quartered at Stow on the Wold and Prince Rupert at Bradwell.

So far, Brereton was totally unaware of these movements towards him. The day after, Friday 9th, they marched to Evesham where they joined with another three thousand three hundred foot under Lord Astley. That day, Parliament sent a letter to Brereton informing him that the King was on the move towards him.

By the next day, the Royalist army had arrived near Worcester. Parliament now started to send out letters for all the northern forces to combine and to order the Scottish army southwards. The House of Lords, mindful of Brereton's impending removal, directed that his cavalry was to be commanded by Colonel Jones and that his infantry was to be commanded by Lothian.

On Sunday 11th, the Royalists had a rendezvous of the whole army, now also including Sir Marmaduke Langdale with his Northern Horse. Later that day, the King and Prince Rupert arrived at Droitwich, the army being camped near Bromsgrove. Brereton had, by now, heard of the King's advance, and started writing letters to the Scots and Lord Fairfax to inform them. Parliament also wrote letters to the Scots urging them to send assistance towards Cheshire. At this point, Oliver Cromwell with seven thousand horse and foot were at Woodstock, following the Royalists from the south. Cromwell had the same problem as Brereton, in that he was due to be removed, being an MP for Cambridge. Parliament started to consider what to do about the Self-Denying Ordinance. Removing these two commanders would leave themselves seriously exposed with such a large Royalist army in the field. The following day, Brereton had his period of command extended by forty days, whilst the King rested his army. By Tuesday, Brereton had started to act. He started to secure and victual his garrisons. However, further south, Cromwell, by now only ten or so miles from Warwick was ordered to cease his pursuit, although he did not immediately comply.

Parliament sent more letters, ordering troop movements. Troops were to be sent from Yorkshire, Derbyshire, Staffordshire, Nottinghamshire and Lincolnshire towards Brereton, and other forces were ordered to be sent towards the Scots. Wednesday 14th saw the King's forces taking the Parliamentary garrison at Hawkesley House without too much effort. The defenders refused to fight when they saw it was the King attacking them. The Royalists gained a large amount of supplies and burnt the house. Brereton was still not having much luck with the Yorkshire Horse. At this point they were at Knutsford but refused to head towards Brereton unless they got paid. This he did the next day, telling them to either now act, or leave. That next day, Thursday 15th May, the Royalists marched from four o'clock in the morning until six in the evening without stopping, and the King arrived at Himley Hall in Staffordshire.

Although Brereton had not yet removed his sieges of Hawarden and Chester, he started the preparations by removing the great artillery piece that was at Hawarden. Friday saw the Royalists arrive at Wolverhampton. Rupert quartered in the town, which was described as **"a handsome town with one fair church in it."**

MD Documents 58, 59, 60, 61, 63, 64, 65, 66, 67, 68 & 69

The King quartered at Bushbury, which was described as **"a private sweet village."** Brereton and his commanders now started talking about removing the troops from the Welsh side of Chester. This included those besieging Hawarden where they had been digging a mine under the walls, although this was not yet near enough completion. On the following day, the army marched through Tong and then to Newport. The King quartered himself at Chetwynd Hall, while Prince Rupert was at the Swan in Newport.

The troops, spread out for their camp were as far north as Cheswardine.

Market Drayton's Civil War

Brereton held a Council of war which almost unanimously voted to withdraw from the sieges of Hawarden and Chester and to retreat into their garrisons. Saturday 17th, Brereton had still not yet decided where best to rendezvous with the Scots who were on their march. The Royalist army had settled down for a rest around Newport. The day after, Brereton ordered all his troops both out of Wales and all garrisons except Tarvin to retreat towards Nantwich. On Monday 19th, with the Royalists still around Newport, Brereton named Barlow Moor as his army's rendezvous point. Then, Barlow moor was an area of moorland near Chorlton-cum-Hardy, but is now a part of the Greater Manchester conurbation. Cromwell, who had still not regarded the Parliament's order to stop the pursuit, was now ordered to join with the Scots if they got that far, otherwise to march as best serves if the King changed his course. Cromwell now wrote to Parliament stating that they were turning back, and the Scots had also decided to not move yet, as they were still uncertain whether the King was indeed heading for Chester or would change course east towards Newark.

The following day, Tuesday 20th was a momentous day for Market Drayton. The Royalist army arrived and encamped in and around the town at places such as Blore Heath, Woore and Moreton Say. Prince Rupert quartered in the town itself, probably at one of the inns. The King, initially in Market Drayton itself where he wrote some letters, then moved to Betton Hall just outside the town, where he set up his court.

Whilst the Royalists were there, Sir Marmaduke Langdale was sent with a party of horse to attempt to surprise Wem, which at this point only had 150 men in it. However, they arrived too late in the day, so seeing no opportunity, they returned.

Brereton carried on preparing for the Parliamentary rendezvous, but he wrote to Parliament expressing dismay that Cromwell and the Scots had not joined him already, thereby making a force easily big enough to defeat the King.

All the intelligence that Brereton had (including from captured Royalists) was that Chester was the target. On Wednesday 21st, the army rested at Market Drayton. We are not told what effect this would have had upon the market, but one can only imagine. Brereton himself put all his foot into his garrisons and headed for Barlow Moor with his horse and dragoons.

MD Documents 70, 71, 72, 73, 74, 75 & 76

Whatever the intelligence, the following day saw the Royalist army march. However, instead of heading towards Chester, they changed direction and headed into Staffordshire, through Loggerheads and Ashley. This is recorded in Ashley's parish register with the phrase **"Serenissimus Rex Carolus per hanc villam de Ashley transiit ad Stone cum magno militum exercitu."** This translates to **"Most Serene King Charles passed through Ashley to Stone with a large army."** That night the Royalists arrived around Stone. Brereton, unaware of the King's departure carried on with his preparations. The following day he wrote that the Royalists were departing east, but not entirely sure whether the intention was to march via Newcastle-Under-Lyme and then via Congleton to Lancashire, or whether they had changed course towards Newark. By Saturday, the Royalist army had got to Uttoxeter. A group of Cheshire committee men urged that instead of the whole army following the King, that some forces be left behind, as there were still Royalist troops in the area, and that they had been emboldened by the raising of the sieges.

Meanwhile, of course, Parliament had not yet heard of the King's change of course, so still carried on sending letters, orders etc. to protect Chester. By Sunday, the Scots had heard of the change of course and so stopped heading towards Brereton, who was on the Lancashire/Cheshire border with his force of horse and dragoons. Brereton had sent Colonel Bowyer to gain intelligence of what the King was up to, but by now the Royalists had got too far for this to be useful. On Monday 26th, Brereton held his rendezvous at Barlow Moor. He ordered Colonel Bowyer to return and was still trying to arrange his troops in case they were ordered to march after the King, but otherwise was at a loss what to do, the King now having disappeared.

13 The routing of Sir Sydenham Poyntz?

May 1645

Brereton continued his rendezvous at Barlow Moor for five or six days, while the King was heading East towards Newark. Letters flew backwards and forwards between the various Parliamentary forces detailing the Royalists movements, but there was no army big enough in the field to prevent his movements. On Thursday 29th, Brereton signalled his intention to return from Manchester. The Chester royalists had been getting bold during their absence and looting the area between Beeston and Chester. He informed Parliament that as the Scots were no further from the King than he was that they should be sent after the King instead. Two days later, the Royalists took Leicester with heavy casualties on both sides. Parliament, who were still trying to combine forces to assault the royalists, issued orders at the start of June to the northern counties to raise troops to march to Sir John Gell to join with the Scots. They specifically requested that Brereton, although to send some troops, was to stay in Cheshire to look after things there. Prince Rupert was, at this time, doing what he did best, charging around the midlands with his cavalry, and visited such places as Daventry, Market Harborough and Wolverhampton. Skirmishes continued all this time between forces from Hereford, Ludlow, Shrewsbury and Chester.

June 1645

Brereton now left Nantwich to head for London as he had been recalled by Parliament. He must now have feared that someone else would be appointed to command in our area. On his way, in Stafford, he sent out Colonel Stone who met with some of the King's forces, and took men and money. On Saturday 14th, one of the most decisive battles of the war took place, at Naseby. Sir Thomas Fairfax routed the royalist forces, capturing all their carriages and ordinance. The King with what remained of his army fled via Lichfield, towards South Wales and safety. Two days later, Parliament wrote to Brereton requesting that he kept his troops in Cheshire as the situation had now changed somewhat. Leicester was now recaptured by the Parliament's forces. More local Parliamentary troops also took many of the garrisons around this time, such as Shrawardine, Caus Castle, Stokesay Castle and Stocklidge House. On Friday 27th, the State Papers record that Brereton and Middleton were due to appear in Parliament the next day, although on the Saturday this was amended to Monday.

July 1645

In late July a Scottish army under Lord Leven besieged Hereford. They did not travel past Market Drayton on the way there, but when they returned, they may well have passed this way, although this is not recorded.

August 1645

At the start of August, Brereton and Middleton were still in London about Parliamentary business. A few days later, the King with the remains of his army set out northwards from Cardiff. On Thursday 7th they arrived at Ludlow travelling from there to Bridgnorth and then Litchfield. In response to this, Parliament appointed Colonel Sir Sydenham Poyntz to command a force to head towards the King. The royalists continued heading East at this point, apparently once again towards Newark, and on Friday 15th Gell wrote to the speaker that the King was at Chatsworth. Gell estimated his strength to be only about two thousand, mostly cavalry although (in his words) **"ill armed and ill horsed."** Receiving intelligence, the King turned and headed into Yorkshire, although how good this intelligence was is open to question, including the untruth that Poyntz had been taken prisoner. On Thursday 28th the speaker wrote to the Committee at Nantwich that their request for assistance in reducing Chester had been deferred until Monday September 8th. Two days later, Prince Rupert lost Bristol. This was almost as huge an issue for the Royalist cause as the defeat at Naseby.

September 1645

It took Parliament until Friday 19th to discuss the business of Chester, and their answer was that they could not spare the forces which would have to be taken from those following the King. Meanwhile the Royalist army was now marching through Wales towards Chester. By Tuesday 23rd, the outworks at Chester were taken by Parliament, and the sword and mace of the city Mayor were taken, which to the Parliamentarians was a good omen. On this day, the King and his army arrived out of Wales. The next day intelligence was received in Chester of a Parliamentary force under the command of Sir Sydenham Poyntz that had arrived in Whitchurch, and was heading towards them. As some of the outworks had already been taken, it was decided that the best form of defence was attack, and a force was sent out to meet them.

This action, known as the Battle of Rowton Heath was a decisive victory for Parliament. Sir Marmaduke Langdale, in command of the Royalist detachment had not informed the King, and as a result the rest of the Royalist soldiers within the city walls did not arrive to support them. As Langdale at first pushed Poyntz back, this could have made for a very different outcome. The King, having been informed what was going on too late to do anything about it, watched from the Phoenix Tower as the rest of his troops sallied out to try and save the day. Over one thousand of the Royalist troops were taken prisoner, with three hundred killed. Gerard and Langdale were both wounded. Chester was now not safe, so the next day the King retreated to Denbigh, via Hawarden with what was left of his army. He remained there for four days, waiting for the stragglers from his force, which when assembled reached only two thousand four hundred. Notwithstanding the Self-Denying Ordinance, on Thursday 25th Parliament voted that Brereton should command forces in Cheshire for another four months.

The Self-Denying Ordinance had not been suspended for Sir Thomas Middleton however, and on the following day, Sir Thomas Mytton was assigned to take his office in Wales with the rank of Colonel. Brereton, meanwhile sent word to Stafford, requesting troops so that he could continue in his efforts to secure Chester.

At this stage, Parliament had not heard about the victory at Rowton, and were busy sending letters to try and press the advantage of the suburbs being taken. The King, meanwhile, was sensible of the danger that Chester was now in, and resolved to keep the Welsh side of the city open, so that supplies could be sent in. That day, Friday 26th, prisoners from Rowton Moor were taken to Nantwich.

The following day, Sir Sydenham Poyntz was still about the suburbs of Chester. At Denbigh, Prince Maurice arrived with his troop and Prince Rupert's horse. Monday 29th saw the King travel to Llandisilio. Poyntz by this time had received intelligence of the King's movements. The following day, Parliament, having now heard of Poyntz's victory sent him money and ordered him to continue to pursue the King and assist the Chester besiegers. The King now travelled with his army to Bridgnorth. Their route took them within three miles of Shrewsbury where they were given several alarms by the Shrewsbury Horse.

October 1645

The King and his force rested at Bridgnorth until Thursday 2nd when they marched to Lichfield. Parliament wrote to the committees of Derbyshire, Shropshire, Lancashire and Staffordshire to send as many horse-mounted troops as they could to assist Poyntz. They also wrote to the committee at York two days later requesting troops to head towards Poyntz.

On Sunday 5th, the King marched towards Newark. Poyntz was ordered to follow him. Parliament finally decided to do something about reducing Chester, and requested troops from Derbyshire, Warwickshire and Staffordshire to march towards Chester.

On Tuesday 7th, Poyntz, presumably not having yet received the orders from Parliament was still about Chester, where on the next day he summoned them to surrender. Their answer was that they were not in such a state that they needed to, but would send a messenger to the King to see what he thought. They requested a ceasefire for two weeks so that they could get a response.

The following day they received their response from Poyntz which was a flat refusal. Chester replied that they were ready to defend themselves. Poyntz almost immediately restarted the attack, reportedly firing three hundred and fifty six cannon shots but it didn't come to anything. However, on Saturday 11th, Poyntz received his orders to march. By Thursday 16th he was between Derby and Nottingham.

MD Documents 77, 78, 79 & 80

And now to the point of this chapter from a Market Drayton viewpoint. A set of letters were sent from Chester, and intercepted by Brereton, giving information that on Wednesday 15th, Poyntz had his quarters at Market Drayton beaten up by Sr William Vaughan or the governor of High Ercall.

Whether this is true or not, or whether Poyntz just retreated towards

Newark due to orders from Parliament, it details the fact that once again Market Drayton was being used as the quarters for a Parliamentarian force.

The rumours may well have started because a skirmish took place as Poyntz was leaving, any news of this sort would have been good news for a besieged city like Chester. Indeed, in Brereton's letter books, intelligence from within the city records that **"most nights at the parade letters of good news are read, that Sir Thomas Fairfax is routed, Maurice and Vaughan with 1,000 and the like."**

Market Drayton's Civil War

14 Events Leading to the Fall of Chester

October 1645

By Saturday 18th Brereton was on his way back from London. Parliament were concentrating on reducing Chester, and they wrote to the committees of Derbyshire, Lancashire, Shropshire, Staffordshire and North Wales to send any provisions they could into the Leaguer. Three days later, Brereton had got as far as Coventry. Another two days travelling saw him at Stafford, where he was expecting to encounter the forces of Colonel Hastings, but Hastings had moved on. The next day, Friday 24th saw him getting involved in the Stafford elections.

Shropshire's committee wrote to the Leaguer on the same day, informing them that the enemy was on the march and expected to get to Bishop's Castle that night. It was estimated that this force consisted of two thousand, except for three hundred horse that had gone to Chirk. They were believed to be planning to relieve Chester on the Welsh side. This was confirmed in a letter to the Shropshire committee the next day which stated that captured men had told them that they were three thousand, mostly horse and that the force was designed to raise a siege.

The Shropshire committee also received the same news from some Shropshire men in Montgomery, but this put the force at between twelve and fifteen hundred horse and foot and further stated that they were ill-armed and had got to Hyssington towards Ruthin. The Montgomery committee repeated this information in a letter to Powis Castle, but breaks the troop numbers down as twelve hundred horse and three hundred foot of which five hundred were **"riff-raff"**. Most of the foot were armed but only a tenth of the horse had pistols. They were expected to quarter that night at Pontesbury.

A large number of Parliamentary letters fly about for the next couple of days, attempting to concentrate what forces they could muster to keep the siege at Chester active with the large Royalist force approaching. One from Monday 27th interests us the most, as it concerns a group of soldiers, the Reformadoes, that we will hear about a bit later in this chapter. Colonel Jones wrote to Adjutant Lothian to hasten the Shropshire horse which by now were at Whitchurch and he urged him to get Mytton to send troops to Wrexham. He added that he required two hundred foot to be sent there, or else the Reformadoes would not abide there.

With the reorganisation of the Parliamentarian army, creating the **"New Model Army"**, a large number of officers ended up without commands of their own. These were formed up into troops and became known as **"Reformadoes"**. One such group was in our area, although over the border in Wales.

So, at this point, a large Royalist force was on its way to relieve Chester, and the Parliamentarians were doing everything they could to continue the siege. This was not made easy by the lack of troops, provisions and money.

Some of the troops already with the Leaguer were ready to mutiny for want of pay. They also received word from Sir Sydenham Poyntz that all his forces were occupied and he could not send any. Sir William Brereton sums it up quite nicely in a single letter written on Thursday 30th October to a member of the Committee of Both Kingdoms in London.

"At Stafford on Wed 22nd Oct I received news of enemy's preparations for relieving Chester. At several requests to do so, I sent post to Gen. Poyntz to procure assistance. On coming to Nantwich I received letters confirming the enemy's approach to relieve Chester. By this time, they were past Salop on their march. I sent despatches to Gloucester, Evesham, Northampton, Coventry, Montgomery, Oswestry, Derby, Lancashire and to Gen. Poyntz. On Monday I went towards the Leaguer and met more messages on the way, and I sent several more. The next morning I went to Chester and so over the water to Dodleston on the Welsh side where we resolved speedily to collect our forces into a body and follow the enemy, which was delayed by a day due to Col. Mytton's forces coming up. On Monday the Cheshire foot who were nearly two months in arrears were in a high mutiny. On my coming to them the next morning, they were not only well appeased but seemed so well satisfied that none demanded any pay. IF IT PLEASE God to enable us to scatter those forces that are now drawn into a body, I hope it will be not long before Chester and Beeston fall into our hands. P.S. I have so little money I daren't pay anyone for fears of others mutinying. We need ten thousand

pounds."

In another letter sent the next day, he gives details of his strength. He stated that he had sent a force of twelve hundred horse and as many foot ten miles towards the enemy under Colonels Jones and Mytton and Adjutant Lothian.

The reason for doing this was so that the forces within Chester could not sally out and join in any fighting that occurred, which was something Brereton learned at Nantwich. He confirmed that Cheshire now had no provisions left to use, and that he had received nothing from the surrounding counties. He also now owed sixteen hundred pounds for ammunition.

Brereton now gives us a list of all the forces under his command at this time. Apart from those sent with Jones, Mytton and Lothian, he listed sixteen hundred horse plus an unspecified number of the Shropshire horse and two thousand nine hundred and sixty foot. He also listed an unspecified number of Reformadoes.

On Friday night, 30th, the force commanded by Mytton, Jones and Lothian, which now included the Reformadoes quartered at Ruthin, where they heard that the enemy was at Denbigh.

November 1645

The next day, Saturday 1st, they marched to meet the enemy. A Forlorn Hope unit was formed which included forty men from each regiment and this was commanded by one of the Reformadoes, a Captain Otter. Captain Otter was described by Nathaniel Lancaster in his report of the battle as **"a gallant soldier"**. The outcome was that the Parliamentarians won the day and the Reformadoes were of great service in a battle that saw the Royalists routed.

This regiment of Reformadoes had marched from London the last time that Brereton returned to Cheshire and was commanded by Colonel Henry Sanderson. Under him were three troops plus a further group of unattached officers labelled "Heteroclytes". Under Sanderson were Major Baker, and Captain Otter (sometimes spelled Potter).

The day after, Brereton wrote to William Lenthall to tell Parliament of the victory. He gives the result as five to six hundred enemy horse taken, three to four hundred prisoners and a hundred enemy slain. He mentions the Forlorn Hope and Captain Otter, calling him **"a very brave and valiant man"**.

On Monday 3rd, the Shropshire committee wrote to Brereton to try and retrieve their horse which had been with him some time, as they were having continuing trouble with the Royalist garrisons at High Ercall, Bridgnorth and Ludlow. They did however let him know that they were sending provisions to Wem from where he could convey them to Cheshire.

The following day, Tuesday 4th, Parliament started to act. They ordered an extra twenty barrels of powder for the siege, six thousand pounds to be raised to pay the troops there and to order the navy to be on the lookout for Royalist troop ships from Ireland. That day, Poyntz wrote to Brereton stating that the King had marched out of Newark with five hundred horse to head towards Chester and that he was sending troops with all speed to assist him. The next day he wrote again confirming that there were three hundred horse with the King and that they had left Newark on the evening of Monday 3rd.

Thursday, Ashurst wrote to Brereton from London, stating that they were dealing with his needs, but that there was no intelligence of any Royalist shipping heading towards him, and that they were trying to acquire both powder and money.

MD Document 81

The following Monday, 10th, Brereton wrote to Colonel Mainwaring who was at Nantwich that he had intelligence that the King was, by this time marching near Oxford, and that Mainwaring's troops should head in his direction, always keeping between the King and Chester, and not too far so that he could interrupt the King or return to Brereton. Mainwaring received this at ten o'clock the following morning and promised to prepare to march by nightfall to Market Drayton and the places thereabouts. The next day, Poyntz wrote to Brereton asking for his troops back as he needed them to try and take Newark.

Market Drayton's Civil War

On Saturday 15th, letters started flying about between the Parliamentarians stating that a small Royalist force of between eighty and one hundred horse and forty foot were on their way from Chirk with provisions to relieve Beeston. With the relieving force in mind, the Parliamentarian besiegers, and the defenders at Beeston signed articles of agreement for the Royalists to give up the castle. Brereton confirms the successful taking of it in a letter to Parliament the next day along with the request that the money and ammunition were needed urgently, but that they had received some provisions from Shropshire and Staffordshire. Also on that day, the Warwickshire committee wrote to Sir William requesting their troops back. He wrote back on Wednesday 19th, stating that he could not spare them, but that Chester could not now hold out long.

In the meantime, on Tuesday 18th, Brereton tried to get Chester to surrender by sending a "summons". In it he stated that if the agreement was not reached then any further harm to both the people and the city would be on their heads, not his. He did not get an answer that day, but a refusal came the next.

On Thursday 20th Brereton wrote to Lenthall about the summons and refusal, mentioning that they had received no provisions from Derbyshire or Lancashire and very little from Wales. However, Derbyshire wrote to Brereton on the following day stating that they could not send any due to a command from Poyntz.

Saturday 22nd saw Brereton writing to the neighbouring county committees that with Beeston taken, the enemy would now send any forces it could muster in an attempt to relieve Chester. He requested intelligence of any enemy movements. He had already received intelligence that a force of fourteen hundred foot and two thousand six hundred horse were near Worcester on their way to join with the other Royalist troops to relieve Chester. By Wednesday 26th, he had received intelligence that this force now estimated at two to three thousand were marching under the command of Vaughan to Ludlow. However, as is usual, there were as many estimates of the enemy's strength as there were letters. The Worcester committee reckoned five hundred foot and two hundred horse. Parliament themselves wrote to Brereton the next day stating that there were a thousand to fifteen hundred horse and that they were now at Leighton Buzzard.

MD Document 82

Also on Thursday, the Reformado officers now at Blakenhall wrote to Brereton, stating "**This morning, according to your order, I drew out our regiment, with all the rest of the horse being drawn up and ready to march. They, hearing they were to march to Drayton, with a unanimous vote absolutely refused...**"

However, this was not a slur on Market Drayton itself. They were complaining that they had no proper base and that they had been marching to and fro while **"inferior men"** were properly quartered. They stated that these inferior men were also constantly paid while they had **"not wherewithal to cover their nakedness nor a penny money in their pockets."** Because their commanders could not get them to march, they stood them down. Major Baker who was at Denbigh was one of the signatories.

By Sunday 30th, news was coming in to Brereton that the Royalists' approach was not imminent. The King was at Oxford. Again, the Shropshire committee requested their troops back stating that in a skirmish at High Ercall, Colonel Vincent Corbet was wounded in the thigh. They promised that if they had them back, they would return them if any large force came his way.

December 1645

However, at the start of December, intelligence kept on arriving of the Royalist force but not necessarily heading his way. On Tuesday 2nd, Major Hungerford wrote from Stokesay Castle to let him know that the following troops were gathering. **"Newark 1,500 horse, Hereford 200; Ludlow and Bridgnorth 150; expecting force from Goring, also from other parts as Lichfield, Dudley, all that can be made besides the horse that came with the King to Oxford. They hope to be ready to march Thursday or Friday. They quarter from Tenbury all the way to Bewdley, so to Worcester and so towards Oxford."**

This may well have been the gathering of an army to march north. Chester was vitally important to the Royalist cause and they would have wanted to relieve it at all costs. Also on that day, Lathom House, which had long been the focus of the Lancashire committee, was taken. They wrote to Brereton two days later offering to send troops to his aid.

On Friday 5th, the rumours seemed to have been confirmed. A messenger captured by Brereton's troops stated that the previous Tuesday (2nd) the Royalists inside Chester had received the news that relief was on its way to them. Brereton immediately wrote to Poyntz and Parliament with the news.

The following day, he sent several letters warning everyone about the King gathering his army, informing of the poor state of Chester and requesting troops and provisions. The Warwickshire committee wrote to Sir William that they needed their troops back, but having heard of the King's intentions they had been spoiling fords and demolishing bridges to slow their march. That day, Staffordshire sent intelligence that five hundred had come through Enville, and that three thousand more were expected to come after them.

The following day, Sunday 7th, Vaughan with fifty horse had entered Bridgnorth. Later that day, the rest of his force, all horse, entered the town. It was reported that they entered five abreast and it took them an hour. More rumours spread the next day, including that the King was at Worcester on his way. The Shropshire committee said he wasn't and in fact, he was still in Oxford.

On Monday 8th, Brereton wrote to Parliament requesting a thousand to fifteen hundred horse from Poyntz. However, Parliament wrote to Brereton to let him know that the King was still at Oxford, and that they had a force of horse to follow him.

On the same day, Poyntz wrote that he only had four hundred horse with him and couldn't send any. He stated that the King was still in Oxford and that he was being kept there by the force Parliament mentioned under Sir Thomas Fairfax. Vaughan, at Bridgnorth wrote to the governor of Dudley, stating that it was his orders to relieve Chester and to send any horse and foot that could be spared.

Tuesday saw intelligence that Vaughan was breaking up his force and sending parties out to the local garrisons as well as Worcester. It was Parliament's opinion that the King would not wear out the horse in winter marches, so it appeared that Chester had been given up as lost. This was apparently confirmed from some captured Royalist soldiers, who stated that it was indeed the case unless they could get more troops sent from Ireland. As a result, the Shropshire committee requested that their troops be sent back. They were keen to stop up High Ercall's Royalist garrison.

One other interesting piece of information from this date in the state papers is that the Reformadoes (who had refused to go to Market Drayton) were still owed money from the committees of Oxfordshire, Buckinghamshire and Berkshire. It seemed that they were having trouble getting paid wherever they went, making their attitude more understandable. However, with money short, no troops were getting all that they should.

On Thursday 11th, Brereton wrote to Lancashire, requesting troops to help him finish off Chester. George Booth had been with the Lancashire troops and said that they would not march without money or provisions. He seemed confident however, that he could persuade them, and the Lancashire committee issued orders for all the Lancashire horse to march towards Chester. The Worcester committee confirmed that there was no large force coming from the King, but contrary intelligence from Benthall garrison stated that two thousand had been on their way from Oxford but had been attacked at Broadway.

The next day, more intelligence came from various sources that suggested that the King's forces were on the move and at Stow-on-the-Wold on their way to Worcester. Parliament concurred and started to organise troops to intercept or slow them down. They also wrote the following day to all the county committees who had troops at the Leaguer at Chester, asking them to keep them there for the moment.

On Sunday 14th the Royalist forces in Bridgnorth were told to be in readiness for marching to join with forces from Worcester to relieve Chester. On the same day, the Shropshire Committee told Brereton that the King could not draw sufficient forces together to do this, requesting their troops back, promising again to send them back if any large force came their way.

The next day saw many letters being sent with intelligence, none of which was from definite sightings. There were rumours aplenty, including that ten thousand were ready to sail from Ireland with two hundred barrels of powder. However, Brereton maintained his siege having stopped up all the routes in and out of Chester as well as he could.

MD Document 83

It is interesting at this point to have a Royalist letter, as most of the information that we have is from the Parliamentarian point of view. This one is from Sir Richard Lloyd at Holt Castle to Sir William Vaughan. **"Intelligence is brought here that this night the enemy is calling all the forces he can together to encounter the principal design for the relief of Chester. In Nantwich they have left but the townsmen and have called some clubmen to defend the town. They gave out that they will fight the King's forces in Shropshire. … At this time all the ditches about Nantwich are frozen. The works are but very slight and low, the river frozen over, where by the mills the entrance to the town lies open over the frost. So, with fifteen hundred foot that place might be taken by surprise, for in three hours from Market Drayton or Whitchurch you might march thither these fair nights. And if it fortuned that place were taken, besides the great booty in all kind, Chester were relieved."**

Poyntz, however, on the same day reported that the Royalists had returned to Banbury. It must have been very difficult deciding which intelligence was accurate.

On Tuesday 16th, a Royalist deserter was questioned by Brereton. He mentioned that he had stated that he would escape Chester if he could to Captain Otter (of the Reformadoes) although how they were in contact is not known. He gives a very good report on the state of Chester. In summary, food was running out, beer was running out (with no malt to make more), and they were down to forty barrels of powder with no sulphur to make it. He stated that most in Chester were wanting to surrender, especially with the nightly bombardment from Sir William's mortar.

The Lancashire Committee now wrote to Sir William informing him that with the fall of Lathom, all their horse and foot were now marching towards him.

Brereton continued examining men who had escaped from Chester. One, Giles Hunt, who had been conscripted by the Royalists described the conditions inside Chester. **"The poor are in very great want and many that have lived well formerly go begging. Little bread or beer left and beef is scarce. Welsh soldiers almost famished and general want amongst all, the gentry excepted. They have sufficient. They are daily expecting relief, but the poor and the soldiers want to surrender but the great men persuade them that relief is coming within a few days."** His opinion was that the city could not hold out for more than two weeks. Another escapee also stated that some of the Welsh soldiers had starved to death.

On Thursday 18th, the accounts record that of the Parliamentary grant, fifteen pounds had at last been paid to the Reformadoes. However, four days later, the Reformado commanders were begging Brereton to lend them two to three hundred pounds, as they had to walk their horses as they had no money to shoe them. Brereton could only promise to make Parliament aware of their plight.

A week later on Christmas Day, a Council of War was held at the Red Lion at Whitchurch. Officers of all the units were present. It had been previously decided to march the army as far as Newport, but for various reasons this was decided to be a bad move. Cheshire and Derbyshire troops were sent into Wales to strengthen that side of the siege along with Colonel Massey's Nantwich Foot and the Firelocks. The rest of the Cheshire foot were commanded to the Cheshire side of the Leaguer to strengthen it there. The rest of the army were ordered to remain at Whitchurch and **"parts adjacent"** until further order.

MD Document 85, 86, 87 & 89

The next day, Brereton sent orders to the party under Col. Bowyer which was around Whitchurch. **"It is this day ordered that the regt of Reformadoes under Maj. Baker, the Warks. Horse under Mj. Hawkesworth, the Lancs horse under Maj. Jackson and the Staffs. Horse under Col. Bowyer shall this night remain in the quarters where they now are, whereof Col. Bowyer with the concurrence of the** majors aforesaid, is to command and dispose of the said horse. If they think fit tomorrow to march to Drayton and to advertise Capt. Stone of their being there, that so he may communicate intelligence with them and, if any advantage offer itself against the enemy, that they may lay hold upon and prosecute the same. And if no such advantage be offered to continue together in their quarters till further order."

He then confirmed his intentions to Captain Stone at Stafford, adding that they were six to seven hundred horse in strength, and that they would head for Market Drayton and thence to Newport.

MD Document 84

Colonels Bowyer (Staffordshire Horse) and Hawkesworth (Warwickshire Horse) wrote from Adderley to Brereton. **"We are concluded of our rendezvous at Moretonwood tomorrow by 10 o'clock and so for Drayton. We came through the quarters of the Reformadoes this night, but they were removed out of them before orders could come to them, so that we do not know how to order them. We shall be at Drayton; we desire your further directions for our regts."**

This appears to indicate that Colonel Bowyer was having trouble communicating with all the troops under his command. The Reformadoes had returned to their old quarters in Cheshire against a direct order.

MD Document 88

Brereton, incensed at the Reformadoes behaviour wrote from Nantwich to Major Baker the next day, Saturday 27th. **"You know it was ordered on Thursday last that the four regts of horse should remain in a body. Also on Friday they were ordered to march towards Drayton and so forwards as there should be occasion. Now I have received letters from Col. Bowyer and Major Hawkesworth that your regt is gone to your old quarters in Cheshire., which I much marvel at, considering that Salop affords so good accommodation and you may with more comfort join with the rest. I pray you so soon as convenient draw your regiment to the rest and receive orders from Col. Bowyer, whereby you will prevent further inconveniences occasioned by your absence** and much satisfy the gents who desire your company. I have received letters from them even now that this night they intend to quarter at Drayton."

The following day, Sunday 28th, Major Baker sent a reply to Brereton from the Reformado quarters at Rode Hall. He claimed that he had not received his orders and that he had been ordered to return to Cheshire by Colonel Jones. He stated that they could not march back to Market Drayton, as forty of his horse were lame for want of shoeing but that he had no money to shoe them. Brereton sent the contents of Major Baker's letter to London stating that they would not march. Sir William gave up trying to order them, perhaps with some sympathy for their plight, but told Major Baker that **"I shall not say any more but I believe your accommodation in Salop would be better than where you are and the duty not hard. The Salop Com. Have sent to me desiring some assistance against High Ercall. I have ordered Col. Bowyer to march unto that county for their assistance and desire you will speedily write to him whether he may expect your coming up to him with your regt."**

Maj Baker wrote back from Rode Hall stating that in their current condition he could not order his men to return. Monday, Brereton wrote back to Major Baker, apologising for their conditions, but unable to help.

January 1645/6

On Thursday 1st, Colonel Bowyer wrote to Brereton that they had now marched to Newport, expecting to meet with the Shrewsbury Committee, but they had not heard from them. As the weather was bad, they were under strength, the Reformadoes not coming up and a large part of the Lancashire forces returning home, they considered that with Vaughan's force at Bridgnorth, other forces being near Kidderminster and Bewdley, and the High Ercall forces being two hundred foot and two hundred horse, they were not safe in their present location and had moved to parts about Newcastle-under-Lyme.

A week and a half later, Sunday 11th, the Reformadoes finally joined with Colonel Bowyer, who by this point was only one hundred foot and two troops of horse. The Warwickshire regiment had not come to Newcastle so far. The following day, Brereton wrote in his accounts that of the ten thousand pounds so far sent up by Parliament, the Reformadoes had by now received thirty-one pounds and seventeen shillings.

On Saturday 17th Byron wrote to Lord Astley that Chester could not hold out above nineteen days. He urged Astley (and Astley further urged Lord Loughborough) to send troops to Bridgnorth where he was assembling an army for Chester's relief to rendezvous on Tuesday 27th. Byron had also received word from Ormonde in Ireland that once the wind had turned, he would be sending three thousand more well-armed foot troops

Two days later, Monday 19th, the start of negotiations for the surrendering of Chester finally started. Brereton sent a message in to the city to start talking about propositions for peaceful handover. When Byron's thirty-six propositions arrived with Brereton, they were much more favourable to the Royalists than the Parliamentarians, so dismissing all but six of them out of hand and ensuring Byron that the preservation of the City was uppermost in his mind, Sir William sent back eight propositions of his own, which they refused to receive.

He confirmed to the Speaker, William Lenthall in a letter of Friday 23rd that Chester was still hopeful of relief and it was this that made their propositions unreasonable.

The following day saw Holt Castle surrendered to Colonel Mytton, and the siege of Ruthin Castle began. Brereton sent the force containing the Reformadoes, The Warwickshire Horse, The Staffordshire Horse and his own dragoons towards Ruthin to be placed under Mytton's command.

On sending Mytton's force towards Ruthin, the Royalist forces in Wales retreated towards Conway, removing hope of Chester's relief.

February 1645/6

On Sunday 1st, after nearly two weeks of negotiations, the surrender of Chester was agreed upon. Two days later, Brereton and his troops occupied the City.

March 1645/6 to April 1646

On or about Monday 16th, High Ercall was surrendered and the following month, Bridgnorth was also surrendered, marking the end of Royalist Shropshire.

May 1646

On Tuesday 5th, King Charles surrendered to the Scots and was held at Southwell near Newark, marking the end of this first part of the Civil War.

15 The Second Civil War

After Chester and the rest of Cheshire and Shropshire had fallen, both now being completely surrendered to the Parliamentarians, the war, what was left of it, moved away from the area and Market Drayton almost completely disappears from the written records for the time being.

However, after King Charles had escaped captivity and fled to the Isle of Wight in 1647, the second Civil War began, seeing Royalist uprisings in England and Wales and an invasion by the Scots, but being very uncoordinated, the Parliament was able to crush them.

I have found a few documents relating to this period, so, not really fitting into a timeline in the same way as previous events, I list them in this final chapter.

May 1648

MD Document 91

Firstly, there is a pamphlet from Friday 26th May 1648 which does not concern us much from the historical aspect, being a religious tract. It is grandly entitled: **"A Testimony of the Ministers in the Province of Salop, to the Truth of Jesus Christ, and to the Solemn League and Covenant, as also against the Errors, Heresies, and Blasphemies of these times, and the toleration of them. Sent up to the Ministers within the Province of London, Subscribers of the first Testimony."**

The reason that this is interesting from our point of view is that nearly sixty ministers from Shropshire signed it, including the ministers of Whitchurch, Hodnet, Prees, Wem, Adderley, Ightfield, Moreton-Say and Cheswardine. However, right at the top of the list and therefore putting himself forward as the main signatory, is Thomas Cook, styled the **"Pastor of Drayton Magna"**.

July 1648

There is a letter from Robert Clive of the Shropshire Committee from his house at Styche written on Saturday 15th July 1648 to William Lenthall, the Speaker of the House of Commons. It details the fact that many men from the county had been lately enlisted for the Royalist cause and that Parliament were failing to recruit enough men locally.

August 1648

Another pamphlet worthy of a mention, even though it does not directly mention Market Drayton is from Tuesday August 8th 1648, and is titled: "**A Great and Bloody Fight in Shropshire: Shrowden surprised by a troop of horse for the King and the Fight with Coll: Mackworth. The Number of the Lord Byron's Army, and their Rendezvous at Brees Heath. Prince Charles, his Instructions, with Sir Marmaduke Langdales Letter to the Lord Byron: The Lord Byron's Declaration to the Kingdom, and his Resolutions. With His Lordships Speech in the Head of his Army at Brees Heath.**"

Brees Heath, is, of course, Prees Heath, so a Royalist army was assembled at this date very near to Market Drayton. It tells the story of how Lord Byron appointed a troop of horse to enter Shrewsbury, which they did, but were driven out again. The rest of his army assembled on Prees Heath between Whitchurch and Market Drayton. Having unsuccessfully tried to take Shrewsbury, the fairly small army (about five hundred horse) marched off into Wales. The pamphlet also contains the speech that Lord Byron made to the troops at Prees Heath.

The incident was mentioned in Parliament on Tuesday 8th August, detailing that it occurred on Thursday August 3rd, where a letter about it from Colonel Mackworth was read. It confirms the details listed in the pamphlet, adding that Parliament's forces were now stationed in and around Wem. He used the incident to request a stronger garrison for Shrewsbury.

MD Document 92

On Thursday 17th the Battle of Preston was fought. This was the beginning of the end for the Second Civil War. It was fought between the forces of Cromwell, and the Scottish Engager Army with the forces of Sir Marmaduke Langdale. Cromwell and the Parliamentarians won the day, and Langdale escaped with some of his force and headed towards Warrington to attempt to join with Lord Byron's Cheshire Royalists.

Market Drayton's Civil War

The Parliamentarians attacking their rear, they marched on towards Malpas. From there they marched to Market Drayton and then to Stone. In the end, pretending to be Parliamentarians, Sir Marmaduke amongst others was captured in a house near Nottingham, and ended up imprisoned in the Castle there.

I have found no more Market Drayton documents between this and the beheading of King Charles I, which is a good point to finish. The other main events happening in Market Drayton shortly after this, the great fire and the story of how Thomas Cook, the vicar of Drayton became a Royalist spy occur in 1651, and that needs to be another work.

Market Drayton's Civil War

Appendix 1 Market Drayton Documents

This is the list of primary source documents specifically mentioning Market Drayton by name (I have included one that mentions Buntingsdale). I have transcribed all the text of each document to include in my research, but I have only reproduced the portion mentioning Market Drayton in the list below. Some of these documents contain many subjects and can be quite long, and without editing, this would be a very large section. Although in my original transcriptions I kept the spelling and grammar as in the original, I have modernised some of it here to make it more readable, while still retaining the original sense.

Document 1

Type:	Parliamentarian Pamphlet
Date:	Saturday 24th September 1642
Reference:	British Library Thomason E.119[5]. pp 3-4
Title:	The Latest Remarkable Truths from Worcester, Chester, Salop, Warwick, Stafford, Somerset, Devon, Yorke, and Lincoln Counties. Most of which was sent up Poste from judicious men, of purpose to be Printed. London, Printed for T.Underhill. 1642.
Notes:	This document details events around the Royalist attack on Nantwich on Saturday 24th September 1642. Transcribed from an original copy in the British Library.
Relevant Text:	The Commissioners of Array in Cheshire met upon Monday last at a house in the Forest of Delamere, and as we hear they combined together by an oath of secrecy to plunder and disarm the town of Nantwich, which they have done by the assistance of about fifteen hundred horse which came from **Drayton** to meet them, under the command of Lord Grandison.

Document 2

Type:	Royalist Letter
Date:	Wednesday 28th September 1642
Reference:	Trans. Shrops. Arch. Nat. Hist. Soc. 2nd Ser. V7 1895 part 2 p249. Ottley 67
Title:	The Ottley Papers Relating to the Civil War (Ed. William Phillips)
Notes:	A letter from Mr John Weaver to Sir Francis Ottley about Royalist plundering around Market Drayton. I have not located the original so this is not my transcription. As this is entirely about Market Drayton I have reproduced the text in its entirety.
Relevant text:	May it please your worship to be advertised, that diverse persons have had their houses plundered by some northern persons (as is conceived that follow the camp) and especially the house of John Weever dwelling in the Parish of **Drayton in Hales** in the county of Salop who is his majesty's most obedient and dutiful subject, whose house the said persons Intended to have plundered upon Monday night last and this last night, being Tuesday they endeavoured to plunder it but were prevented by reason he did suspect them then coming thither. That same night they did hurt and

did much violence to a poor man and two of his sons that had little or nothing to lose, whereof his majesties most obedient and faithful subjects humbly pray redress in that behalf. Diverse other persons have received the like revenge in these parts that are no Roundheads but most dutiful subjects to his majestie.

Document 3	
Type:	Parliamentarian Pamphlet
Date:	Friday 14th October 1642
Reference:	British Library Thomason E.123[16]
Title:	A Wonderful deliverance or God's abundant mercy in preserving from the Cavaliers the town of **Drayton** in the county of Hereford. Declaring how many troops of the Cavaliers came against the said town, with an intent to have plundered it and put the inhabitants to the sword, men, women, and children. Also manifesting how they were happily discovered by a scout of our dragoons, who gave an alarm to several troops of horse and foot, which were quartered in the adjoining villages, by whose assistance the town was preserved, and a wonderful victory obtained over the Cavaliers. Being the true copy of a letter sent from Mr. Tho. Kittermaster of Hereford, to Mr. William Knowles in Holborn, dated Octob. 14. 1642. London: printed by T.F. for I.H., October 20. 1642.
Notes:	This pamphlet purports to be an attack on the town of **Drayton** in Herefordshire. No such town exists, and the printer of the pamphlet, being based far away in London, may well be assuming that as the letter came from Herefordshire, that is where the event took place. The writer of the letter, Thomas Kittermaster, does not state that it is in that county, and although there is no guarantee that this is Market Drayton, it is the most likely place, especially as the King and Prince Rupert were in the area at the time. (The King's army left Shrewsbury on 12th October). Of course, it is always a possibility that it is a complete work of fiction for propaganda purposes. Transcribed from an original copy in the British Library. As this is entirely about Market Drayton, I have reproduced it almost in its entirety.
Relevant text:	Prince Rupert with his troops did intend to plunder **Drayton**, but our commanders having intelligence of his purpose sent forces to intercept him which was as followeth. They having intelligence by a scout of dragoons, six troops of horse and a thousand foot were sent to intercept them. Betwixt whom held a dangerous skirmish for the space of an hour, yet being at that onset over-pressed with odds upon Prince Rupert's party, which had not their courage been answerable to their cause and minds, in rights behest of King and Parliament, they alone had not been lost but the town also, who likewise lent their aid and assistance, otherwise they had been plundered and utterly ruined. But God, who still guards the fighters of his battles, did likewise to their courage add their victory. For they with undaunted resolution (to whose aid was brought two troops more of horse, with two hundred dragoons) assailed them on the right wing of Prince Rupert's Army, which new refreshing, (they supposing more supplies were ready for to back them) began by degrees to retreat, which our party perceiving, with fiery resolution redoubled their former courage and with joyful acclamations, symptoms of a hopeful victory, which did so dismay the adverse party with fear, that we got ground of them and forced them to a present flight. In which flight a worthy gentleman not to be forgotten for his brave courage and approved valour Mr John Ramsey cornet, behaved

himself so bravely, that he deserves to have our loves and future memory; for he not only dismounted Prince Rupert's cornet, but further broke into their ranks, slew a lieutenant, and so bravely behaved himself which gained him many followers as envious of his fame to gain themselves like honour, in which flight Prince Rupert's horse was shot under him, and he was forced to take a trooper's horse to save him from their pursuit, and had not this aforesaid worthy gentleman Mr John Ramsey Cornet, received a dangerous wound in the thigh, he questionless had slain Prince Rupert or fallen in the attempt, yet howsoever this to his fame be it spoke, he brought the trophy of the other cornet which he dismounted to his Colonel, who so with love received him for his service, and gave him a lieutenant's place. And had not the evening prevented the pursuit of Prince Rupert's army they had given them a greater overthrow. The number of slain on the other side as yet I cannot send you…

Document 4

Type:	Parliamentarian Pamphlet
Date:	Wednesday 11th January 1642/43
Reference:	British Library Thomason E84[37].
Title:	The Unfaithfulness of the Cavaliers and Commissioners of Array in keeping their Covenants, by which may be discerned the issue of all future treaties and agreements with them; fully discovered in a true narration of the inhumane carriages of the Earl Rivers, Lord Cholmondeley, Colonel Hastings, and their party, during the treaty of pacification in Cheshire, and after it was concluded; In their plundering at Tarporley, and the parts adjacent.
Notes:	This pamphlet deals with the 'Bunbury Agreement' and the Parliamentarian view of the Royalists' behaviour around the event. Transcribed from an original copy in the British Library.
Relevant text:	They heard of great forces on their march to strengthen their adversaries, which proved true; for besides that they brought in Colonel Hastings, with about three hundred horse into the county, they had other companies at Whitchurch and **Drayton**, which might grievously infest the County, though they feared not the loss of their garrison towns.

Document 5

Type:	Royalist Letter
Date:	Sunday 29th January 1642/3
Reference:	Trans. Shrops. Arch. Nat Hist. Soc. Ser. 2. Vol. VI. 1894. Pp 67-8. Ottley 45.
Title:	The Ottley Papers Relating to the Civil War (Ed. William Phillips)
Notes:	This letter is from Sir Vincent Corbet, the commander of the Shropshire Dragoons, at Market Drayton to Sir Frances Ottley at Shrewsbury at 6 a.m. I have not located the original, so this is not my transcription.
Relevant text:	This, in haste, is only to give you notice of a skirmish we have had with Brereton's and the Nantwich forces. I cannot as yet certify of any particular passage; only thus far be satisfied for the present. The relation of it is not very good, neither is it very bad. This much I would request you; that with all speed you will send unto Whitchurch all the surgeons you can possibly provide, for we are in great want of them. So I rest, Yours to serve you, V. Corbet. **Drayton**, Sunday morning at six o'clock

Document 6

Type:	Parliamentarian Diary Entry
Date:	Monday 10th April 1643
Reference:	Cheshire Record Office CRO/ DCC/11 1651
Title:	A breefe & true Relacon of all suche passages & things as happened & weire donne in and aboute Namptwich in the Countie of Chester & in other places of the same Countie. Together wth some other things in other Counties (not farr distant) acted and donne by some of the Com'anders officers & Soldiers of the said Towne of Namptwiche. (after the same was made a Garrison, for Kinge & Parliamt.) scythens the xth of August, 1642. Soe truelie as the wryter hereof cold come by the knowledge of the same. Thomas Malbon.
Notes:	This entry details the capture of young Mr. Bulkeley of Buntingsdale Hall. Transcribed from the original in the Cheshire Record Office.
Relevant text:	The news thereof being brought to Nantwich, some companies, being speedily ready, marched towards Whitchurch, thinking to have met them before they had gotten into the town, but they came half an hour too late: Yet notwthstanding, they met with some of their company, slew three of them, took twelve oxen, some arms which they had thrown away in their flight, and fifteen prisoners whereof young Mr Bulkeley of **Buntingsdale** was one.

Document 7

Type:	Parliamentarian Diary Entry
Date:	Monday 10th April 1643
Reference:	British Library Add. MS 5851 f52 et seq.
Title:	Mr Burghall, Vicar of Acton in Cheshire: his ms intituled Providence Improved
Notes:	This entry details the capture of young Mr. Bulkeley of Buntingsdale Hall. Transcribed from an 18th century copy in the British Library. (Original's whereabouts unknown)
Relevant text:	...these Souldiers came and plundered Captain Massey, afterwards Colonel Massey of the Moss House [in Audlem], and took from him sixty head of cattle, and some of his household goods, and horses from many others; which Nantwich soldiers having intellegence of, speedily pursued, hoping to have rescued them: but they came half an hour too late: yet they overtook some of their companies, and slew three of them, took eleven oxen, some arms which they had thrown away in flying, and brought back fifteen prisoners, whereof young Bulkeley of **Buntingsdale** was one.

Document 8

Type:	Royalist Letter
Date:	Wednesday 3rd May 1643
Reference:	H.M.C., Hastings Papers, vol. 2 (1930), p.99
Title:	Report on the manuscripts of the late Reginald Rawdon Hastings, Esq.
Notes:	This is a letter from Lord Capel at Whitchurch to Col. Hastings at 9 o'clock (a.m. or p.m. not specified). I have not seen the original, so this is not my transcription.
Relevant text:	I conceive that the work is not to be done by any of us in the case we stand or while we intend the particular defence of peculiar places only, but must be compassed by a joined force and by marching with a power able to divert the enemy from his designs and meet him in the field, to which

purpose if you shall think fit to come to **Drayton** in Salop with your strength, I shall by such time as I can receive your resolution be ready there and then we may meet and conclude to proceed as the occasion and state of these parts shall then require.

Document 9

Type:	Parliamentarian Pamphlet
Date:	Thursday 4th May 1643
Reference:	British Library MSS Harl 2125 f141
Title:	Unknown
Notes:	The pamphlet from which this is taken is unknown, being cut out and mounted on another sheet of paper. It precisely dates the Battle of Drayton to Thursday 4th May 1643, whereas all other extant contemporary documents do not. It was printed in 1646. Transcribed from an original copy in the British Library.
Relevant text:	The surprising, taking, and routing six troops of Horse of Sir Vincent Corbets, at **Drayton** in Shropshire, many prisoners horse and arms taken, Sir Vincent escaping narrowly, May 4. 1643.

Document 10

Type:	Parliamentarian Diary Entry
Date:	Thursday 4th May 1643
Reference:	Cheshire Record Office CRO/ DCC/11 1651
Title:	A breefe & true Relacon of all suche passages & things as happened & weire donne in and aboute Namptwich in the Countie of Chester & in other places of the same Countie. Together wth some other things in other Counties (not farr distant) acted and donne by some of the Com'anders officers & Soldiers of the said Towne of Namptwiche. (after the same was made a Garrison, for Kinge & Parliamt.) scythens the xth of August, 1642. Soe truelie as the wryter hereof cold come by the knowledge of the same. Thomas Malbon.
Notes:	Malbon's account of the attack on the Shropshire dragoons based at Merket Drayton. Transcribed from the original in the Cheshire Record Office.
Relevant text:	**Drayton** Battle. On Thursday at Night in May 1643, some horse and foot about midnight marched forth of Nantwich towards **Drayton**, where Sir Vincent Corbet and about three hundred cavaliers horse and foot lay, beginning to make some works (for their safety) about the town: But a little after sunrise, Nantwich forces coming thither, on the sudden (before they were forth of their beds), entered the town (they having neither guard nor scouts abroad), but secure (as they thought); And killed nine of them, took many prisoners, horses and arms; so that all or most of Nantwich foot soldiers were horsed home and many of them had two, three, or four muskets and carbines apiece, beside apparel and other goods of theirs. And also three ensigns, four drums, and other weapons. But Sir Vincent fled in his shirt and waistcoat leaving his apparel behind him, which Captain Whitney had with his money and many letters in his pocket. Captain Kynnaston and Captyn Sandford were there slain (being cavaliers). Nantwich forces did no wrong nor harm to the town, but only threw down their works, after the cavaliers were all fled and slain, and taken prisoners, and then returned back to Nantwich in safety without loss of any man, saving some few common soldiers about three or four which were hurt in the streets with shots forth of windows

Document 11

Type:	Parliamentarian Diary Entry
Date:	Thursday 4th May 1643
Reference:	British Library Add. MSS 5851 f52 et seq.
Title:	Mr Burghall, Vicar of Acton in Cheshire: his ms intituled Providence Improved
Notes:	Burghall's account in this case is a rewording of Malbon's. Transcribed from an 18th century copy in the British Library. (Original's whereabouts unknown)
Relevant text:	Much about this time some horse and foot went out of Nantwich towards **Drayton**, where Sir Vincent Corbet and some others of the King's party were, to the number of three hundred, or thereabouts, beginning to entrench themselves, and make works about the town. But they were prevented of that design: for the Roundheads came suddenly upon them soon after sunrise, when they in **Drayton** were in bed, entered the town, having neither guard nor scouts abroad, killed some nine of them, took many prisoners, and horses, and arms: so that the foot soldiers were horsed back, and many of them had three or four muskets or carbines apiece, besides apparel, and other goods. There was taken three ensigns, four drums, and other weapons. Sir Vincent fled away in his shirt and waistcoat, leaving his clothes behind him, which Captain Whitney took, with all his money, and many letters found in his pockets. Here Captain Kinnaston and Captain Sandford were slain of the King's party. After the Nantwich forces had thrown down their works, the enemies being subdued, they returned home in safety, without the loss of any, or doing the townsmen any hurt; only three or four of the common soldiers were shot out of the windows, but not slain.

Document 12

Type:	Parliamentarian Newspaper
Date:	Thursday 4th May 1643
Reference:	British Library Thomason E.101(15)
Title:	Mercurius Civicus, London's Intellegencer or, Truth impartially related from thence to the whole Kingdome, to prevent misinformation. Iss. 1.
Notes:	Parliamentarian newspaper report of the battle at Market Drayton. Transcribed from an original copy in the British Library.
Relevant text:	...the Parliament's forces under the command of Sir William Brereton, have had a far greater success at **Drayton** in Shropshire, where they have routed the whole regiment of dragoons, under the command of Sir Vincent Corbet, taken most of his chief officers, (himself hardly escaping) and many of his common soldiers with eight hundred arms:

Document 13

Type:	Parliamentarian Book
Date:	Thursday 4th May 1643
Reference:	
Title:	England's Worthies under whom all the civill and Bloudy Warres since Anno 1642, to Anno 1647, are related. Wherein are described, the several Battails, Encounters, and Assaults of Cities, Townes, and Castles at severall times and Places; so that the Reader may behold the time, yeare, and event of every Battle, Skirmish and Assault. Wherein London-apprentices had not

the least share. As also, Severall Victories by Sea, by the Noble Admirall, Robert Earle of Warwick. London, Printed for J. Rothwell, at the Sun and Fountain, in Pauls Church-yeard, 1647. By John Vicars.

Notes: This is from the section on Sir William Brereton. Transcribed from a copy found online.

Relevant text: He also bravely beat the Earl of Derby at Stockton Heath; and Sir Vincent Corbet also a second time at **Drayton** in Shropshire, and took from him many prisoners, horse and arms.

Document 14

Type: Royalist Newspaper

Date: Thursday 4th May 1643

Reference: British Library Thomason E.104(21)

Title: Mercurius Aulicus: the twentieth Weeke, Saturday, May 20 1643.

Notes: This is the Royalists take on the Drayton Battle, stating that it is 'fake news'. Transcribed from an original copy in the British Library.

Relevant text: That Sir William Brereton hath had a greater successe at **Drayton** in Shropshire, (then that of His Majesties at Banbury) having routed a whole regiment of dragoons of Sir Vincent Corbet, taken most of his officers, many of his common soldiers, with eight hundred arms, of which there is not one word true;

Document 15

Type: Royalist Letter

Date: Approx Friday 5th May 1643

Reference: William Salt Library, S.MS.488

Title:

Notes: This letter is from Lord Capel at Shrewsbury to Prince Rupert. It is estimated to be from May-June 1643. Elliot Warburton, in his 'Memoirs of Prince Rupert and the Cavaliers. Vol. I', places it on 5th May 1643. It certainly cannot have been from before that date. It was in the William Salt library, but has since been reported as missing. Neither I nor the library have managed to find a transcript, so the only content we have is from Warburton and the description from the library catalogue entry.

Relevant text: Catalogue: Letter from Arthur Lord Capel to Prince Rupert. 'Relating to the movements of the rebels, who have possessed themselves of **Drayton**, one of the principal market towns of the county... , and requiring aid to join with the forces in these parts to drive the rebels out. Warburton: Rebels have now possessed themselves of **Drayton**;

Document 16

Type: Royalist Letter

Date: Sunday 19th June 1643

Reference: Trans. Shrops. Arch. Nat. Hist. Soc. Ser. 2. Vol. VI. 1894. Pp 67-8. Ottley 163

Title: The Ottley Papers Relating to the Civil War (Ed. William Phillips)

Notes: William Young to Sir Francis Ottley from Caynton House near Shifnal.

Relevant text: Sir, I am bold to crave your favour concerning a horse and arms wherewith my Lord Capel wrote to have me send in to Salop [Shrewsbury] this day. I have at this present horse and arms now in Sir Vincent Corbet's troop, and I know his quartermaster Ambrose Kinaston will testify so much. I had one other horse and arms being a dragoon, under Captain Thomas Piggott which were taken away at **Drayton** when their commander was in bed, and I protest before God I have not any more arms left, but only a birding-piece to kill auckesmeat; neither do I know how to come by any…

Document 17

Type:	Royalist newspaper
Date:	Thursday 22nd June 1643
Reference:	
Title:	Mercurius Aulicus Week 25, 18-24 June 1643
Notes:	I found this late on, and have not obtained a copy of the original, so this is not my transcription.
Relevant text:	…Sir Richard Willys Serjeant Major Generall to the Lord Capel, pursuing those orders which his Lordship left at Wrexham with him, to draw the horse towards **Drayton** and Newport to make incursions into Cheshire and Staffordshire, upon whose moving from Wrexham he understood that about four hundred of the rebel's horse and dragoons were plundering Sir Thomas Hanmer's house in Flintshire, Sir Richard therefore hasted thither…

Document 18

Type:	Parliamentarian Diary Entry
Date:	Thursday 14th September 1643 to Friday 22nd September 1643.
Reference:	Cheshire Record Office CRO/ DCC/11 1651
Title:	A breefe & true Relacon of all suche passages & things as happened & weire donne in and aboute Namptwich in the Countie of Chester & in other places of the same Countie. Together wth some other things in other Counties (not farr distant) acted and donne by some of the Com'anders officers & Soldiers of the said Towne of Namptwiche. (after the same was made a Garrison, for Kinge & Parliamt.) scythens the xth of August, 1642. Soe truelie as the wryter hereof cold come by the knowledge of the same. Thomas Malbon.
Notes:	Malbon titles this **"The whole army removed to Wem."** Transcribed from the original in the Cheshire Record Office
Relevant text:	And the next night, they quartered at **Drayton** and in all the towns and villages thereabouts, keeping their rendezvous there until Tuesday next following, and then, sending forth their warrants, they called in all that country thereabouts to a General Muster and continued at **Drayton** until Friday the 22nd of September next following. And then all the whole army marched thence to Wem and fortified that town, quartering their army in all the towns and places next adjoining.

Document 19

Type:	Parliamentarian Diary Entry
Date:	Thursday 14th September 1643 to Friday 22nd September 1643
Reference:	British Library Add. MSS 5851 f52 et seq.
Title:	Mr Burghall, Vicar of Acton in Cheshire: his ms intituled Providence Improved
Notes:	Parliament's army moves to occupy Wem, after a stop at Market Drayton to recruit. Transcribed from an 18th century copy in the British Library. (Original's whereabouts unknown)
Relevant text:	… and they went the same Night to **Drayton**, and were billeted there, and in all the towns and places adjoining, keeping their rendevouz there till

Tuesday following, when they called in all the country to a general muster, and continued at **Drayton** till Friday September 22nd; and then the whole camp marched to Wem and fortified that town, quartering the soldiers in all the towns and places thereabouts.

Document 20

Type: Parliamentarian Pamphlet
Date: Wednesday 27th September 1643
Reference: British Library Thomason E.75[9]
Title: Shropshires Misery and Mercie. Manifested in the defeat given to the Lord Capels ravenous and devouring Armie, by the Forces of Cheshire and Shropshire, under the Conduct of those valient and unanimous Commanders, Sir William Brereton, Sir Tho: Middleton, and Col: Mytton. Together with the names of the Officers and Common Souldiers, hurt, kild, and taken prisoners on both sides. Faithfully related by those who were employed in the service, and presented to publicke view, as a monument of Gods power and providence in taking the wise in their own craftinesse. November. 8. London, Printed, for Tho: Vnderhil. 1643.
Notes: Transcribed from an original copy of the pamphlet in the British Library.
Relevant text: That whilst we quartered at **Drayton**, as we were on our march to assist Sir Thomas Middleton, and the rest, upon Wednesday night, September 27th. When there came with all possible speed no less (as was reported) than one thousand horse from Shrewsbury to have surprised us in our quarters, they were repelled, and beaten back by a party of thirty or fourty horse and dragoons commanded by Captain Muncke, there being divers of them slain and the rest pursued by our horse …

Document 21

Type: Parliamentarian Book
Date: Wednesday 27th September 1643
Reference: British Library Thomason 51:E.312[3]. p63
Title: Gods Arke Overtopping the Worlds Waves, or the Third Part of the Parliamentary Chronicle. Containing a successive Continuation and exact and faithful Narration of all the most materiall Parliamentary Proceedings & Memorable Mercies wherewith God has crowned this famous present ment and their Armies in all the severall parts of the Land; The famous Seiges, Defeats, Battails, Victories and Prizes obtained and taken by Land & Sea; etc.
Notes: Transcribed from an original copy of the book in the British Library.
Relevant text: That while we quartered at **Drayton**, as we were on our march to assist Sir Thomas Middleton, and the rest; when there came with all possible speed upon us no less (as was credibly reported) than a thousand horse from Shrewsbury, to have surprised us in our quarters; they were all repelled, and beaten back again, by only a party of thirty or forty horse and dragoons, commanded by Captain Munck, there being divers of them slain, and the rest pursued by our horse many miles towards Shrewsbery;

Document 22

Type: Parliamentarian Diary Entry
Date: Friday 29th September 1643
Reference: Cheshire Record Office CRO/ DCC/11 1651
Title: A breefe & true Relacon of all suche passages & things as happened &

weire donne in and aboute Namptwich in the Countie of Chester & in other places of the same Countie. Together wth some other things in other Counties (not farr distant) acted and donne by some of the Com'anders officers & Soldiers of the said Towne of Namptwiche. (after the same was made a Garrison, for Kinge & Parliamt.) scythens the xth of August, 1642. Soe truelie as the wryter hereof cold come by the knowledge of the same. Thomas Malbon.

Notes: Transcribed from the original in the Cheshire Record Office

Relevant text: On Friday, being Michaelmas day, the trained bands of Nantwich hundred marched towards Wem, in assistance of the parliament forces there, with a case of drakes [cannon]; and quartered the first nighte at **Drayton**, and the next day after to Wem.

Document 23

Type: Parliamentarian Diary Entry

Date: Friday 29th September 1643

Reference: British Library Add. MSS 5851 f52 et seq.

Title: Mr Burghall, Vicar of Acton in Cheshire: his ms intituled Providence Improved

Notes: Transcribed from an 18th century copy in the British Library. (Original's whereabouts unknown)

Relevant text: Upon Friday, being Michaelmas day, the trained bands of Nantwich Hundred marched towards Wem, to aid the parliament forces there, with one case of drakes [cannon]; lodged the first Night at **Drayton**, the second at Wem...

Document 24

Type: Parliamentarian Pamphlet

Date: Tuesday 17th October 1643

Reference: British Library Thomason E.77[4].

Title: A True Relation of a Great Victory Obtained by The Parliaments forces Against The Cavaliers neere Chester. With the number of Colonels, Sergeant-Majors, Captaines, Lieutenants, that were slaine at Wem and at Lee-Bridge in this Fight by the Parliaments Forces. As it was sent in a Letter from one that was in the fight to M. James Waters in Newgate Market, and received the 24 of November 1643. Novemb. 27. Printed by E.P. 1643.

Notes: Transcribed from an original copy of the pamphlet in the British Library.

Relevant text: ...and it fell out so that Sir William Brereton had false intelligence, that he came by **Drayton**, and so by Woore, and missed coming in the rear of them, ...

Document 25

Type: Parliamentarian Letter

Date: Saturday October 21st 1643

Reference: Bodleian Library Nalson III f57.

Title:

Notes: This is Brereton and Middleton's own version of events at Wem mentioned in the pamphlet above. The text is from the Manuscripts of the Duke of Portland Volume I pp141-3. I have not seen the original so this is not my transcription.

Relevant text: ... and marched on the right hand from a town called Ash in Shropshire unto **Drayton**, and thence again after a short repast advanced for Nantwich whither with all our forces we came by break of day upon Tuesday morning last for the towns relief.

Document 26

Type:	Parliamentarian Account
Date:	Tuesday 17th October 1643 to Wednesday 18th October 1643
Reference:	Warwickshire Record Office CR2017/C10/60
Title:	Earl of Denbigh's Civil War Letter Books
Notes:	This is Basil Fielding's (Earl of Denbigh) version of events at Lord Capel's attack on Wem. Transcribed from the original in the Warwickshire Record Office.
Relevant text:	Our force that night had they gone into Whitchurch betwixt them and us and either forced them to fight or else to retreat to Chester and so have preserved us, did not but marched to **Drayton**, seven miles wide of Whitchurch and there lay Monday night.

Document 27

Type:	Royalist Letter
Date:	Thursday 29th February 1643/4
Reference:	British Library Add. MS. 18981, f69.
Title:	Untitled
Notes:	This letter is from Sir Vincent Corbet at Moreton Corbet to Sir Thomas Dallison (a Colonel of horse under Prince Rupert). Transcribed from the original in the British Library.
Relevant text:	Colonel Mytton's, Captain Floyd's and Captin Mackwood's [forces] quarter in Ightfield town and have barricaded the avenues with carts: only in Ightfield Hall which is a brick moated house there are eighty dragoons. There is a report that five of Sir Thomas Fairfax's troops are to quarter this night in **Drayton**: there are warrants sent out to Prees and the country thereabouts to come in to Wem tomorrow and those that do not are to leave their livings:

Document 28

Type:	Parliamentarian Diary Entry
Date:	Monday 4th March 1643/4
Reference:	Cheshire Record Office CRO/ DCC/11 1651
Title:	A breefe & true Relacon of all suche passages & things as happened & weire donne in and aboute Namptwich in the Countie of Chester & in other places of the same Countie. Together wth some other things in other Counties (not farr distant) acted and donne by some of the Com'anders officers & Soldiers of the said Towne of Namptwiche. (after the same was made a Garrison, for Kinge & Parliamt.) scythens the xth of August, 1642. Soe truelie as the wryter hereof cold come by the knowledge of the same. Thomas Malbon.
Notes:	Transcribed from the original in the Cheshire Record Office
Relevant text:	Colonell Mytton's march to **Drayton**. On Monday night the fourth of March 1643, Colonel Mytten and Sir William Fairfax, with some of their troops of horse being quartered at **Drayton**, were set upon by Prince Rupert's forces. But being too weak for them, they retired and fled away disorderly.

Document 29

Type:	Parliamentarian Diary Entry
Date:	Monday 4th March 1643/4
Reference:	British Library Add. MSS 5851 f52 et seq.
Title:	Mr Burghall, Vicar of Acton in Cheshire: his ms intituled Providence Improved
Notes:	Transcribed from an 18th century copy in the British Library. (Original's whereabouts unknown)
Relevant text:	Upon Monday night, March 4th, Colonel Mytton, and Sir William Fairfax, with some of their troops of horse, being quartered at **Drayton**, were set upon by Prince Rupert's forces, and being too weak for them, retired, and fled away disorderly.

Document 30

Type:	Royalist Diary Entry
Date:	Monday 4th March 1643/4
Reference:	ISBN 1 898621 14 4
Title:	Memoranda of Mr Francis Sandford. Prior to his capture at Shrewsbury, February 1645.
Notes:	This diary is in unknown private hands, and therefore Transcribed from the edition printed by Jacobus Publications, edited by John Lewis in 1996.
Relevant text:	March. The 4th of this month in the night, being Shrove Monday, Prince Rupert with five hundred foot and three hundred horse met with the rebels near **Drayton**, upon Tyrley Heath, routed them and chased through the town to their body of horse stood in the feild near Shifford's Bridge. Upon the Prince's pursuit they all fled into Tunstall [Hall] ground and locked up the gate with a chain, but the Prince broke through and chased them through Betton and Norton and Bearstone; in which pursuit he took thirty four prisoners and killed divers of them. [The Prince] lay in **Drayton** all night, and the next day returned to Shrewsbury.

Document 31

Type:	Royalist Diary Entries
Date:	Friday 1st March 1643/4 to Wednesday 6th March 1643/4.
Reference:	Bodleian Library MS Clarendon 28 f 134
Title:	Prince Rupert's Journal in England
Notes:	Transcribed from the original in the Bodleian Library
Relevant text:	4th Monday, some foot sent before. The Prince marched all night towards **Drayton**. 5th Shrove Tuesday, he beat Mytton and Fairfax from thence and quartered there that night. 6th Ash Wednesday after dinner, home to Shrewsbury

Document 32

Type:	Royalist Newspaper
Date:	Monday 4th March 1644 to Tuesday 5th March 1644
Reference:	British Library Thomason E.39[3].
Title:	Mercurius Aulicus: Series 2, the tenth week.
Notes:	Transcribed from an original copy of the newspaper in the British Library.
Relevant text:	For on Monday night last, his Highness marched with about eight hundred horse, and six hundred foot towards **Drayton**, fourteen miles from Shrewsbury, where the Lord Denbigh's regiment of horse, Colonel

Mytton's horse, Sir Thomas and Sir William Fairfax's horse were all quartered, Sir William being in person there, but the rebels had notice of the design before the Prince came thither, (which was by eight of the clock on Tuesday morning) where he found the rebels drawn out in expectation of his coming, and confident to deal with him, advanced with a party of their horse through **Drayton** town to meet him, but were quickly beaten back, their commander in chief was there taken prisoner, with many others; then his Highnesse himself charged through the town, where the rebels were drawn up into a body, and this he did with two troops only (most of his horse being with the foot two miles behind) but as soon as they saw the rest of his horse appear, they all ran shamefully; the Prince pursuing them only with his own troop at least five miles near to Eccleshall Castle: in this pursuit (besides what he had taken before) his Highness took above forty prisoners, whereof one Captain, and one Lieutenant, took also Sir Thomas Fairfax's Major's colours, whose Motto forsooth was FOR REFORMATION ; killed twenty two, took one hundred horse, and lay all night in the town of **Drayton**, where the rebels durst never visit his Highness, who came back to Shrewsbury the next day, having killed and taken above one hundred and twenty rebels, without the loss of any one man.

Document 33

Type:	Royalist Newspaper
Date:	Sunday 10th March 1643/4
Reference:	British Library Thomason E.40[6]
Title:	Mercurius Aulicus: Series 2, the eleventh week
Notes:	Transcribed from an original copy of the newspaper in the British Library. Relates to events on Monday 4th March 1644 and Tuesday 5th March 1644
Relevant text:	…who in the late fight at **Drayton** in Staffordshire, most prudently changed their field-word three times; the first was "FAIRFAX" (their confidence being in Sir Thomas and Sir William's troops, which were both present), and after "FAIRFAX" they chose "THE LORD OF HOSTS"; and lastly, when they had been twice well cudgelled, they changed again into "GOD'S WILL BE DONE", that all might answer Sir Thomas's motto, "FOR REFORMATION".

Document 34

Type:	Royalist Letter
Date:	Sunday 7th April 1644
Reference:	British Library Add. MS. 18981 f.137.
Title:	
Notes:	Lord Byron at Chester to Prince Rupert at Shrewsbury. Transcribed from the original letter in the British Library.
Relevant text:	Whensoever your Highness shall intend to march towards Lankashire, your best way from Shrewsbury, will be to Whitchurch and **Drayton** and thence to Knutsford, which will be a convenient place for me to wait upon your Highness, with those forces I have here.

Document 35

Type:	Parliamentarian Diary Entry
Date:	Saturday 18th May 1644
Reference:	Cheshire Record Office CRO/ DCC/11 1651

Title: A breefe & true Relacon of all suche passages & things as happened & weire donne in and aboute Namptwich in the Countie of Chester & in other places of the same Countie. Together wth some other things in other Counties (not farr distant) acted and donne by some of the Com'anders officers & Soldiers of the said Towne of Namptwiche. (after the same was made a Garrison, for Kinge & Parliamt.) scythens the xth of August, 1642. Soe truelie as the wryter hereof cold come by the knowledge of the same. Thomas Malbon.

Notes: Transcribed from the original in the Cheshire Record Office.

Relevant text:. And drawing all his forces to Holt, Farn, Malpas, Whitchurch, and all that country, upon the 18th of May 1644 he advanced from Whitchurch to **Drayton**; and on Sunday the 19th of May his army consisting of about ten thousand, most of theim horse, advanced over the water of Weaver unto Audlem, Buerton, Hankelow and Woore, plundering all the country as they went (being near Nantwich)

Document 36

Type: Parliamentarian Diary Entry

Date: Saturday 18th May 1644

Reference: British Library Add. MS 5851 f52 et seq.

Title: Mr Burghall, Vicar of Acton in Cheshire: his ms intituled Providence Improved

Notes: Transcribed from an 18th century copy in the British Library. (Original's whereabouts unknown)

Relevant text: He advanced towards **Drayton**: the next Day his Army of 10,000, most Horse, came over the Water to Audlem, Buerton, Woore, etc. and plundered all the country.

Document 37

Type: Royalist Diary

Date: Saturday 18th May 1644 to Tuesday 21st May 1644

Reference: Bodleian Library MS Clarendon 28 f 135

Title: Prince Rupert's Journal in England

Notes: Transcribed from the original in the Bodleian Library.

Relevant text:. 18th Saturday, to Whitchurch.
20th Monday, to **Drayton**.
21st Tuesday, to Betley in Staffordshire

Document 38

Type: Parliamentarian Pamphlet

Date: Sunday 23rd June 1644

Reference: British Library Thomason E.53[3]

Title: Two Great Victories: On Obtained by the Earl of Denbigh at OSWESTRY: And how he took 10 Gentlemen of Wales. 1 Lievtenent Colonell. Divers Captains and other officers. 200 prisoners. 100 Musquets. 500 pound composition. 300 Cows and Welch Roonts. Many Swords and Pistols. Divers Arms. A Barrell of Powder. A quantitie of Bulletts. The Church. The Towne. The Castle. Besides divers hurt. Some slain. Certified by letters from the Earl of Denbigh his Quarters. The other Victory by Colonell Mytton, with a List of the Prisoners by him taken: Certified by Letters from Colonell Mytton. Published according to Order. LONDON. Printed by I.Coe, 1644.

Market Drayton's Civil War

Notes: Transcribed from an original copy of the pamphlet in the British Library.

Relevant text: That night we marched not far by reason of great rain: but my Lord of Denbigh, early the next day got to horse, and leaving all our foot at **Drayton**, we marched to Wem, and our horse to Ellsemere, and two hundred foot and a troope of horse under the command of Colonel Mytton.

Document 39

Type: Parliamentarian Book

Date: Sunday June 23rd 1644

Reference:

Title: Historical Collections. The second Volume of the third part. Containing the principal matters which happened from the meeting of the parliament, November the 3d, 1640. To the end of the year 1644. Wherein is a particular account of the rise and progress of the civil war to that period: impartially related. Setting forth only matter of fact in order of time, without observation or reflection. By John Rushworth late of Lincolns-Inn, Esq; Fitted for the press in his lifetime. Volume the fifth. London: Printed for D.Browne, J.Walthoe, J.Knapton, R.Knaplock, J. and B.Sprint, B.Tooke, E.Bell, J.Darby, D.Midwinter, J.Tonson, S.Buckley, B.Cowse, J.Osborne, R.Robinson. J.Round, S.Burrows, F.Clay, E.Symon, and T.Wotton. M. DCC. XXI.

Notes: Transcribed from a copy in the author's collection

Relevant text: …with the Advice and Assistance of Colonel Mytton Governor of Wem, marched to **Drayton**, where leaving a good reserve, he advanced to Oswestry…

Document 40

Type: Parliamentarian Book

Date: Sunday June 23rd 1644

Reference: British Library Thomason 51:E.312[3]. p63

Title: Gods Arke Overtopping the Worlds Waves, or the Third Part of the Parliamentary Chronicle. Containing a successive Continuation and exact and faithful Narration of all the most materiall Parliamentary Proceedings & Memorable Mercies wherewith God has crowned this famous present ment and their Armies in all the severall parts of the Land; The famous Seiges, Defeats, Battails, Victories and Prizes obtained and taken by Land & Sea; etc.

Notes: Transcribed from an original copy of the book in the British Library.

Relevant text: … with the advice of Colonell Mytton, marched toward **Drayton**, where he left a good reserve; and so advanced to Oswestry; …

Document 41

Type: Parliamentarian Letter

Date: Tuesday 25th June 1644

Reference: Warwickshire Record Office CR2017 C09 137

Title: Earl of Denbigh's Civil War Letter Books Vol 1

Notes: A letter from Thomas Middleton to the Earl of Denbigh written at 8pm. Transcribed from the original in the Warwickshire Record Office.

Relevant text: I shall only presume to present you some directions for your march, as concieving it most convenient for quarter and to meet with the other forces (though some what about) for all those forces that are at Wem and

173

Drayton, to march to Woore; and so thence to Newcastle [under-Lyme] where you may meet with the other forces of Staffordshire;

Document 42

Type:	Parliamentarian Letter
Date:	Wednesday 19th March 1644/5
Reference:	Cheshire Record Office CRO/DDX/428 f.25
Title:	Sir William Brereton's Letter Books
Notes:	This entry is a letter from Sir William Brereton at Middlewich to Major Braine at Wem. Transcribed from a scan of the original (which is in private hands) kept at the CRO.
Relevant text:	I cannot therefore but apprehend Whitchurch a place of danger where they may be surprised and therefore I shall be very unwilling to encourage you thereunto : It is conceived by some that **Drayton** may be more safe as being more remote from the enemy and more ready to join with us.

Document 43

Type:	Royalist Diary Entry
Date:	Thursday 20th March 1644/5 to Friday 21st March 1644/5
Reference:	British Library Add. MS. 11331 f.141
Title:	Sir William Brereton's Letter Books.
Notes:	This entry is from a captured Royalist diary. Transcribed from the original in the British Library.
Relevant text:	Thursday 20th We marched from Whitchurch to **Drayton.** Friday 21st from **Drayton** to Newport.

Document 44

Type:	Parliamentarian Order
Date:	Friday 21st March 1644/5
Reference:	Cheshire Record Office CRO/DDX/428 f.37
Title:	Sir William Brereton's Letter Books
Notes:	This entry is an order from the Council of War at Middlewich to Lt. Gen. Lesley. Transcribed from a scan of the original (which is in private hands) kept at the CRO.
Relevant text:	Resolved and is the opinion of all the officers at a Council of War and that it is the best and advantageous course for the whole army to march towards **Drayton** where the enemy quartered yesterday night to the end the enemy may not at his pleasure waste that part of the country, …Which if it be thought fit by the Lieutenant General of the Scottish Army, then we conceive Sandbach and Beetchson will be the best quarters for their foot or if they will march four miles further, then to Betley and Wrine Hill, seven miles from **Drayton.**

Document 45

Type:	Parliamentarian Letter
Date:	Saturday 22nd March 1644/5
Reference:	Cheshire Record Office CRO/DDX/428 f.32
Title:	Sir William Brereton's Letter Books
Notes:	This is a letter from Sir William Brereton at Middlewich to Lt. Gen Lesley at Sandbach. Transcribed from a scan of the original (which is in private hands) kept at the CRO.
Relevant text:	Sir William Brereton's letter and motion to Lieutenant General Lesley to

march to **Drayton** after the Princes. ...I Humbly offer this for your advice whether it were not best that the horse under Colonel Rossiter conceived about eighteen hundred should advance towards Litchfield on the left of Stafford and that your army or at least your horse with all mine that can possibly be spared advance to **Drayton** and so forwards towards the edge of Staffordshire, whereby we are not likely to receive any engagement ... I desire your advice touching the advance of my own horse and foot to **Drayton** where they shall expect a rendezvous with your army at such time as we shall agree upon.

Document 46

Type:	Parliamentarian Letter
Date:	Sunday 23rd March 1644/5
Reference:	Cheshire Record Office CRO/DDX/428 f.32
Title:	Sir William Brereton's Letter Books
Notes:	This is a letter from Sir William Brereton at Middlewich to the Committee of Both Kingdoms. Transcribed from a scan of the original (which is in private hands) kept at the CRO.
Relevant text:	But the enemy's march was very quick and sudden in their return: upon Thursday night they quartered at **Drayton** and marched the next day through Newport towards Bridgnorth ...

Document 47

Type:	Parliamentarian Letter
Date:	Sunday 23rd March 1644/5
Reference:	Cheshire Record Office CRO/DDX/428 f.33/4
Title:	Sir William Brereton's Letter Books
Notes:	This is a letter from Sir William Brereton at Middlewich to Major General Crawford at 7a.m. Transcribed from a copy of the original (which is in private hands) kept in the Cheshire Record Office.
Relevant text:	The Enemy quartered on Wednesday night at Whitchurch; on Thursday night at **Drayton;** on Friday night at or behind Newport in Shropshire which is about sixteen or seventeen miles from Nantwich.

Document 48

Type:	Parliamentarian Letter
Date:	Friday 28th March 1645
Reference:	Cheshire Record Office CRO/DDX/428 ff.52
Title:	Sir William Brereton's Letter Books
Notes:	This is a letter from Sir William Brereton at Nantwich to John Swinfen, one of the Parliamentary Committee of Staffordshire. Transcribed from a scan of the original (which is in private hands) kept at the CRO.
Relevant text:	Collonel Bethell quartered at Newcastle and **Drayton** until heereturned toward the Leaguer of Pontefract by order from my Lord Fairfax who sent them to us.

Document 49

Type:	Parliamentarian Account
Date:	Saturday 29th March 1645
Reference:	British Library Add. MS. 11331 f.47
Title:	Sir William Brereton's Letter Books
Notes:	This is Sir William Brereton's account of the movement of the Cheshire

troops. Transcribed from the original in the British Library.

Relevant text: The enemy retreated from Tarporley March 19th to Whitchurch and from Whitchurch to **Drayton** and Newport March 20th, and from thence to Newport March 21st and there remained three days.

Document 50

Type:	Parliamentarian Letter
Date:	After Tuesday 1st April 1645
Reference:	British Library Add. MS. 11331 f.46
Title:	Sir William Brereton's Letter Books
Notes:	This is a letter from Sir William Brereton to Lt. Gen. Lesley. Transcribed from the original in the British Library.

Relevant text: It is true also I did much desire that our forces might have advanced toward **Drayton** after them if you had thought so fit but yourself desired that Lieutenant General Crawford might come up unto us before we did engage:

Document 51

Type:	Parliamentarian Letter
Date:	Tuesday 8th April 1645
Reference:	Cheshire Record Office CRO/DDX/428 ff.67-8
Title:	Sir William Brereton's Letter Books
Notes:	This is a letter from Sir William Brereton at Dodleston to William Ashurst, one of the Parliamentary Committee of Lancashire. Transcribed from a scan of the original (which is in private hands) kept at the CRO.

Relevant text: Therefore it is earnestly desired that Major General Crawford may be ordered to lie near or about Coventry or about Leicester and that both the forces under the command of Lieutenant General Lesley now at Halifax and that Crawford's may be appointed to meet about **Drayton** or Whitchurch upon the first notice of the Princes' motions this way

Document 52

Type:	Royalist Diary Entry
Date:	Thursday 10th April 1645 to Saturday 19th April 1645
Reference:	Bodleian Library MS Clarendon 28 f130
Title:	Prince Rupert's Journal in England
Notes:	The dates are somewhat confused, and the compiler of the journal excuses this by stating that "My notes of the marche to relieve Beeston Castle are lost: these following I tooke out of Mercurye". Therefore, having a gap in events, he resorted to old newspapers. The result is a very large amount of travelling in a very short space of time. The entry of the 19th is obviously wrong. The following Tuesday was the 15th, and by the 19th he was back in Bristol. Transcribed from the original in the Bodleian Library

Relevant text:. 10. Thursday, to Wenlock
- To **Drayton**
- To Whitchurch
- To a little village

19. Tuesday, Prince Maurice joined on Stimmye Heath and Sir William Brereton after seventeen weeks seige, left Beeston castle. (Valett Governor). The Prince quartered a day or two by it – whence back, -
- To Whitchurch
- To **Drayton**
- To ~~Newport~~ my Ld Newports howse, at High Arkall.

To Newport in Shropshire, where hearing of the ~~Shropshire~~ Worcester & Herefordshire Associations, he marched

Document 53

Type:	Parliamentarian Letter
Date:	Friday 11th April 1645
Reference:	Cheshire Record Office CRO/DDX/428 ff.86-7
Title:	Sir William Brereton's Letter Books
Notes:	This is a letter from Sir William Brereton at the leaguer near Chester to Alexander Lesley, Earl of Leven , the Commander-in-Chief of the Scots army in England. Transcribed from a scan of the original (which is in private hands) kept at the CRO.
Relevant text:	For prevention whereof I know nothing would be more advantageous than that these forces which are Intended for our relief in that case might have timely order to advance so as we might give the enemy meeting about **Drayton** or Newport then our garrisons would be left secure in the rear so as we might be able to draw into the field more than two thousand serviceable foot.

Document 54

Type:	Parliamentarian Letter
Date:	Tuesday 15th April 1645
Reference:	Cheshire Record Office CRO/DDX/428 ff.98-9
Title:	Sir William Brereton's Letter Books
Notes:	This is a letter from Sir William Brereton to Lord Montgomery at Halifax at noon. Transcribed from a scan of the original (which is in private hands) kept at the CRO.
Relevant text:	The like letter was written to Lord Fairfax and likewise to Lord Leven desiring that these forces at Halifax might timely advance to our assistance: so as we might meet. The enemy could be encountered about **Drayton** or Newport: so should we be able to draw a greater strength into the field leaving our garrisons secure in the rear.

Document 56

Type:	Parliamentarian Letter
Date:	Friday 25th April
Reference:	British Library Add. MS. 11331 f.21
Title:	Sir William Brereton's Letter Books
Notes:	A letter from Sir William Brereton at Dodleston to Sir David Lesley. Transcribed from the original in the British Library.
Relevant text:	I therefore propose and desire (if you concur therein) that you will speedily advance with your forces to lie nearer to this work: I conceive **Drayton,** Whitchurch, Newport or Wellington and that part of Shropshire will be most convenient for your quarters.

Document 57

Type:	Parliamentarian Letter
Date:	Thursday 1st May 1645
Reference:	British Library Add. MS. 11331 f.45/6
Title:	Sir William Brereton's Letter Books
Notes:	A letter from Sir William Brereton to the Committee of Both Kingdoms. Transcribed from the original in the British Library.

Relevant text: March 20th the Scotch forces came to Knutsford upon whose approach the Prince drew off his army, of which we had certain intelligence and that he lay at **Drayton** March 20th and moved thence to Newport March 21st, where some reported he intended to fortify. ... To that end it was resolved by my self and the rest of the Cheshire and Lancashire commanders at a council of war held at Middlewich March 21st, which I have sent here enclosed, and that the whole army should march toward **Drayton** in pursuit of the enemy who then lay still at Newport, seven miles distant from **Drayton**:

Document 58

Type:	Parliamentarian Letter
Date:	Monday 19th May 1645
Reference:	British Library Add. MS. 11331 ff.133-4
Title:	Sir William Brereton's Letter Books
Notes:	A letter from Sir William Brereton at Nantwich to Lord Leven. Transcribed from the original in the British Library

Relevant text: ... the next day being Saturday last the King marched and quartered at Mr. Piggott's of Chetwynd a mile on this side of Newport, sixteen miles from Nantwich: the two Princes at the Swan in Newport, Shifnal and there abouts, and part of them towards **Drayton,** twelve miles from Nantwich upon which night the same troop of mine consisting of about eighty and some other horse to the number of two hundred horse fell upon their guard which was very strong guard and killed some twenty at least; took some prisoners and sixty horse without any loss, only one man is wanting.

Document 59

Type:	Parliamentarian Book
Date:	Tuesday 20th May 1645
Reference:	
Title:	Historical Collections of Private Passages of State. Rushworth
Notes:	Transcribed from a copy in the author's collectrion

Relevant text: From Newport his Majesty marched to **Drayton** (on the borders of Cheshire) and by that time the army came within twenty miles of Chester. The Lord Byron with some troops of horse came from that City, and assured his Majesty of the raising of that siege, and that Sir William Brereton was retreated into Lancashire.

Document 60

Type:	Parliamentarian Letter
Date:	Tuesday 20th May 1645
Reference:	British Library Add MS 11331 f.144
Title:	Sir William Brereton's Letter Books
Notes:	Letter from Sir William Brereton at Nantwich to Lord Fairfax. A similar letter was sent to Lord Leven at 10 o'clock. Transcribed from the original in the British Library.

Relevant text: ... this morning it is generally reported that the Kings forces marched this day and quartered this night at and about **Drayton** and the foot upon Bloor Heath ten miles from this town ... Since the writing of the lines above some of my scouts are returned and have taken prisoner near **Drayton** some officers, who inform that the army was upon the march and intends this night to quarter at **Drayton** ten miles hence, Morton [possibly Moreton

Say but more likely Norton-in-Hales] and other places seven or eight miles hence.

Document 61

Type:	Royalist Diary
Date:	Saturday 17th May 1645 to Thursday 22nd May 1645
Reference:	Bodleian Library MS Clarendon 28 f 137).
Title:	Prince Rupert's Journal in England
Notes:	Transcribed from the original in the Bodleian Library

Relevant text:. 17th Saturday, the King to Chetwynd Hall : Prince [Rupert] to Newport in Shropshire.

20th Tuesday, the King to Betton : Prince [Rupert] to **Drayton**

22nd Thursday, King to Park Hall : Prince to Stone

Document 62

Type:	Parliamentarian Letter
Date:	Tuesday 20th May 1645
Reference:	British Library Add. MS. 11331 f.139
Title:	Sir William Brereton's Letter Books
Notes:	Letter from Sir William Brereton at Nantwich to Lord Fairfax. Transcribed from the original in the British Library.

Relevant text: King at **Drayton**. The enemy is at **Drayton** and Woore within six miles of Nantwich;

Document 63

Type:	Parliamentarian Letter
Date:	Tuesday 20th May 1645
Reference:	British Library Add. MS. 11331 f.140
Title:	Sir William Brereton's Letter Books
Notes:	Letter from Sir William Brereton at Nantwich to the Committee of Both Kingdoms. Transcribed from the original in the British Library.

Relevant text: … the King's forces marched this day from Newport, (where they have stayed ever since Saturday refreshing themselves) unto **Drayton,** ten miles hence. Many of them quarter this night at Whitchurch, at Woore and other villages within six miles of this garrison, …

Document 64

Type:	Parliamentarian Letter
Date:	Tuesday 20th May 1645
Reference:	British Library Add. MS. 11331 f.138
Title:	Sir William Brereton's Letter Books
Notes:	Letter from Sir William Brereton at Nantwich to Sir Robert King. Transcribed from the original in the British Library.

Relevant text: The Kings army has continued ever since Saturday night, within sixteen miles of Nantwich; the King himself at Mr Piggott's of Chetwynd, the two Princes at the Swan in Newport; their whole army thereabouts, some of them have been taken at **Drayton:**

Document 65

Type:	Royalist Diary
Date:	Tuesday 20th May 1645
Reference:	British Library MS. Harl. 911 ff18-19

Market Drayton's Civil War

Title: The Marches & moovings & Actions of the Royall Army His majestie being personally present. From his coming out of his winter quarter Quarter at Oxford May 7, 1645 till the end of August following. (Richard Symonds Diary)

Notes: Transcribed from the original in the British Library.

Relevant text: Tuesday, May 20th, 1645. His Majesty with his army removed from Chetwynd through **Drayton** in Shropshire, and lay a mile further. The Earl of Lichfield etc. at Norton, at a house sometimes the habitation of Grosvenor, now Cotton's. The King lay at Church's house in **Drayton** parish.

Document 66

Type: Parliamentarian Letter

Date: Wednesday 21st May 1645

Reference: British Library Add. MS. 11331 f.146

Title: Sir William Brereton's Letter Books

Notes: Letter from Sir William Brereton at Knutsford to the Committee of Both Kingdoms. Transcribed from the original in the British Library.

Relevant text: The King's march is slow and with much ease as well knowing there is no army near to disturb and annoy them He marched yesterday seven miles from Newport to **Drayton** and the adjacent parts. Which way he may incline this day you shall hear speedily.

Document 67

Type: Parliamentarian Diary

Date: Wednesday 21st May 1645

Reference: Cheshire Record Office CRO/ DCC/11 1651

Title: A breefe & true Relacon of all suche passages & things as happened & weire donne in and aboute Namptwich in the Countie of Chester & in other places of the same Countie. Together wth some other things in other Counties (not farr distant) acted and donne by some of the Com'anders officers & Soldiers of the said Towne of Namptwiche. (after the same was made a Garrison, for Kinge & Parliamt.) scythens the xth of August, 1642. Soe truelie as the wryter hereof cold come by the knowledge of the same. Thomas Malbon.

Notes: Transcribed from the original in the Cheshire Record Office

Relevant text: But on Wednesday Night the King lay at **Drayton**, and his army at Mucklestone, Bellaport, Bloor and all the country thereabouts; and the same day an alarm was given at Nantwich, (but without cause).

Document 68

Type: Parliamentarian Diary

Date: Wednesday 21st May 1645

Reference: British Library Add. MS 5851 f52 et seq.

Title: Mr Burghall, Vicar of Acton in Cheshire: his ms intituled Providence Improved

Notes: Transcribed from an 18th century copy in the British Library. (Original's whereabouts unknown)

Relevant text: The King came on very slowly: on Wednesday night he lay at **Drayton** and his army quartered in the country thereabout.

Market Drayton's Civil War

Document 69

Type:	Parliamentarian Letter
Date:	Thursday 22nd May 1645
Reference:	British Library Add. MS. 11331 f.142
Title:	Sir William Brereton's Letter Books
Notes:	A letter from Sir William Brereton at Knutsford to Lord Leven. Transcribed from the original in the British Library.
Relevant text:	These lines may give your Excellence this assurance that I am upon my march towards the rendezvous upon Barlow Moor, this day according to your excellence's and Lord Fairfax's command having left the enemy's body yesterday at **Drayton** and betwixt that place and Nantwich where I do believe they either rested yesterday or removed to Whitchurch, seven miles from Nantwich ...

Document 70

Type:	Royalist Diary
Date:	Thursday May 22nd 1645
Reference:	British Library MS. Harl. 911 ff18-19
Title:	The Marches & moovings & Actions of the Royall Army His majestie being personally present. From his coming out of his winter quarter Quarter at Oxford May 7, 1645 till the end of August following. (Richard Symonds Diary)
Notes:	Transcribed from the original in the British Library.
Relevant text:	We marched from **Drayton** to Stone in Staffordshire.

Document 71

Type:	Parliamentarian Letter
Date:	Thursday 22nd May 1645
Reference:	British Library Add. MS. 11331 f.150
Title:	Sir William Brereton's Letter Books
Notes:	A letter from Sir William Brereton at Manchester to Lord Leven. Transcribed from the original in the British Library.
Relevant text:	I do therefore humbly offer to your Excellence's consideration whether it might not be requisite to make your march the near and speedie way least the circumference intended for your march may give advantage to the enemy (who still stayes at **Drayton** or Whitchurch within fourteen miles of Chester for anything I can hear) to wheel about and make an attempt upon Yorkshire.

Document 72

Type:	Parliamentarian Letter
Date:	Friday 23rd May 1645
Reference:	British Library Add. MS. 11331 f.151
Title:	Sir William Brereton's Letter Books
Notes:	A letter from Sir William Brereton at Manchester to the Committee of Both Kingdoms. Transcribed from the original in the British Library.
Relevant text:	... and quarter in much security having rested three nights at Newport and three nights at **Drayton** whence this morning (as I am informed) they are preparing to remove, but whither I have not yet heard.

Document 73

Type:	Parliamentarian Letter
Date:	Friday 23rd May 1645
Reference:	British Library Add. MS. 11331 f.158
Title:	Sir William Brereton's Letter Books
Notes:	A letter from Sir William Brereton at Manchester to the Speaker. Transcribed from the original in the British Library.
Relevant text:	I have marched with all my forces that possibly could be spared out of my garrisons into Lancashire to the rendezvous at Barlow Moor near Manchester: the enemy advancing with all their forces near us to **Drayton,** Whitchurch, Woore and the adjacent villages within six miles of Nantwich and according to their own letters, and my best intelligence, being on their march for Chester there to recruit their army out of Wales.

Document 74

Type:	Parliamentarian Letter
Date:	Saturday 24th May 1645
Reference:	British Library Add. MS. 11331 f.148
Title:	Sir William Brereton's Letter Books
Notes:	A letter from Sir William Brereton at Stockport to the Committee of Lincolnshire. Transcribed from the original in the British Library.
Relevant text:	After he had with his army hovered for divers days about **Drayton** and that part on Cheshire side and given us strong inducement to believe, both by letters intercepted and assertions of the Lieutenant of his own troop and other commanders taken prisoners, that his march was resolved for Chester, there to augment his army out of Wales and march thence through Lancashire into the north, upon Thursday last he removed thence to Newcastle in Staffordshire.

Document 75

Type:	Parliamentarian Letter
Date:	Saturday 24th May 1645
Reference:	British Library Add. MS. 11331 f.148
Title:	Sir William Brereton's Letter Books
Notes:	A letter from Sir William Brereton at Stockport to the Committee of Both Kingdoms. Transcribedr from the original in the British Library.
Relevant text:	Yesterday I sent a messinger away from Manchester that might inform you the certainty of the enemy's removal from **Drayton,** Whitchurch and those parts of Cheshire where he had continued divers days, and intended to march thence to Chester, stay there a while and hence to Lancashire as their own letters and several letters assured us: but contrary to all thoughts and expectation upon Thursday last (the same or the next day that the Scots broke up their Leaguer, and marched towards Westmorland this way) the enemy marched the contrary way to Newcastle in Staffordshire:

Document 76

Type:	Parliamentarian Letter
Date:	Monday 26th May 1645
Reference:	British Library Add. MS. 11331 f.159
Title:	Sir William Brereton's Letter Books
Notes:	A letter from Sir William Brereton at Barlow Moor to Lesley, Callander and Montgomery. Transcribed from the original in the British Library.

Relevant text: Upon Thursday 22nd of this instant, the King altered his course from what was expected and marched from **Drayton** to Newcastle and Trentham, the next night to Stone, himself quartering at Mr Crompton's house in the Park and upon the Saturday they marched towards Uttoxeter.

Document 77

Type:	Royalist Letter
Date:	Friday 17th October 1645
Reference:	British Library Add. MS. 11332 f.81
Title:	Sir William Brereton's Letter Books
Notes:	A Captured letter entered into Sir William Brereton's letter book from Lt. Col. Peter Griffith at Chester to his wife. Transcribed from the original in the British Library.

Relevant text: As for news, Poyntz horse were beaten at **Drayton** by Sir William Vaughan and so routed insomuch as the Staffordshire horse and the Lincolnshire horse as many as escaped are gone home.

Document 78

Type:	Royalist Letter
Date:	Friday 17th October 1645
Reference:	British Library Add. MS. 11332 f.96
Title:	Sir William Brereton's Letter Books
Notes:	A Captured letter from Lt. Col. Peter Griffith at Chester to to Thomas Whitley, his uncle. Transcribed from the original in the British Library.

Relevant text: We have had intelligence that Poyntz was routed by Sir William Vaughan at **Drayton**, it was the beating of his quarter but it was a full one:

Document 79

Type:	Royalist Letter
Date:	Friday 17th October 1645
Reference:	British Library Add. MS. 11332 f.82
Title:	Sir William Brereton's Letter Books
Notes:	A captured letter from Col. Roger Mostyn at Chester to Thomas Vaughan, Lt. Gov. Flint Castle. Transcribed from the original in the British Library.

Relevant text: Poyntz upon Tuesday night last was well beaten by Armourer, governour of High Arcall, at **Drayton** in Shropshire …

Document 80

Type:	Royalist Letter
Date:	Friday 17th October 1645
Reference:	British Library Add. MS. 11332 f.82
Title:	Sir William Brereton's Letter Books
Notes:	A captured letter from 'Your assured servant' at Chester to 'Mai:'. Transcribed from the original in the British Library.

Relevant text: I have no news to send you but what came to my Lord General Poyntz. His quarters was beaten up by Sir William Vaughan at **Drayton** with the loss of five or six hundred men at least …

Document 81

Type:	Parliamentarian Letter
Date:	Tuesday 11th November 1645
Reference:	British Library Add. MS. 11332 f.74

Title:	Sir William Brereton's Letter Books
Notes:	A letter from Col. Rob. Mainwaring at Nantwich to Sir William Brereton. Transcribed from the original in the British Library.
Relevant text:	...God willing I will march this night to **Drayton** and the places thereabouts and so according as I have intelligence I shall not neglect any opportunity ...

Document 82

Type:	Parliamentarian Letter
Date:	Thursday 27th November 1645
Reference:	British Library Add. MS. 11332 f.107
Title:	Sir William Brereton's Letter Books
Notes:	A letter from the Reformado officers at Blakenhall to Sir William Brereton. Transcribed from the original in the British Library.
Relevant text:	This morning according to your Honour's order, I drew out our regiment with all the rest of the horse being drawn up and ready to march: They hearing they were to march to **Drayton**, with an unanimous vote absolutely refused saying they were infinitely injured, saying also that inferior men were countenanced and laid in secure quarters, have their pay constantly paid and they constantly put upon out quarters: having not wherewithal to cover their nakedness nor a penny money in their pockets. Truly I must confess if I had not been an eye witness I should hardly have believed it.

Document 83

Type:	Royalist Letter
Date:	Monday 15th December 1645
Reference:	British Library Add. MS. 11333 f.37
Title:	Sir William Brereton's Letter Books
Notes:	A captured letter from Sir Rich. Lloyd at Holt Castle to Vaughan at 9 pm. Transcribed from the original in the British Library.
Relevant text:.	At this time all the ditches about Nantwich are frozen. The works are but very slight and low and the river frozen over, where, by the mills the entrance to the town lies open over the frost so as with fifteen hundred foot that place might be taken by surprise, for in three houres from **Drayton** or Whitchurch you might march thither these fair nights ...

Document 84

Type:	Parliamentarian Letter
Date:	Friday 26th December 1645
Reference:	British Library Add. MS. 11333 f.70
Title:	Sir William Brereton's Letter Books
Notes:	A letter from Col John Bowyer and Maj. Jos. Hawkesworth at Adderley to Sir William Brereton. Transcribed from the original in the British Library.
Relevant text:	We are concluded of our rendezvous at Moretonwood tomorrow by 10 o' clock and so for **Drayton.** We came through the quarters of the Reformados this night but they were removed out of them before orders could come to them so that we doe not know how to order them. Sir, we shall be at **Drayton**. We desire your further directions for our regiments.

Document 85

Type:	Parliamentarian Order
Date:	Friday 26th December 1645

Market Drayton's Civil War

Reference: British Library Add. MS. 11333 f.67
Title: Sir William Brereton's Letter Books
Notes: Sir William Brereton's orders to party under Col. Bowyer sent from Whitchurch. Transcribed from the original in the British Library.
Relevant text: Whereof Colonell Bowyer is to take charge and command; who, with the concurrence of the Majors aforesaid shall command and dispose of the said horse. And if they think fit to march tomorrow to **Drayton** and to advertise Captain Stone of their being there that so he may communicate intelligence with them and if any advantage offer itself against the enemy that they may lay hold upon and prosecute the same.

Document 86
Type: Parliamentarian Letter
Date: Friday 26th December 1645
Reference: British Library Add. MS. 11333 f.67
Title: Sir William Brereton's Letter Books
Notes: A letter from Sir William Brereton at Whitchurch to Captain Stone. Transcribed from the original in the British Library
Relevant text: I have now sent six or seven hundred horse at least who are to quarter hereabouts this night, tomorrow towards **Drayton** and afterwards to Newport as they shall have intelligence.

Document 87
Type: Parliamentarian Letter
Date: Friday 26th December 1645
Reference: British Library Add. MS. 11333 f.69.
Title: Sir William Brereton's Letter Books
Notes: A letter from Sir William Brereton at Whitchurch to the Committee of Lancashire. Transcribed from the original in the British Library.
Relevant text: We have returned all our foot to the Leaguer and some horse also and have placed your horse under the command of Major Jackson. The regiment of Reformadoes, the Warwickshire regiment and the Staffordshire regiments in very good and safe quarters betwixt Whitchurch and Newport and about **Drayton** where they are very convenient and may perform good service in order to our grand design.

Document 88
Type: Parliamentarian Letter
Date: Saturday 27th December 1645
Reference: British Library Add. MS. 11333 f.70
Title: Sir William Brereton's Letter Books
Notes: A letter from Sir William Brereton at Nantwich to Maj. Baker. Transcribed from the original in the British Library.
Relevant text: You know it was ordered on Thursday last that the four regiments of horse should remain in a body. Also on Friday they were ordered to march toward **Drayton** and so forwards as there should be occasion. Now I have received letters from Colonel Bowyer and Major Hawkesworth that your regiment is gone to your old quarters in Cheshire … I have received letters from them even now that this night they intend to quarter at **Drayton**.

Document 89

Type: Parliamentarian Statement of Letters
Date: Saturday 27th December 1645
Reference: British Library Add. MS. 11333 f.70
Title: Sir William Brereton's Letter Books
Notes: A statement of letters received and sent between Sir William Brereton, Col. Bowyer and Maj. Baker. Transcribed from the original in the British Library.
Relevant text: Letter was likewise written to Colonel Bowyer that whereas intelligence was sent from Captain Stone that the enemy was gone on the other side the rivers as there was no hopes of falling upon them that he should remain in his quarters about **Drayton** and those parts until further order according to the said order of the 24th December.

Document 90

Type: Parliamentarian Letter
Date: Sunday 28th December 1645
Reference: British Library Add. MS. 11333 f.72
Title: Sir William Brereton's Letter Books
Notes: A letter from Sir William Brereton at Nantwich to the Committee of Salop. Transcribed from the original in the British Library.
Relevant text: Though I dare not promise to myself that they will obey this order yet notwithstanding in pursuance hereof the Warwickshire and Staffordshire horse came yesternight to **Drayton.** The Reformados are marched to their old quarters in Cheshire, but I ordered them to come up unto the rest and I hope the Lancashire horse will join with them, though I am not certain thereof.

Document 91

Type: Parliamentarian Pamphlet
Date: Tuesday May 16th 1648
Reference: British Library Thomason E.442[18]
Title: A Testimony of the Ministers in the Province of Salop, to the Truth of Jesus Christ, and to The Solemn League and Covenant; as also Against the Errors, Heresies, and Blasphemies of these times, and the Toleration of them. Sent up to the Ministers within the Province of London, Subscribers of the First Testimony. London: Printed by F.N. for Tho: Underhill at the Bible in Woodstreet. M.DC.XLVIII (1648)
Notes: Transcribed from the original in the British Library.
Relevant text: **This pamphlet contains religious argument that tells us nothing about Market Drayton, with the exception of the list of subscribers, headed by the pastor of Market Drayton, and including other local pastors among which are:**
Thomas Cook Pastor of **Drayton magna.**
Tho: Porter Pastor of Whitchurch.
Francis Boughey Pastor of Hodnet.
Aylmer Houghton Pastor of Prees.
Andrew Parson Pastor of Wem.
Peter Niccols Pastor of Adderley.
Robert Benny Rector of Ightfield.
Henry Vaughan Pastor of Moreton-Say.
John Malden Pastor of Cheswardine.

Document 92

Type:	Parliamentarian Pamphlet
Date:	Tuesday September 26 1648
Reference:	British Library Thomason E.464[42].
Title:	An impartiall Relation of the late Fight at Preston. Being the Copy of a Letter, written (as the Tenour of it importeth) By Sir Marmaduke Langdale. Printed in the Year, 1648.
Notes:	Transcribed from the original in the British Library.

Relevant text: From Malpas they marched to **Drayton** and to Stone. In their march from thence to Uttoxeter, the Parliament forces fell upon the rear, and took Lieutenant-General Middleton.

Market Drayton's Civil War

Appendix 2 Parish Register 1642 to 1649

The full transcription and translation of the Market Drayton Parish Registers is now long overdue. However, it is a long and onerous task, the earlier entries being in Latin and not always as readable as would be desired, certainly at the time this book is dealing with. That being stated, any study of Market Drayton that attempts to deal with the lives of the ordinary citizens at this period must take these invaluable snapshots of family life into consideration.

I have therefore made an initial translation of the years 1642 to 1649, the years covered by the largest part of this book. I do not guarantee the accuracy of the results; translating names from their Latin versions does not always get back to the original. As an example, the Latin name Jacobus could either be Jacob or James. The recording of the entries themselves can be variable as to their accuracy. The document that now exists cannot always have been written on a day-by-day basis. For one thing, the writing hand and the ink colour are generally too consistent. For another, sometimes the person writing does not know the name of a child that has been baptized, and in one case even the sex, an omission that surely could not have happened if the writing had taken place soon after the event. The entries are also occasionally not in consecutive order. It is possible that the recorder was lax in entering events in a reasonable timeframe. It is also a possibility that what we have is fair copy, copied up from notes, and some entries may not have been readable some time after the original events. It must have been written around the time, however, as the writing conforms to the style of the period. Occasionally an entry is inserted subsequently in a different hand using different ink.

There are various locations recorded, most of which are obvious:

Adderley	Hales	Moreton Say
Almington	Hankshurst	Oakley
Betton	Heckmondwike	Ridgewardine
Blore	Hinstock	Shephards Bridge
Blore Heath	Knowle Wood	Spoonley
Brockley Moor	Lancashire	Styche
Cheshire	Little Drayton	Sutton
Chipnall	Little Heath	Tern Hill
Cox Oke	Little Heath Green	Tunstall
Derihowse	London	Tyrley
Drayton	Longford	Woodseaves

Market Drayton's Civil War

Drayton Field   Longslow

Similarly, there are various occupations recorded:

Arms-bearer	Farmer	Miller
Bailiff	Feltmaker	Servant
Butcher	Glover	Shoemaker
Chapman	Haberdasher	Soldier
Clerk	Joiner	Soldier
Clothier	Mercer	Vicar

As an example of transcription and translation, I will take an entry of each type, transcribe it and then translate it.

Male Burial

Quinto die Sepultus fuit John' Preston de little Heath greene
The fifth day John Preston of Little Heath Green was buried.

Female Burial

Eodem die Sepulta fuit Francisi Wade uxor Ricard Wade de Allmington
The same day Francis Wade wife of Richard Wade of Almington was buried.

Male Baptism

Vicessimo nono die baptizatus fuit Galfridus Shore filius Galfridi Shore et Bridget uxoris eius
The twenty ninth day [of the month] Geoffrey Shore son of Geoffrey Shore and Bridget his wife was baptized.

Female Baptism

Decimo quarto die Baptizata fuit Susanna Eaton filia Will'm Eaton et uxo' e'
The fourteenth day [of the month] Susanna Eaton daughter of William Eaton and his wife was baptized.

Marriage

Ultimo die nuptie celebrate fuerunt inter Will'm' Drury et Margret Allcraft

On the last day [of the month] the marriage of William Drury and Margaret Allcraft was celebrated.

I have listed the entries as date, type and names as this makes it easier to understand. I have anglicized forenames where the registrar has latinised them, and where known, modernized the spelling of place names. I would recommend that anyone researching family history should return to the original. As with all other dates in this book, I have included the day of the week. I have recorded the family names as written. Anywhere a word is obviously missing, where a gap has been left I have recorded [blank]. Where a word is used that I am unsure of I have also used square brackets, but a question mark followed by what I can make of the word, e.g. [?mno]. Where extra text is used to make the meaning clear, it is also in square brackets as in the examples above, e.g. [of the month].

January 1641/2

Sat 1st	Baptism	Richard Smith son of Humphrey Smith and Katherine his wife
Sun 9th	Baptism	Roger Jackson son of John Jackson and Mary his wife
Sun 9th	Baptism	Jane Pursell daughter of John Pursell and Margaret his wife
Sun 9th	Burial	Margaret Pursell wife of John Pursell
Mon 10th	Baptism	John Butterton son of Thomas Butterton and Elizabeth
Thu 13th	Marriage	Richard Teler and Mary Brodhurst
Sun 16th	Baptism	Samuel Betchcot son of Thomas Betchcot and Deborah his wife
Sun 16th	Baptism	James Scarrat son of Thomas Scarrat and [blank]
Sat 22nd	Burial	Moode Boulton wife of William Boulton
Wed 26th	Baptism	Elizabeth Deakin daughter of Robert Deakin and Margaret his wife of Ridgewardine
Mon 31st	Baptism	Mary Frende daughter of Thomas Frende and Mary his wife

February 1641/2

Sun 6th	Baptised	Robert Eaton son of George Eaton and Dorothy his wife
Sun 13th	Batpised	Joan Eaton daughter of Robert Eaton and Joan his wife
Wed 16th	Burial	Dorothy Robi daughter of Edward Robi and Dorothy his wife
Thu 17th	Baptism	Gideon Hande son of Thomas Hande and Anne his wife
Sat 19th	Burial	Alexander Tut son of Mr Richard Tut and Eleanor his wife
Thu 24th	Baptism	Alice Boeth daughter of James Boeth and Mary his wife

Mon 28th	Burial	Alice Boeth daughter of James Boeth and Mary his wife

March 1641/2

Fri 4th	Baptism	Mary Silleto daughter of Moses Silleto and Margaret his wife
Sun 6th	Baptism	Mary Salt daughter of Francis Salt and Timinson his wife
Wed 16th	Burial	Katheren Meddins wife of William Meddins
Sat 19th	Baptism	Anne Brodhurst daughter of James Brodhurst and Anne his wife
Sun 20th	Baptism	Susanna Lewis daughter of Hugh Lewis and Jane his wife
Wed 23rd	Baptism	Emme Meaninge daughter of John Meaninge and Emme his wife

March 1642

Thu 31st	Baptism	Margaret Robinson daughter of Francis Robinson and Alice his wife
Thu 31st	Marriage	Thomas Cha'berlin and Mary Steventon

April 1642

Fri 1st	Baptism	Frances Eaton daughter of Ralph Eaton and [blank]
Wed 6th	Baptism	Mary Phillips daughter of David Phillips and [blank]
Sun 10th	Baptism	Bartholomew Cooke son of John Cooke and Jane his wife
Tue 12th	Burial	Thomas Bradley of Drayton Field
Fri 15th	Burial	Robert Brasnell
Fri 15th	Baptism	Ellen Poole daughter of Thomas Poole and Alice his wife
Sat 16th	Burial	John Jackson of Sutton farmer
Sat 16th	Baptism	Ellen Hill daughter of Henry Hill and Mary his wife
Wed 20th	Burial	John Jenckes son of Elizabeth Jenckes widow [?good]
Thu 21st	Baptism	Edward Baker son of Richard Baker and [blank]
Sat 23rd	Baptism	John Rennolds son of Thomas Rennolds of Spoonley in the parish of Adderley and [blank]
Sat 23rd	Baptism	Matthew Holliday son of Matthew Holliday and Anne his wife
Sat 23rd	Marriage	Edward Embry and Margaret Bostock

May 1642

Sun 1st	Burial	Alice Poole wife of Robert Poole of Almington
Mon 2nd	Burial	Anne Cresswall wife of William Cresswall
Thu 5th	Burial	Elizabeth Preston widow of Almington
Fri 6th	Burial	Mr Humphrey Gouldston of Drayton
Mon 9th	Burial	Mathew Holliday son of Mathew Holliday and Anne his wife
Fri 13th	Burial	Thomas Lesseter of Little Drayton
Thu 19th	Baptism	Thomas Grinsell son of Richard Grinsell and Anne his wife
Thu 19th	Baptism	Roger Henderson son of Thomas Henderson and Elizabeth his wife
Thu 19th	Burial	Katherine Hasselhurst of Sutton widow
Fri 20th	Baptism	Mary Hamnett daughter of Richard Hamnett and Margaret his wife

Tue 31st	Burial	Andrew Jervis of Blore Heath

June 1642

Sat 4th	Baptism	Dorothy Jones daughter of Richard Jones and Sarah his wife
Tue 7th	Burial	John Holliday son of Isabelle Holliday widow
Thu 9th	Burial	Thomas Wythers of Little Drayton
Fri 10th	Burial	Alice Johnson wife of Hugh Johnson
Tue 14th	Burial	Margaret Shore wife of Jeffrey Shore of Drayton
Fri 24th	Baptised	Clara Morrey daughter of John Morrey and Katherine his wife of Betton

July 1642

Thu 7th	Baptism	Elizabeth Leech, daughter of James Leech and Elizabeth his wife
Sun 10th	Baptism	George Gueste son of George Gueste and Mary his wife
Thu 21st	Baptism	Wiiliam Wardley son of William Wardley of Betton and Margaret his wife of Betton
Thu 21st	Baptism	Edward Benbo son of John Benbo of Blore and [blank] his wife
Sun 24th	Baptism	Jane Prince daughter of Robert Prince and Anne his wife
Thu 28th	Marriage	John Growcoke and Maria Shocklich
Sun 31st	Baptism	Thomas Preston son of John Preston of Chipnall in Cheswardine parish and Jane his wife
Sun 31st	Burial	Bartholomew Cooke son of John Cooke and Jane his wife

August 1642

Thu 4th	Baptism	Elizabeth Peat daughter of John Peat and Sarah his wife
Fri 5th	Burial	George Jebb of Hales
Sat 6th	Burial	Mary Cooke daughter of John Cooke and Jane his wife
Sun 7th	Baptism	Roland Hatchet son of John Hatchet and Anne his wife
Wed 10th	Burial	Elizabeth Peat daughter of Mary Peat illegitimate birth
Wed 10th	Burial	[blank] Robinson daughter of Francis Robinson and Alice his wife
Sun 14th	Baptism	Elizabeth Johnson daughter of William Johnson and Jane his wife
Tue 23rd	Burial	Roland Hatchet son of John Hatchet and Anne his wife
Thu 25th	Burial	Margaret Preston wife of William Preston
Sat 27th	Burial	Ralph Brodhurst of Woodseaves
Wed 31st	Burial	Margaret Massey daughter of Robert Massey of Almington

September 1642

Sat 3rd	Baptism	John Sargant son of Hugh Sargant and Margaret his wife
Mon 12th	Burial	Richard Felton son of Mr Thomas Felton cleric
Wed 14th	Baptism	William Rennolds son of Hugh Rennolds and Anne his wife
Sun 18th	Baptism	William Wrich son of James Wrich and Anne his wife
Wed 21st	Baptism	Elizabeth Dew daughter of Christopher Dew and [blank]
Thu 22nd	Burial	Maria Naginton daughter of John Naginton

Fri 23rd	Burial	Dorcus Humston daughter of John Humston and his wife
Sun 25th	Baptism	Lawrence James son of Thomas James and Anna his wife
Sun 25th	Burial	Maria Kenricke daughter of Ralph Kenricke and Anne his wife
Wed 28th	Burial	Richard Creswall of Almington
Thu 29th	Baptism	Mary Quicquick daughter of Bartholomew Quicquick and Mary his wife of London

October 1642

Mon 3rd	Burial	Alice Cresswall daughter of John Cresswall
Wed 5th	Burial	Mary Loe wife of Francis Loe
Wed 5th	Burial	Margaret Cowper daughter of John Cowper and Katherine his wife
Thu 6th	Baptism	Margaret Bate daughter of Humphrey Bate and Jane his wife
Thu 6th	Baptism	Anne Frend daughter of Thomas Frend and Mary his wife
Thu 6th	Burial	John Naginton son of John Naginton and Timinson his wife
Fri 7th	Marriage	Edward Allen and Elizabeth Wade
Fri 14th	Baptism	Eleanor Botman daughter of John Botman and Rebecca
Sat 15th	Burial	Edward Benboe son of John Benbo and his wife
Sun 16th	Burial	William Holliday son of Matthew Holliday and Anne his wife
Wed 19th	Baptism	Mary Porter daughter of John Porter and Sarah his wife
Thu 20th	Burial	Isabelle Meredeth daughter of Richard Meredeth and Anne his wife
Sat 22nd	Burial	William Huxley son of Thomas Huxley
Sun 23rd	Baptism	Mary Richardson daughter of George Richardson
Tue 25th	Burial	John Tomson son of Lawrence Tomson [?]
Thu 27th	Burial	Lawrence Tomson son of the same Lawrence
Fri 28th	Baptism	Mary Meredeth daughter of Richard Meredeth and Anne his wife
Sun 30th	Baptism	Anne Lightfoot daughter of Humphrey Lightfoot and Elizabeth his wife
Mon 31st	Burial	Jane Colly daughter of Walter Colly and Eleanor his wife

November 1642

Tue 1st	Baptism	Elizabeth Eicke daughter of Anne Eicke and alleged father William Skattergoode
Sun 6th	Baptism	Priscilla Cooke daughter of Richard Cooke and Joan his wife
Sun 6th	Baptism	Roland Cowper son of John Cowper and Katherine his wife
Tue 8th	Burial	Simon Cowper of Drayton
Sun 13th	Baptism	Anne Stonhurst daughter of Ambrose Stonhurst and Anne his wife
Sun 13th	Burial	William Minton son of Margaret Minton widow

Sun 13th	Burial	[blank] Davis of Betton widow
Tue 15th	Burial	John Cooke son of Richard Cooke and Joan his wife
Tue 15th	Burial	Eleanor Boulton daughter of William Boulton
Sun 20th	Burial	Anne Smith daughter of Thomas Smith [?mno'] of Blore
Fri 25th	Baptism	Thomas Nealer son of Thomas nealer and Anne his wife
Sat 26th	Burial	Lawrence Wixstid of Betton
Sun 27th	Burial	Elizabeth Eike daughter of Anne Eike and alleged father William: Skattergoode
Tue 29th	Baptism	Ambrose Rea son of Mr Richard Rea and Anne his wife
Wed 30th	Marriage	Thomas Lockett and Elizabeth Jackson

December 1642

Thu 1st	Marriage	James Booth and Susanna Wade
Fri 2nd	Baptism	Roger Adames son of Richard Adames and Elizabeth
Wed 7th	Marriage	William Yerdsley and Anne Moure
Sun 11th	Burial	Thomas Cooke son of Mr Thomas vicar of Drayton
Sat 17th	Burial	Richard Watson son of Richard Watson and his wife
Sat 17th	Burial	Eleanor Randell wife of William Randell
Sat 17th	Burial	Emme Meaninge daughter of John Meaninge and his wife
Sun 18th	Baptism	Thomas Cartwright son of Thomas Cartwright and Bridget his wife
Tue 20th	Burial	Robert Bodington son of John Bodington
Tue 20th	Burial	Mary Hamnet daughter of Richard Hamnet and his wife
Thu 22nd	Burial	Thomas Leavit of Blore
Thu 22nd	Burial	[blank] Browne daughter of John Browne
Thu 22nd	Burial	Anne Stenson wife of Virgil Stenson
Fri 23rd	Burial	Richard Smith son of Humphrey Smith
Mon 26th	Burial	The son of Thomas Chamberlin unbaptised
Tue 27th	Baptism	Katherine Masson daughter of Thomas Masson
Wed 28th	Baptism	Alice Nealer daughter of William Nealer and Mary his wife

January 1642/3

Thu 5th	Burial	Joan Bridge widow of Drayton
Fri 6th	Burial	Thomas Benboe son of John Benboe
Fri 6th	Baptism	Jane Parrock daughter of John Parrock and Elizabeth
Fri 6th	Baptism	William Lateworth son of William Lateworth
Sat 7th	Burial	William Hampton of Drayton
Sun 8th	Marriage	Richard Higgin and Margaret Suker
Sun 15th	Baptism	Alice Smith daughter of Richard Smith and Margaret his wife
Sun 22nd	Baptism	Sarah Powell daughter of Bartholomew Powell and Frances his wife
Sun 29th	Baptism	Richard Allcraft son of John Allcraft and Margaret his wife

February 1642/3

Thu 2nd	Baptism	[blank] Willot son of William Willat and Eleanor his wife
Fri 3rd	Burial	William Wordley son of John Wordley and Margaret his

		wife
Sun 5th	Baptism	Elizabeth Barker daughter of Mr George Barker and Elizabeth
Sun 5th	Marriage	Richard Kennett and Margaret Rogers
Thu 9th	Baptism	Mary Higgin daughter of John Higgin and Margaret his wife
Thu 9th	Marriage	William Adames and Margaret Poole
Thu 9th	Marriage	Edward Bate and Elizabeth Arnett
Fri 10th	Baptism	James Booth son of James Booth and Mary his wife
Sun 12th	Baptism	Mary Greene daughter of Mr John Greene and Sylvie
Mon 13th	Burial	John Small son of Katherine Small widow
Mon 20th	Baptism	John Roberts son of Richard Roberts and [blank]
Thu 23rd	Burial	Reynold Betchcott son of Thomas
Mon 27th	Baptism	Parnel Pursell daughter of Roger Pursell and Parnel his wife

March 1642/3

Wed 1st	Baptism	[blank] Bruse daughter of John Bruse and Margaret
Thu 2nd	Burial	Richard Allcraft son of John Allcraft and Margaret
Thu 9th	Burial	Joan Triner of Tyrley widow
Fri 10th	Baptism	Thomas Evanson son of George Evanson and Margaret his wife
Sun 12th	Baptism	Joan Harrington daughter of John Harrington and his wife
Thu 23rd	Burial	Roland Cowper son of John Cowper and his wife
Fri 24th	Burial	Anne Hope wife of William Hope of Little Drayton

March 1643

Sun 26th	Burial	Anne Wrich wife of James Wrich
Tue 28th	Baptism	Anne Bull daughter of Thomas Bull and Anne his wife
Fri 31st	Baptism	Mary Nettels daughter of John Nettels and Mary his wife

April 1643

Fri 7th	Burial	Anne Bull daughter of Thomas Bull and Anne his wife
Fri 7th	Baptism	Michael Hope son of Michael Hope and Elizabeth his wife
Sun 23rd	Baptism	Mary Jackson daughter of John Jackson and Mary his wife
Sun 23rd	Burial	Roger Williams of Ridgwardine
Wed 26th	Baptism	Ralph Brodhurst son of John Brodhurst of Betton

May 1643

Mon 1st	Baptism	Anne Thomas daughter of William Thomas and his wife
Sat 6th	Baptism	Mary Peele daughter of Richard Peele and his wife
Thu 11th	Baptism	George Colley son of Walter Colley and Eleanor his wife
Thu 11th	Baptism	Humphrey Bedworth son of Humphrey Bedworth and his wife
Fri 12th	Burial	John Hopp of Drayton
Sat 13th	Burial	George Colley son of Walter Colley
Mon 15th	Baptism	William Simister son of Charles Simister
Fri 19th	Baptism	Isabelle Steventon daughter of Mr George Steventon and

		Mary his wife of Drayton
Sun 21ˢᵗ	Burial	Thomas Brockton
Mon 22ⁿᵈ	Baptism	William Holliday son of Matthew Holliday and Anne his wife
Tue 23ʳᵈ	Burial	Joan Dorington widow of Almington
Thu 25ᵗʰ	Burial	Elizabeth Allcraft widow
Fri 26ᵗʰ	Baptism	Jane Bowles daughter of Mr Thomas Bowles and Frances his wife
Sat 27ᵗʰ	Burial	Joan Pickin wife of William Pickin
Sun 28ᵗʰ	Baptism	John Cowper son of Randal Cowper
Wed 31ˢᵗ	Baptism	Roland Yerdsley son of Roland Yerdsley

June 1643

Fri 2ⁿᵈ	Burial	John Dod of Brockley Moor
Sat 3ʳᵈ	Burial	Ralph Hilldich of Longslow
Tue 6ᵗʰ	Baptism	Thomas Poole son of Henry Poole and Elizabeth his wife
Sat 10ᵗʰ	Burial	Elizabeth Simister wife of Thomas Simister
Tue 13ᵗʰ	Burial	Thomas Meakin of Drayton
Tue 13ᵗʰ	Burial	John Davis of Knowle Woode servant
Tue 20ᵗʰ	Burial	Thomas Holmes of Little Drayton Joiner
Sat 24ᵗʰ	Baptism	Margaret Grice daughter of Evan Grice and Margaret his wife
Fri 30ᵗʰ	Baptism	Alice Clutton daughter of William Clutton and Grace his wife

July 1643

Fri 7ᵗʰ	Burial	Mary Nettells daughter of John Nettells and Mary his wife
Sat 8ᵗʰ	Baptism	Thomas Venables son of Elizabeth Vennables and alleged father William Eaton
Sun 9ᵗʰ	Baptism	Anne Growcocke daughter of John Growcocke and Mary his wife
Sun 9ᵗʰ	Baptism	Mary Wright daughter of John Wright and [blank]
Mon 10ᵗʰ	Burial	Son of Robert Blakewey not baptised
Sat 15ᵗʰ	Burial	Matthew Holliday of Drayton
Sun 16ᵗʰ	Baptism	Eleanor Preston daughter of Richard Preston and Jane his wife
Sun 23ʳᵈ	Baptism	Margaret Davison daughter of Thomas Davison and Margaret his wife
Thu 27ᵗʰ	Baptism	Elizabeth Cowfeild daughter of Henry Cowfeild
Fri 28ᵗʰ	Burial	Joan Bate wife of George Bate alias Farmer
Mon 31ˢᵗ	Burial	Anne Smith wife of Thomas Smith alias Turner

August 1643

Sun 6ᵗʰ	Burial	[blank] Wolley wife of William Wolley of Woodseaves
Thu 10ᵗʰ	Baptism	Margaret Cooke daughter of John Cooke and Jane his wife
Fri 11ᵗʰ	Baptism	Edward Bate son of Edward Bate and [blank]
Sat 12ᵗʰ	Baptism	John Eaton son of William Eaton

Thu 17th	Burial	Anne Davenport wife of Mr [blank] Davenport
Thu 17th	Burial	Thomas Poole son of Henry Poole and Elizabeth
Fri 18th	Baptism	Margaret Lockett daughter of Thomas Lockett and Elizabeth
Wed 30th	Baptism	Mary Higgin daughter of Humphrey Higgin and Elizabeth his wife
Wed 30th	Baptism	Margaret Bate daughter of John Bate and Isabelle his wife of the parish of Adderley

September 1643

Fri 1st	Burial	Richard Whitworth of Drayton
Sun 3rd	Baptism	John Wade son of William Wade and [blank]
Sun 3rd	Burial	Ralph Willat of Betton [?w....]
Sun 3rd	Burial	William Holliday son of Matthew Holliday
Wed 6th	Baptism	William Naginton son of John Naginton and [blank]
Thu 7th	Burial	Mary Bayly daughter of Roger Bayly and his wife
Wed 13th	Baptism	Anne Wade daughter of George Wade and Elizabeth his wife
Wed 13th	Baptism	Elizabeth Barley daughter William Barley and Anne his wife
Fri 29th	Baptism	William Peat son of William Peat
Fri 29th	Baptism	Mary Davis daughter of John Davis

October 1643

Wed 11th	Burial	Mary Naginton of Drayton
Wed 11th	Burial	William Gooddian soldier
Thu 19th	Baptism	Priscilla Peat daughter of Francis Peat and Mary his wife
Thu 19th	Burial	Katherine Wright wife of William Wright

November 1643

Sat 4th	Burial	Roger Madley of Longford
Tue 14th	Burial	[blank] Hills daughter of Jeffrey Hills
Tue 14th	Baptism	Ursula Laton daughter of Robert Laton and his wife
Wed 15th	Burial	Elizabeth Lightfoote wife of Humphrey Lightfoote
Thu 16th	Baptism	William Ackis son of John Ackis and Jane his wife
Thu 16th	Baptism	Eleanor Hurdman daughter of John Hurdman and his wife
Thu 23rd	Baptism	Mary Browne daughter of John Browne of Blore
Fri 24th	Burial	Richard Cooke of Drayton mercer
Fri 24th	Baptism	Ralph Williamson son of Richard Williamson
Thu 30th	Baptism	Alice Mosse daughter of Thomas Mosse and Jane his wife

December 1643

Tue 5th	Baptism	Isabelle Church daughter of Mr Thomas Church and Mary his wife of Betton
Wed 6th	Baptism	Alice Hill daughter of Mr Phillip Hill and Elizabeth his wife
Sat 9th	Baptism	Margaret Constandine daughter of Thomas Constandine and Elizabeth his wife
Fri 22nd	Baptism	Thomas Rogers son of Thomas Rogers

Fri 22nd	Baptism	George Wade son of George Wade of Sutton
Sun 24th	Baptism	Richard Peeke son of John Peeke of Sutton
Sun 24th	Burial	Roland Davison Butcher and Alice his wife
Tue 26th	Baptism	Edward Bate son of Edward Bate of Blore and [blank] his wife
Fri 29th	Burial	Mary Cresswall of Almington widow
Fri 29th	Burial	Mary Nealer wife of William Nealer
Sun 31st	Marriage	John Bayly and Jane Drury*

January 1643/4

Tue 2nd	Baptism	Joseph Podmore son of John Podmore and Katherine his wife of Moreton Say parish
Tue 2nd	Burial	Ralph Williams son of Richard Williams and his wife
Mon 8th	Burial	Hugh Johnson of Hakshurst
Thu 11th	Baptism	Mary Felton daughter of Thomas Felton and Mary his wife
Sun 14th	Burial	William Chade of Almington
Wed 17th	Burial	Isabelle Duker widow
Sat 20th	Baptism	Judith Massey daughter of Thomas Massey and Judith his wife of Moreton Say parish
Sun 21st	Baptism	Richard Leech son of James Leech and Elizabeth his wife
Fri 26th	Baptism	Elizabeth Meaninge daughter of John Meaninge and Em his wife
Sat 27th	Baptism	Mary Eaton daughter of Robert Eaton and Joan his wife
Sat 27th	Baptism	Anne Whitingam daughter of Thomas Whitingam and [?Jecs] his wife

February 1643/4

Thu 1st	Burial	Thomas Pitchford of Derihowse
Fri 2nd	Baptism	Margaret Turner daughter of William Turner and Elizabeth his wife
Sun 4th	Baptism	Thomas Salt son of Francis Salt and Timinson his wife
Tue 6th	Burial	Edward Bate son of Edward Bate and his wife
Wed 7th	Baptism	Thomas Turner son of Richard Turner and Anne his wife
Wed 7th	Baptism	Mary Bechcot daughter of Thomas Bechcot and Deborah his wife
Sat 10th	Burial	John Berdmore son of James Berdmore
Sat 10th	Burial	Richard Rabon of Drayton
Sat 17th	Baptism	Jane Deakin daughter of Robert Deakin and Margaret his wife
Tue 20th	Burial	Richard Caddy
Thu 22nd	Baptism	Thomas Wilkinson son of Lawrence Wilkinson and Mary his wife
Thu 22nd	Baptism	Thomas Mendlove son of Richard Mendlove and Isabelle his wife of Longford in Morton Say parish
Thu 22nd	Burial	Isabelle Steventon daughter of George Steventon
Thu 22nd	Baptism	Alice Cotton daughter of Thomas Cotton and Margaret his wife

Fri 23rd	Burial	Richard Caddie
Mon 26th	Burial	Thomas Person
Mon 26th	Burial	Anne Bayly widow of Blore Heath

March 1643/4

Sun 3rd	Burial	Thomas Hope of Drayton
Mon 11th	Burial	James Witworth of Drayton
Tue 12th	Burial	Anne Browne wife of John Browne
Thu 14th	Burial	Eleanor wife of George Richardson
Mon 18th	Burial	Thomas Peat son of Frances Peat
Tue 19th	Burial	Jeffrey Hills of Drayton
Fri 22nd	Burial	Robert Poulride of Heckmondwicke in the parish of Birstall in the county of York clothier
Sat 23rd	Burial	[blank] Thomas daughter of William Thomas
Sat 23rd	Baptism	Roland Lateworth son of William Lateworth
Sun 24th	Burial	Jane Barker wife of John Barker [?mno]

March 1644

Fri 29th	Baptism	Richard Hills son of Jeffrey Hills and Matilda his wife
Sat 30th	Burial	Phillip Cartwright of Drayton Shoemaker
Sat 30th	Baptism	Francis Triner son of Robert Triner and his wife
Sat 30th	Baptism	John Cowper son of John Cowper and Katherine his wife

April 1644

Sat 6th	Baptism	William Worldley son of John Wordley and Margaret his wife
Sun 7th	Baptism	Elizabeth Blomer daughter of William Blomer and his wife
Sat 13th	Burial	Margaret Robinson widow of Woodseaves
Sun 14th	Baptism	John Whitney son of Robert Whitney of Longford in Morton Say parish
Sun 14th	Baptism	Thomas Mosse son of Edward Mosse and Bridget his wife of Hinstock parish
Mon 22nd	Baptism	Margaret Brodhurst daughter of James and Joan his wife
Sat 27th	Baptism	George Wade son of William Wade and Jane

May 1644

Wed 1st	Baptism	Eleanor Booth daughter of James Booth
Thu 2nd	Burial	Timinson Naginton wife of John Naginton
Fri 3rd	Burial	Joan Poole of Drayton spinster
Sat 4th	Burial	Robert Gouldswine
Sun 5th	Baptism	John Browne daughter of Thomas Browne and his wife
Sun 5th	Baptism	Sarah Eales daughter of John Eales and Elizabeth his wife
Sun 5th	Burial	Anne Meredeth daughter of Richard Meredeth and Anne his wife
Fri 10th	Baptism	John Wetherell son of Mr John Wetherell
Sun 12th	Burial	[blank] Bechcote daughter of Thomas Bechcot and Deborah his wife

Sun 12th	Marriage	Ralph Watson and Mary Bridge
Sat 18th	Baptism	Eleanor Adames daughter of James Adames and Margaret
Sat 18th	Burial	Elizabeth Hoggins wife of Thomas Hoggins
Wed 22nd	Burial	Anne Hill wife of George Hill of Woodseaves
Fri 24th	Burial	Mary Lea wife of Ralph Lea
Fri 24th	Baptism	Mary Lea daughter of Ralph Lea and before mentioned Mary his wife
Thu 30th	Burial	John Masson of Drayton
Thu 30th	Burial	Jane Deakin daughter of Robert Deakin and Margaret his wife

June 1644

Tue 4th	Burial	John Preston of Little Heath Green
Tue 4th	Burial	Francis Wade wife of Richard Wade of Almington
Thu 13th	Baptism	William Massey son of Peter Massey and [blank]
Thu 13th	Baptism	Eleanor Higgin illegitimate daughter of Joan Higgin
Fri 14th	Baptism	Susannah Eaton daughter of William Eaton and his wife
Fri 14th	Baptism	Sarah Phillips daughter of David Phillips and Elizabeth his wife
Sat 15th	Baptism	Mary Wolley daughter of Humphrey Wolley and Joan his wife
Wed 26th	Baptism	Anne Johnson daughter of Thomas Johnson and Elizabeth his wife
Sat 29th	Baptism	Geoffrey Shore son of Geoffrey Shore and Bridget his wife
Sun 30th	Marriage	William Drury and Margeret Allcroft

July 1644

Tue 9th	Burial	Katherine Growcoke of Hales widow
Wed 10th	Burial	Elizabeth Smith daughter of Richard Smith and Margaret his wife
Fri 19th	Baptism	Roger Bayly son of Roger Bayly and Margaret
Mon 22nd	Baptism	Isabelle Farmer daughter of Abraham Farmer and Anne
Sat 27th	Marriage	Richard Hoggins and Elizabeth Cramer

August 1644

Mon 5th	Baptism	Hugh Lewis son of Hugh Lewis and Alice his wife
Wed 7th	Burial	Alice Morton wife of Thomas Morton
Sun 11th	Baptism	William Preston son of William Preston and Elizabeth his wife
Sun 11th	Burial	Elizabeth Preston wife of William Preston of Hales
Mon 19th	Baptism	Robert Nealer son of Thomas Nealer and Anne
Tue 20th	Baptism	Margaret Growcoke daughter of Thomas Growcoke[?mno] and Alice his wife
Thu 29th	Burial	John Jones pauper
Thu 29th	Baptism	Sarah Phillips daughter of Mr William Phillips and [?Jennet] his wife of Tunstall
Sat 31st	Burial	Alice wife of Humphrey Smith

September 1644

Sun 1st	Baptism	Margaret Brodhurst daughter of John brodhurst of Betton
Sun 1st	Baptism	[blank] Challener daughter of William Challener and Elizabeth his wife
Thu 5th	Burial	Mary Peat daughter of Thomas Peat and Margaret his wife
Fri 6th	Burial	Roger Frend of Drayton Bailiff
Sun 8th	Burial	Isabelle Denteth of Drayton spinster
Sat 14th	Baptism	John Botman son of Elizabeth Botman widow
Sun 15th	Baptism	Anne Grinsell daughter of Richard Grinsell and Anne his wife
Sun 15th	Baptism	Mary Wilde daughter of Ralph Wilde of Longslow
Sun 15th	Baptism	Margaret Baylie daughter of Roland Bayly of Blore Heath
Sat 21st	Baptism	Martha Wythers daughter Roger Wythers and Alice his wife
Sat 28th	Baptism	[blank] Benboe [fili*] of John Benboe of Blore * Not only was the name not known, the sex wasn't either. The word 'fili' with a space after it has been written instead of the usual 'filius' for son or 'filia' for daughter.
Mon 30th	Baptism	Richard Nettles son of John Nettles of Little Drayton
Mon 30th	Baptism	Elizabeth Leech daughter of William Leech and Elizabeth his wife

October 1644

| Mon 7th | Baptism | Mary Botman daughter of John Botman and Rebecca his wife |
| Sun 20th | Baptism | Jane Longshawe daughter of William Longshawe of Blore |

November 1644

Fri 8th	Baptism	Joanna Bube daughter of Thomas Bube and Anne his wife
Sat 9th	Burial	Margaret Salman wife of John Salman
Sun 10th	Burial	Eleanor Higgin daughter of William Higgin and Anne
Sun 10th	Baptism	Mary Brodhurst daughter of James Brodhurst
Fri 15th	Baptism	Humphrey Cresswall son of Robert Cresswall
Sun 17th	Baptism	Mary Bowles daughter of Mr Thomas Bowles and his wife
Wed 20th	Burial	Sarah Phiilips daughter of Mr William Phillips and Eleanor his wife
Fri 22nd	Baptism	Anne Pursell daughter of Roger Pursell and Parnel his wife

December 1644

Sun 8th	Baptism	Robert Rea son of Mr Richard Rea and Anne his wife
Mon 9th	Baptism	Andrew Bate son of Edward Bate and Elizabeth his wife
Mon 9th	Baptism	Richard Hamnett son of Richard Hamnett and Elizabeth

		his wife
Sat 14th	Baptism	George Porter son of John Porter and Sarah his wife
Sat 14th	Baptism	Mary Baker daughter of Richard Baker of Blore
Wed 18th	Burial	Richard Steventon of Drayton
Thu 19th	Burial	Margaret Wetherell wife of John Wetherell
Fri 20th	Burial	Peter Cause of Drayton
Wed 25th	Burial	John Wordley of Betton
Thu 26th	Burial	Ralph Lea son of Ralph Lea
Tue 31st	Baptism	Sarah Charles daughter of [blank] Carles illegitimate birth

January 1644/5

Wed 1st	Baptism	Mary Adams daughter of Richard Adams and Elizabeth his wife
Thu 2nd	Baptism	Mary Jones daughter of Richard jones and Sarah his wife
Thu 2nd	Burial	John Henderson of the County of Lancaster
Fri 3rd	Burial	Humphrey Cresswall son of Robert Cresswall
Mon 6th	Baptism	Isabelle Remedeth daughter of Richard Remedeth
Mon 6th	Marriage	Richard Peret and Mary Axson
Fri 10th	Marriage	John Bayly and Jane Drury
Sun 12th	Burial	Margaret Sargant wife of Hugh Sargant
Sat 18th	Baptism	Ralph Eaton son of Ralph Eaton and Anne
Thu 23rd	Baptism	Margaret Stannelley daughter of Richard Stannelley and Mary
Fri 24th	Marriage	William Cresswall and Mary Davis
Sun 26th	Baptism	Henry Neavit son of Thomas Neavit and Mary
Sun 26th	Marriage	William Heamis and Eleanor Daker

February 1644/5

Sat 1st	Baptism	Lawrence Norcopp son of Lawrence Norcopp and Mary his wife
Tue 4th	Burial	William Grome of Spoonley in Adderley parish
Sun 9th	Baptism	Alice Preston daughter of George Preston and [blank]
Mon 10th	Burial	[blank] Frances of Hales widow
Thu 13th	Marriage	Thomas Cartwright and Sarah Hues
Fri 14th	Baptism	Ambrose Stele son of Ambrose Stele and his wife
Fri 14th	Baptism	Jane Poole daughter of Henry Poole and Elizabeth his wife
Tue 25th	Baptism	Anne Pursell daughter of John Pursell and Margaret

March 1644/5

Sun 2nd	Burial	Elizabeth Hurdman of Almington widow
Thu 6th	Baptism	John Derington son of Thomas Derington and Elizabeth his wife
Thu 6th	Baptism	Elizabeth Bro'ninge daughter of Robert Bro'ninge and Elizabeth his wife
Thu 6th	Baptism	Elizabeth Preston daughter of Richard Preston and Jane his wife
Sat 8th	Baptism	Elizabeth Edwards daughter of Owen Edwards and Elizabeth
Tue 11th	Baptism	Elizabeth Phillips daughter of Thomas Phillips and

		Dorothy
Thu 13th	Baptism	Phyllis Cowfeild daughter of Henry Cowfeild and his wife
Fri 14th	Burial	Alice Hickcoke of Almington
Mon 17th	Burial	Anne Jackson daughter of William Jackson of Sutton
Sun 23rd	Baptism	Jonathan Smith son of Richard Smith and his wife

March 1645

Tue 25th	Burial	Joyce Watson [?aglascarrier]
Thu 27th	Baptism	Eleanor Peel daughter of Richard Peele and his wife
Fri 28th	Baptism	Anne Orton daughter of Randal Orton and his wife
Sun 30th	Baptism	Mary Jackson daughter of John Jackson and Mary his wife
Sun 30th	Baptism	Mary Booth daughter of James Booth and Mary his wife

April 1645

Tue 1st	Baptism	Mary Cowper daughter of Ralph Cowper and Mary
Wed 2nd	Burial	Roger Withers
Mon 7th	Baptism	Alice Cartwright daughter of Ralph Cartwright of Betton
Mon 14th	Burial	Eleanor Hildich of Longslow spinster
Wed 16th	Burial	Frances Floyd wife of John Floyd
Wed 16th	Marriage	Hugh Sargant amd Margaret Johnson
Mon 21st	Burial	Thomas Nealer of Drayton turner
Fri 25th	Baptism	Thomas Clutton son of William Clutton of Little Drayton
Sun 27th	Baptism	Eleanor Masson daughter of Thomas Masson and Mary his wife
Sun 27th	Baptism	Mary Peate daughter of William Peate and Anne his wife
Mon 28th	Burial	Anne Flint of Hales widow
Mon 28th	Burial	Eleanor Kenricke of Drayton spinster

May 1645

Thu 8th	Burial	Edward Massey of Ockley miller
Fri 9th	Baptism	Abigail Blakwey daughter of Robert Blakwey and Anne his wife
Fri 9th	Baptism	Sarah Frend daughter of Thomas Frend and Dorothy his wife
Tue 20th	Baptism	Mary Barker daughter of Mr George Barker and Elizabeth
Sun 25th	Burial	John Weever of Tern Hill gentleman
Tue 27th	Baptism	Thomas Cowper son of Thomas Cowper and Elizabeth his wife
Tue 27th	Baptism	George Eaton son of George Eaton and Mary his wife
Tue 27th	Baptism	Eleanor Davison daughter of Thomas Davison and Margaret his wife
Tue 27th	Baptism	Mary Rennolds daughter of Hugh Rennolds
Sat 31st	Baptism	Walter Griffin son of Walter Griffin a soldier

June 1645

Thu 5th	Baptism	Thomas Wright son of John Wright and Joan his wife
Thu 12th	Burial	Mary Jackson daughter of John Jackson and Mary his

wife

Fri 13th	Baptism	Margaret Parrocke daughter of John Parrocke and Anne his wife
Sat 14th	Baptism	Dorcus Peat daughter of Francis Peat and Mary
Sun 15th	Marriage	Richard Challener and Eleanor Gravener
Sun 22nd	Marriage	Richard Lee and Mary Poole
Tue 24th	Burial	Elizabeth Larton daughter of Elizabeth Larton widow
Tue 24th	Burial	Elizabeth Leech daughter of William Leech and Elizabeth

July 1645

Tue 1st	Burial	George Browne son of John Browne
Wed 2nd	Marriage	Robert Browne and Margaret Boulton widow
Sat 5th	Baptism	Thomas Watkin son of Thomas Watkin and Jane his wife
Mon 14th	Burial	[blank] Dod widow of Spoonley in Adderley parish
Mon 14th	Burial	Richard Hamnett son of Richard Hamnett
Thu 17th	Marriage	Richard Adames and Katherine Melsin
Wed 23rd	Marriage	Richard Pickin and Margaret Bate
Mon 28th	Burial	John Cox son of William Cox and Margaret his wife

August 1645

Wed 6th	Baptism	Adam Chetwine son of Thomas Chetwine and Eleanor his wife
Wed 6th	Burial	Abigail Blakwey daughter of Robert Blakwey and Anne his wife
Sun 10th	Baptism	Priscilla Roberts daughter of Richard Roberts and Ursula his wife
Wed 20th	Baptism	Aristarcus James son of Thomas James and Anne
Sun 24th	Baptism	Eleanor Huxley daughter of William Huxley and Eleanor

September 1645

Sun 14th	Burial	George Unton person of Hinstock
Thu 18th	Baptism	Margaret Huxley daughter of Katherine Huxley illegitimate birth
Mon 22nd	Baptism	Anne Cloues daughter of John Cloues and [blank]
Tue 23rd	Burial	Elizabeth Barley daughter of John Barley of Almington
Wed 24th	Marriage	Thomas Yomans and Margaret Pursell

October 1645

Thu 9th	Baptism	Richard Thomas son of William Thomas and his wife
Sat 11th	Baptism	Eleanor Sellito daughter of Moses Sellito and Margaret his wife
Sun 12th	Burial	Robert Pearsall a soldier
Wed 15th	Baptism	Mary Peret daughter of Richard Peret and Mary his wife
Fri 24th	Burial	William Preston of Hales
Sat 25th	Burial	Mary Povey wife of Mr John Povey
Sat 25th	Burial	George Wade son of William Wade of Little Heath
Tue 28th	Burial	Jane Parrocke daughter of John Parrocke and [blank]
Wed 19th	Burial	Katherine Trulove widow

November 1645

| Wed 5th | Baptism | Richard Yerdsley son of Roland Yerdsley |

Mon 24th	Baptism	Andrew Higgin son of John Higgin of Little Drayton
Wed 26th	Burial	Anne Blakwey wife of Robert Blackwey

December 1645

Mon 1st	Baptism	Joan Morton daughter of Lawrence Morton and Joan his wife
Mon 8th	Baptism	Margaret Poole daughter of Thomas Poole and Alice his wife
Mon 8th	Baptism	Anne Hope daughter of William Hope and [blank]
Wed 10th	Burial	Ralph Hatchet of Longslow
Thu 11th	Burial	Thomas Jervis of Blore Heath
Fri 12th	Burial	Andrew Barker of Longslow [?gensou]
Wed 17th	Burial	Thomas Mosse of Drayton
Thu 18th	Burial	Andrew Higgin son of John Higgin
Fri 19th	Burial	Roger Pursell of Drayton
Sun 21st	Baptism	Richard Church son of Mr Thomas Church and Mary his wife of Betton
Sun 21st	Burial	Richard Baylie son of Roland Baylie
Mon 22nd	Baptism	Bridget Smith daughter of Mr James Smith and Sarah his wife

January 1645/6

Wed 7th	Baptism	Margaret Higgin daughter of Humphrey Higgin and [blank] his wife
Thu 8th	Burial	Robert Gravener of Drayton
Sat 17th	Burial	John Frend of Drayton pauper
Tue 20th	Baptism	John Bruse daughter of John Bruse of Little Drayton
Fri 24th	Baptism	Mary Guest daughter of George Guest and Mary his wife
Tue 28th	Baptism	Elizabeth Wade daughter of George Wade and Elizabeth
Tue 28th	Marriage	John Espley and Anne Botman

February 1645/6

Mon 16th	Baptism	Frances Wilkinson daughter of Lawrence Wilkinson and Mary his wife
Tue 24th	Baptism	John Barley son of William Barley and Anne his wife
Fri 27th	Baptism	Thomas Mosse son of Thomas Mosse and Jane his wife

March 1645/6

Sun 1st	Burial	Anne Barley wife of William Barley of Almington
Wed 4th	Baptism	Thomas Wade son of George Wade and Elizabeth his wife
Wed 4th	Baptism	Anne Adames daughter of John Adames and Dorothy his wife
Sun 8th	Marriage	Richard Lee and Margaret Wolley
Wed 18th	Baptism	Mary Malkin daughter of John Malkin and Anne his wife
Wed 18th	Baptism	Katherine Cresswall daughter of Robert Cresswall and Elizabeth his wife
Tue 24th	Baptism	Elizabeth Constandine daughter of Thomas Constandine and Elizabeth his wife

March 1646

Tue 31st	Marriage	Thomas Piggott and Mary Wolley

April 1646

Wed 1st	Baptism	Margaret Adames daughter of James Adames and Margaret his wife
Fri 3rd	Baptism	Mary Leech daughter of James Leech and Elizabeth Leech
Sat 4th	Baptism	Thomas Locket son of Thomas Locket and Elizabeth his wife
Sun 5th	Baptism	Thomas Yomans son of Thomas Yomans and Margaret his wife
Mon 6th	Burial	Thomas Clutton son of William Clutton of Little Drayton
Thu 9th	Baptism	Margaret Goulborne daughter of John Goulburne and Margaret his wife
Thu 9th	Baptism	Elizabeth Skriven daughter of Elizabeth Skriven widow of Drayton
Fri 10th	Burial	Mr John Cooke of Drayton mercer
Fri 10th	Burial	Richard Maddox of Drayton
Mon 13th	Burial	Anne Locket wife of John Locket
Thu 16th	Baptism	Martha Jackson daughter of John Jackson and Mary his wife
Sat 18th	Baptism	John Barker son of Mr John Barker and Anne his wife
Sun 19th	Baptism	William and Elizabeth Richards twin son and daughter of Owin Richards and Elizabeth his wife
Wed 22nd	Burial	Alice Ashley wife of Thomas Ashley of Blore Heath
Thu 23rd	Baptism	Alice Adames daughter of Richard Adames and Katherine his wife
Thu 23rd	Burial	Margaret Melfin daughter of Owin Melfin and Katherine his wife
Fri 24th	Burial	Elizabeth Richards daughter of Owin Richards [?pd]
Thu 30th	Baptism	Jane Rider daughter of John Rider and Elizabeth his wife
Thu 30th	Baptism	Warber Johnson daughter of Thomas Johnson and Elizabeth his wife

May 1646

Sun 3rd	Burial	William Cresswall of Blore Heath
Mon 4th	Burial	Margaret Bradley of Blore widow
Thu 7th	Baptism	Priscilla Baylie daughter of John Baylie and Jane his wife
Thu 14th	Baptism	Robert Holme son of Nathaniel Holme and Mary his wife
Thu 14th	Baptism	Eleanor Lee daughter of Richard Lee and Mary his wife
Thu 14th	Burial	Thomas Tewe of Almington
Wed 20th	Baptism	James Perbin son of Roland Perbin and Elizabeth his wife
Fri 22nd	Baptism	Thomas Hoggins son of Richard Hoggins and Elizabeth his wife
Fri 22nd	Baptism	Margaret Tufte daughter of William Tuft and Anne his

wife

Sun 24th	Baptism	Thomas Pursell son of Roger Pursell and Parnel his wife
Wed 27th	Burial	Thomas Allcraft of Drayton feltmaker
Thu 28th	Baptism	James Cowper son of Thomas Cowper and Elizabeth his wife
Thu 28th	Baptism	Margaret Chamberline daughter of Thomas Chamberline and Mary

June 1646

Fri 5th	Baptism	William Pickin son of Richard Pickin and Margaret
Fri 5th	Baptism	Mary Benboe son of John Benboe and Elizabeth
Fri 5th	Baptism	George Greene son of Thomas Greene of Styche
Fri 12th	Baptism	Elizabeth Wade daughter of William Wade and Jane his wife
Fri 12th	Baptism	Elizabeth Ackis daughter of John Ackis and Jane his wife
Fri 26th	Baptism	James Boeth son of James Boeth and Susannah his wife
Fri 26th	Burial	Katherine Price pauper
Sun 28th	Baptism	Thomas Lewis son of Hugh Lewis and Susannah his wife

July 1646

Sun 5th	Baptism	Margaret Triner daughter of Robert Triner and Margaret his wife
Tue 7th	Burial	William Mertin of Drayton
Wed 22nd	Burial	George Evanson
Fri 24th	Burial	Eleanor Jones spinster
Sun 26th	Baptism	Robert Thomas son of John Thomas and Ermin his wife
Mon 27th	Baptism	William Ackis son of John Ackis
Fri 31st	Burial	Elizabeth Ackis daughter of John Ackin

August 1646

Mon 3rd	Baptism	Isabelle Steventon daughter of George Steventon and Mary his wife
Tue 4th	Burial	Mary Benboe daughter of John Benboe
Sun 9th	Baptism	Mary Lochard daughter of David Lochard and Ursula his wife
Sun 9th	Baptism	Isabelle Masson daughter of Richard Masson and Anne
Sun 9th	Baptism	James Baylie son of James Baylie and Elizabeth his wife
Sun 16th	Baptism	Daniel Higgins son of Edward Higgins and Margaret his wife
Sun 16th	Baptism	George Grinsell son of Richard Grinsell and Anne his wife
Tue 18th	Baptism	Mary Bate daughter of John Bate and Alice his wife
Tue 18th	Burial	Mary Witworth of Drayton widow
Sat 22nd	Marriage	William Swan and Elizabeth Jackson
Mon 31st	Baptism	William Willat son of William Willat and Eleanor his wife
Mon 31st	Baptism	Margaret Rogers daughter of Thomas Rogers and Anne
Mon 31st	Baptism	Richard Wright son of John Wright and Constance his wife

September 1646

| Mon 28th | Baptism | Roland Lee son of John Lee and Margaret his wife |

Mon 28th	Burial	John Ashley of Almington

October 1646

Sat 10th	Baptism	Thomas* Wetherell son of John Wetherell gentleman and Susannah his wife
		* A later hand has crossed out Thomas and written something that looks like Samuel
Sat 10th	Baptism	Mary Williams daughter of Roland Williams and Katherine his wife
Tue 13th	Burial	Eleanor Backster daughter of Thomas Backster haberdasher
Wed 14th	Baptism	Eleanor Phillips daughter of Mr William Phillips and Eleanor his wife
Sun 18th	Baptism	John Frend son of Thomas Frend and Mary his wife
Mon 19th	Burial	Richard Hoggins of Drayton shoemaker
Sun 25th	Baptiam	Mark Botman son of John Botman
Fri 30th	Baptism	Eleanor Remedeth daughter of Richard Remedeth**
		** A later hand has added 'or Meredeth'

November 1646

Fri 13th	Burial	John Menley of Little Drayton
Wed 18th	Baptism	Elizabeth Menley daughter of John Menley and Elizabeth
Sun 22nd	Baptism	Susannah Baker daughter of Richard Baker of Blore
Sat 28th	Baptism	Margaret Harrington daughter of Humphrey Harrington
Sat 28th	Burial	Jane Blakewey wife of Robert Blakewey

December 1646

Wed 2nd	Baptism	Robert Poole son of Robert Poole and Margaret his wife
Wed 2nd	Baptism	Mary Mole daughter Richard Mole and Anne his wife
Thu 10th	Burial	John Bund of Almington
Sun 13th	Baptism	William Turner son of William Turner and Elizabeth his wife
Fri 18th	Burial	James Yeomans
Fri 25th	Burial	John Allcraft son of John Allcraft

January 1646/7

Wed 6th	Burial	Margaret Frith wife of William Frith of Little Drayton
Mon 25th	Baptism	John Weston son of Thomas Weston and [blank]
Mon 25th	Baptism	John Bate son of Edward Bate and Elizabeth
Sun 31st	Baptism	Anne Cowfeild daughter Henry Cowfeild and Elizabeth his wife

February 1646/7

Thu 4th	Baptism	Edward* Browne son of John Browne and Elizabeth his wife
		* A later hand has underlined Edward and written Andreas nearby
Thu 4th	Baptism	Dorothy Bate daughter of Edward Bate and Rebecca his wife
Wed 10th	Burial	Elizabeth Challener wife of William Challener
Thu 25th	Burial	Mary Jarvis daughter of Edward Jarvis
Fri 26th	Baptism	Margaret Adames daughter of Richard Adames and

		Elizabeth his wife
Sat 27th	Baptism	Richard Lateworth son of William Latworth and his wife

March 1646/7

Mon 1st	Marriage	Robert Felton* and Margaret Locket
		* An inky fingerprint makes Felton difficult to read, so may be incorrect
Sun 7th	Baptism	Thomas Preston son of Richard Preston and Jane his wife
Sun 7th	Baptism	Sarah Porter daughter of John Porter and Sarah his wife
Thu 11th	Baptism	John Eaton son of George Eaton and Mary his wife
Tue 16th	Burial	Margaret Handford
Thu 18th	Baptism	Sarah Mounford daughter of Richard Mounford and Elizabeth
Thu 18th	Baptism	Mary Hills daughter of Mode Hills and alleged father Nicholas Bickerstaff
Sat 20th	Baptism	Thomas Piggott son of Thomas Piggott and Mary his wife
Sat 20th	Baptism	Roland Baylie son of Roland Baylie and Elizabeth his wife

April 1647

Thu 1st	Baptism	William Stone son of Ambrose Stone and Anne his wife
Thu 1st	Burial	William Wolley of Cox Oak
Fri 16th	Baptism	Robert Espley son of John Espley and Anne his wife
Fri 16th	Baptism	John Davis son of Edward Davis and Katherine his wife
Fri 23rd	Burial	Mark Botman son of John Botman

May 1647

Thu 6th	Marriage	William Podmore and Margaret Wright
Thu 6th	Baptism	Margaret Cresswall daughter of James Cresswall and Margaret his wife
Thu 6th	Burial	Francis Piggott gentleman
Fri 7th	Marriage	Roland Maddox and Rose Evans
Thu 13th	Burial	Elizabeth Frend wife of Thomas Frend
Thu 13th	Baptism	Margaret Williams daughter of Richard Williams and Mary his wife
Sat 15th	Burial	Daniel Higgins son of Edward Higgins
Sun 16th	Baptism	Dorcus Clutton daughter of William Clutton of Little Drayton
Mon 17th	Burial	Margaret Lochard wife of John Lochard
Tue 18th	Burial	Mary Weever daughter of Jane Weever widow
Thu 20th	Baptism	Mary Bedworth daughter of Humphrey Bedworth and Eleanor his wife
Sun 30th	Baptism	Anne Masson daughter of Thomas Masson and Isabelle his wife

June 1647

Fri 4th	Burial	Ralph Orton of Drayton
Mon 7th	Baptism	Thomas Hurdman son of John Hurdman and Eleanor his wife

Wed 9th	Baptism	Thomas Bull son of Thomas Bull and Anne his wife
Wed 9th	Baptism	John Grinsell son of William Grinsell and Mary his wife
Wed 9th	Baptism	Mary Cley daughter of John Cley and Elizabeth his wife
Wed 9th	Burial	Elizabeth Billit gentlewoman spinster
Thu 10th	Burial	[blank] Laton son of Robert Laton of Little Drayton
Sun 13th	Baptism	Mary Preston daughter of John Preston and Mary his wife
Sun 13th	Baptism	[blank] Hope daughter of Michael Hope and Elizabeth his wife
Thu 24th	Baptism	[blank] Simester daughter of Charles Simester and Elizabeth
Sun 27th	Baptism	Margaret Boeth daughter of James Boeth and Mary his wife
Mon 28th	Burial	Mary Steventon wife John Steventon

July 1647

Sun 4th	Marriage	Owin Rennolds and Mary Cowper
Mon 5th	Burial	John Cowper of Little Drayton
Thu 8th	Baptism	Andrew Barker son of George Barker gentleman and Elizabeth
Tue 13th	Burial	William Barratt of Little Drayton
Thu 15th	Baptism	Thomas Watkin son of Thomas Watkin and Jane
Thu 15th	Burial	Isabelle Bate wife of John Bate of Spoonley
Wed 21st	Marriage	William Gilby and Mary Forgam
Thu 29th	Baptism	Anne Parrocke daughter of John Parrocke and Anne his wife
Thu 29th	Burial	Ralph Cunny of the County of Cheshire
Sat 31st	Baptism	Thomas Longshaw son of William Longshaw and Margaret

August 1647

Sun 1st	Baptism	William Bowles son of Thomas Bowles and Frances his wife
Thu 12th	Baptism	Richard Eules son of John Eules and Katherine
Thu 12th	Baptism	Elizabeth Cowper daughter of Thomas Cowper and Elizabeth his wife
Fri 20th	Burial	Richard Eules son of John Eules and Katherine his wife
Sun 29th	Marriage	William Chalener and Martha Watkin
Tue 31st	Burial	Robert Stringer alias Horsman

September 1647

Tue 10th	Baptism	Richard Boeth son of James Boeth and Susannah his wife
Wed 11th	Burial	Anne Jarvis of Blore Heath widow
Fri 20th	Baptism	Jane and Mary Grice daughters of Evan Grice
Sun 29th	Baptism	Anne Adames daughter of Richard Adames and Katherine his wife
Mon 30th	Burial	Christopher Wolley of Blore

October 1647

| Wed 6th | Baptism | Elizabeth Cox daughter of William Cox and Margaret his wife |

Mon 11th	Burial	John Peat of Drayton
Mon 11th	Burial	Elizabeth Cox daughter of William Cox and Margaret his wife
Tue 19th	Burial	John Pursell of Little Drayton
Thu 21st	Baptism	Roland Perbin son of Roland Perbin
Thu 21st	Baptism	Robert Malkin son of John Malkin of Betton [?Coppie]
Thu 21st	Burial	Thomas Ashley of Blore Heath
Sat 23rd	Burial	William Bowles son of Thomas Bowles
Sat 23rd	Burial	Mary Davison alias Stich of Betton
Sun 24th	Baptism	Thomas Cowper son of Lewis Cowper
Sun 31st	Baptism	Thomas Preston son of Thomas Preston and Dorothy his wife
Sun 31st	Baptism	Dorothy Blakwey daughter of Margaret Blakwey

November 1647

Mon 1st	Burial	[blank] Lewis son of Hugh Lewis
Thu 11th	Baptism	Arthur Baylie son of Arthur Baylie and Margaret
Thu 11th	Baptism	Alice Benboe daughter of John Benboe and Margaret
Mon 15th	Burial	James Hoggins gentleman
Tue 16th	Burial	John Salmon pauper
Thu 18th	Baptism	John Smith son of James Smith and Sarah his wife
Mon 29th	Baptism	William Eaton son of Robert Eaton and Jane Ermin

December 1647

Wed 1st	Burial	Frances Robinson of Almington
Thu 2nd	Baptism	Rebecca Poole daughter of Henry Poole and Elizabeth his wife
Thu 9th	Burial	Thomas Hurdman son of John Hurdman
Wed 15th	Burial	Simon Poole of Woodseaves
Sat 25th	Baptism	John Nettells son of John Nettells and his wife
Sat 25th	Burial	Elizabeth Davis of Tyrley widow
Tue 28th	Baptism	John Wright son of John Wright and Joan his wife of Longslow
Wed 29th	Burial	Thomas Unton arms-bearer of Drayton

January 1647/8

Wed 5th	Burial	Elizabeth Cley wife of Thomas Cley
Thu 6th	Marriage	Randal Brodbery and Margaret Holliday
Fri 7th	Baptism	Andrew Bently son of James Bently and Elizabeth his wife
Fri 7th	Baptism	[blank]
Wed 12th	Burial	Elizabeth Ford wife of William Ford
Thu 20th	Baptism	Jane Harrison daughter of William Harrison and Margaret
Thu 20th	Baptism	Anne Holme daughter of Nathaniel Holme and Mary
Sun 30th	Baptism	Thomas Benboe son of Francis Benboe and Katherine his wife

February 1647/8

Tue 1st	Burial	Abigail Bulkley wife of Mr Richard Bulkley
Tue 1st	Burial	Mary Cowper daughter of William Cowper glover

Thu 3rd	Baptism	Mary Lee daughter of Richard Lee and Mary his wife
Thu 10th	Burial	Arthur Peat
Fri 11th	Burial	Moses Sillitoe
Sat 12th	Marriage	Phillip Cartwright and Sarah Triger
Sat 12th	Marriage	William Phillips and Elizabeth Tomson
Sun 13th	Baptism	John Cloues son of John Cloues and Mary his wife
Sun 13th	Baptism	Mary Wade daughter of George Wade and Elizabeth
Sun 20th	Baptism	Thomas Felton son of Robert Felton and Mary
Sat 26th	Burial	[blank] Adames daughter of Richard Adames
Sun 27th	Baptism	Eleanor Leech daughter of James Leech and Elizabeth

March 1647/8

Fri 3rd	Burial	Roger Watkin of Drayton butcher
Sat 4th	Burial	William Yonge of Little Drayton
Sun 5th	Baptism	Richard Botman son of John Botman and Rebecca his wife
Sat 11th	Baptism	William Church son of Mr Thomas Church and Margaret his wife
Sat 11th	Baptism	Sarah Tuft daughter of William Tuft and Anne his wife
Mon 13th	Burial	Thomas Cley of Drayton
Mon 20th	Baptism	Mary Charles daughter of Robert Charles
Thu 23rd	Baptism	Mary Wade daughter of George Wade and Elizabeth

March 1648

Sun 26th	Baptism	Robert Edwards son of Owin Edwards
Sun 26th	Baptism	Anne Maddoxe daughter of Roland Madoxe and Rose
Wed 29th	Baptism	Andrew Jones daughter of Richard Lones
Fri 31st	Burial	Cicely Cartwright daughter of Ermin Cartwright Gentleman

April 1648

Mon 10th	Burial	Margaret Bickerton of Drayton widow
Mon 10th	Burial	[blank] Jackson daughter of John Jackson of Sutton
Sun 16th	Burial	Ralph Growcoke of Blore
Thu 20th	Baptism	Roland Davison alias Stich son of George Davison alias Stich and Mary his wife
Fri 28th	Baptism	Joan Luke daughter of John luke
Sun 30th	Baptism	Henry Henderson son of Thomas Henderson

May 1648

Thu 4th	Burial	Anne Weever of Tern Hill widow
Sat 6th	Burial	Mary Wade daughter George Wade and Elizabeth his wife
Thu 11th	Baptism	John Jackson son of John Jackson and Mary his wife
Wed 17th	Marriage	Edward Adney and Elizabeth [?Thursten]
Wed 17th	Baptism	Thomas Garvis son of Thomas Garvis
Mon 22nd	Burial	Anne Axson widow
Wed 24th	Marriage	William Waller and [blank]

June 1648

Thu 1st	Baptism	Elizabeth Locket daughter of Thomas Locket and Elizabeth his wife

Thu 1st	Burial	Jane Beavan wife of James Beavan
Sat 3rd	Burial	Thomas Monford chapman
Sat 10th	Baptism	Thomas Smith son of William Smith and Jane
Sat 10th	Baptism	Jane Davison daughter of Thomas Davison and Margaret
Thu 15th	Baptism	Ralph Guest son of George Guest and Mary his wife
Wed 21st	Baptism	Daniel Laton son of Robert Laton of Little Drayton
Thu 22nd	Baptism	Elizabeth Cresswall daughter of Robert Cresswall
Thu 29th	Burial	James Cowper son of Ralph Cowper

July 1648

Mon 3rd	Burial	Anne Person of Betton spinster
Wed 5th	Marriage	William Bate and Isabelle Eike widow
Sat 15th	Baptism	Edward Morton son of Lawrence Morton and his wife
Sat 15th	Baptism	Anne Blakewey daughter of Robert Blakewey and Katherine his wife
Sat 15th	Marriage	Richard Forgam and Margaret Silleto
Thu 20th	Baptism	George and William Bowles sons of George Bowles and Anne his wife of Drayton
Sat 29th	Burial	Isabelle Holliday of Drayton widow
Sun 30th	Baptism	Henry Cowfeild son of Henry Cowfeild and Elizabeth his wife of Little Drayton

August 1648

Thu 3rd	Baptism	Francis Weston son of Thomas Weston and Jane his wife
Thu 3rd	Baptism	Hugh Johnson son of Thomas Johnson and [blank]
Thu 3rd	Baptism	Margaret Baylie daughter of James Baylie and Elizabeth his wife
Thu 3rd	Baptism	Mary Allcraft daughter of John Allcraft and [blank]
Wed 9th	Marriage	John Dicke and Elizabeth Hardinge
Thu 10th	Baptism	John Caust son of William Caust and Mary his wife
Wed 16th	Baptism	Anne Cowper daughter of Ralph Cowper and [blank]
Thu 17th	Baptism	William Eiley son of Thomas Eiley and Jane his wife
Sun 20th	Marriage	Thomas Steventon and Margaret Poole
Thu 24th	Marriage	Richard Espley and Elizabeth Leavit
Thu 31st	Baptism	Elizabeth Trever daughter of Thomas Trever and Mary his wife

September 1648

Thu 14th	Baptism	Thomas Smith son of Robert Smith and Mary
Fri 22nd	Baptism	John Yerdsley son of Roland Yerdsley and Elizabeth his wife
Fri 22nd	Baptism	Jane Baylie daughter of John Baylie and Jane his wife
Fri 29th	Baptism	Mary Growcoke daughter of William Growcoke and Elizabeth
Sat 30th	Baptism	Mary James daughter of Thomas James and Anne his wife

October 1648

Thu 5th	Baptism	Elizabeth Nettels daughter of Samuel Nettels and Joan
Sun 22nd	Burial	Fouke Morgan pauper
Thu 26th	Baptism	John Cox son of William Cox and Margaret his wife

Thu 26th	Baptism	Richard Lewis son of Hugh Lewis and Jane
Sun 29th	Burial	Mary Cox wife of William Cox
Sun 29th	Burial	Thomas Hoggins of Drayton Shoemaker

November 1648

Thu 2nd	Baptism	Robert Browning son of Robert Browning
Mon 6th	Burial	Thomas Smith alias Turner
Wed 8th	Burial	Jane Cartwright wife of Richard Cartwright
Fri 10th	Burial	William Cresswall of Hankshurst
Fri 17th	Marriage	Roger Witworth and Isabelle Perbin
Sat 18th	Baptism	Elizabeth Remedeth daughter of Richard Meredeth and Anne
Thu 30th	Marriage	Thomas Frend and Margaret Bradley

December 1648

Sun 3rd	Burial	[blank] Minton spinster
Thu 7th	Baptism	George Preston son of George Preston and Alice his wife
Fri 8th	Burial	Dorothy Cresswall widow of Hankshurst
Tue 26th	Marriage	William Nealer and [?feles] Mullener

January 1648/9

Mon 1st	Burial	Jane Pursell of Drayton widow
Thu 18th	Baptism	Henry Jones son of Edward Jones and Katherine his wife
Fri 19th	Burial	Margaret Clutton widow of Little Drayton
Mon 22nd	Burial	Elizabeth Goulborne widow
Thu 25th	Baptism	Edward Benboe son of Francis Benboe and Katherine

February 1648/9

Thu 1st	Burial	Margaret Barker widow of Little Drayton
Thu 8th	Baptism	Elizabeth Lee daughter of John Lee and Margaret his wife
Sat 10th	Marriage	John Picford and Mary Bennion
Sun 11th	Burial	Hugh Bloure feltmaker
Wed 14th	Marriage	James Payne and Anne Espley
Wed 14th	Marriage	Edward Cotton and Jane Dickin
Thu 15th	Burial	Margaret Cresswall daughter* of James Cresswall * The registrar has written 'filius', i.e. 'son of' at this point.
Mon 19th	Burial	Arthur Proud son of James Proud Gentleman
Mon 19th	Burial	Dorothy Eldershawe widow
Tue 20th	Marriage	William Humpton and Margaret Redrope
Fri 23rd	Baptism	Mary Perkin daughter of [?Bengem] Perkin

March 1648/9

Fri 2nd	Burial	Thomas Adames son of Richard Adames
Fri 2nd	Burial	Elizabeth Adames wife of Richard Adames
Mon 5th	Baptism	Thomas Boeth son of James and Susannah his wife
Mon 12th	Burial	Thomas Lockett of Drayton
Tue 13th	Burial	Thomas Smith son of William Smith
Sun 18th	Baptism	Samuel Preston son of Richard Preston
Mon 19th	Burial	James Blakeborne son of John Blakborne

March 1649

Wed 28th	Burial	Margaret Bowles widow
Thu 29th	Baptism	Samuel Porter son of John Porter
Thu 29th	Baptism	Bridget Cowper daughter of Thomas Cowper

April 1649

Sat 7th	Baptism	John Wilde son of Ralph Wilde and Anne his wife
Tue 10th	Baptism	Anne Weever daughter of Mr George Weever and Jane his wife of Tern Hill
Wed 11th	Burial	Robert Poole of Almington

May 1649

Tue 1st	Burial	Edward Bate of Blore
Thu 3rd	Baptism	Richard Eales son of William Eales and Elizabeth his wife
Sat 5th	Baptism	Joanna Mosse daughter of Thomas Mosse and Jane his wife
Sun 6th	Marriage	Thomas Yomans and Margaret Jackson
Tue 8th	Burial	Mary Tew of Betton [?Coppie]
Sat 12th	Burial	Elizabeth Hope wife of Michael Hope
Sun 13th	Burial	[blank] Bradley of Shephards Bridge
Mon 14th	Baptism	Francis Forgam daughter of Richard Forgam
Tue 15th	Baptism	Mary Adames daughter of James Adames
Thu 24th	Burial	John Brerihurst of Betton
Thu 24th	Burial	Anne Evanson wife of William Evanson of Drayton
Thu 31st	Baptism	Samuel Espley son of John Espley and Anne his wife
Thu 31st	Baptism	Thomas Dicke son of John Dicke and Elizabeth his wife
Thu 31st	Baptism	Thomas Blakwey son of Margaret Blakwey* * Added in different ink

June 1649

Fri 1st	Burial	Roland Poole of Longslow
Tue 5th	Burial	John Benboe of Blore
Tue 5th	Burial	Eleanor Badnall wife of William Badnall
Fri 8th	Burial	John Upton of Betton
Fri 8th	Burial	Anne Brasnell of Drayton widow
Fri 8th	Burial	John Wixstid son of [blank]
Sun 10th	Baptism	William Bate son of Andrew Bate
Sun 10th	Baptism	John Mulleners of Drayton
Sun 10th	Baptism	William Bate son of Andrew Bate of Blore
Mon 11th	Burial	Thomas Bull son of Thomas Bull
Thu 14th	Baptism	Isabelle Rider daughter of John Rider
Wed 20th	Baptism	William Wilkinson son of Lawrence Wilkinson
Mon 25th	Burial	Mary Barker daughter of Mr George Barker
Thu 28th	Baptism	Sarah Colley daughter of Walter Colley and Eleanor his wife
Fri 29th	Burial	[blank] Higgin daughter of Andrew Higgin and Mary
Sat 30th	Burial	Francis Bowles wife of Mr Thomas Bowles
Sat 30th	Baptism	Mary Pickin daughter of Richard Pickin of Blore

Market Drayton's Civil War

July 1649

Sat 7th	Baptism	Mary Peate daughter of Francis Peate and Mary his wife
Sat 7th	Burial	Thomas son of James Boeth of Sutton
Sun 8th	Burial	William Preston of Almington
Tue 10th	Burial	Aristarchus James son of Thomas James
Wed 11th	Burial	Bartholomew Porter
Thu 12th	Baptism	Thomas Wythers son of Lawrence Wythers
Sun 15th	Burial	[blank] Mosse daughter of Thomas Moss and Jane his wife
Sun 22nd	Burial	Andrew Barker son of Mr John Barker
Mon 23rd	Burial	John Smith of Drayton

August 1649

Sat 4th	Baptism	Elizabeth Derington daughter of Thomas Derington
Sun 5th	Baptism	Thomas Triner son of Steven Triner
Thu 9th	Baptism	Ralph Boeth son of James Boeth
Mon 13th	Burial	Mary Pitchford widow of Derihowse
Sat 18th	Burial	Anne Stone daughter Ambrose Stone
Wed 22nd	Burial	Isabelle Steventon daughter of Mr George Steventon
Thu 23rd	Burial	Francis Wilkinson daughter of Lawrence Wilkinson
Wed 29th	Burial	Ambrose Henderson daughter of Thomas Henderson
Thu 30th	Burial	Isabelle Meredeth daughter of Richard Meredeth and [?A..]
Fri 31st	Burial	Joshua Cowper
Fri 31st	Baptism	Robert Felton son of Robert Felton and Mary his wife

September 1649

Sat 1st	Burial	Thomas Dicke son of John Dicke and Elizabeth
Sat 8th	Burial	Margaret Boeth daughter of James Boeth and Mary his wife
Mon 17th	Burial	Richard Sherrat of Drayton
Mon 17th	Burial	George Bate alias Francis
Mon 17th	Burial	Richard Small son of Thomas Small
Tue 18th	Burial	Thomas Preston son of Richard Preston
Wed 19th	Burial	Margaret Browne daughter of John Browne
Thu 20th	Baptism	Midleton Hope son of Henry Hope and [blank]
Thu 27th	Baptism	Roland Frend son of Thomas Frend

October 1649

Mon 1st	Burial	John Steventon of Sutton
Thu 4th	Burial	Samuel Preston son of Richard Preston
Thu 4th	Burial	Joan Richards wife of Richard Richards of Little Drayton
Fri 5th	Marriage	Richard Adames and Margaret Weston
Fri 5th	Burial	James Baylie son of James Baylie
Mon 8th	Burial	Elizabeth Trever daughter of Thomas Trever and Mary
Tue 9th	Marriage	Richard Sallower and Joan Tomson
Thu 11th	Baptism	Mary Davison daughter of Thomas Davison and Margaret his wife
Sat 13th	Marriage	John Bromford and Joan Midelton
Tue 16th	Baptism	William Grinsell son of William Grinsell and Mary

Tue 23rd	Burial	[blank] Smith son of George Smith
Thu 25th	Burial	Margaret Spire of Woodseaves widow

November 1649

Thu 1st	Marriage	John Morris and Margaret Eales
Sat 3rd	Burial	Edward Smith son of George Smith
Sat 3rd	Baptism	Alice and Anne Massie daughters of Thomas Massy
Sun 4th	Baptism	Joseph Barker son of Mr George Barker
Sat 17th	Burial	Thomas Wolley of Woodseaves
Tue 20th	Burial	Joseph Barker son of Mr George Barker
Wed 21st	Burial	Isabelle Bate daughter of Edward Bate
Sun 25th	Baptism	Mary Blakwey daughter of Robert Blakwey
Thu 29th	Baptism	Jane Bubb daughter of Thomas Bubb
Thu 29th	Baptism	George Preston son of William Preston
Thu 29th	Burial	Elizabeth Cresswall daughter of Robert Cresswall

December 1649

Mon 5th	Baptism	Robert Jarvis son of Robert Jarvis
Mon 5th	Baptism	Mary Brager daughter of John Brager and Mary his wife
Mon 12th	Burial	Eleanor Roberts alias Hunt
Fri 16th	Baptism	Thomas Adames son of Richard Adames and Katherine his wife
Sat 17th	Marriage	Thomas Bosworth and Margaret Hills
Sat 17th	Marriage	Thomas Locket and Mary Ashley
Tue 20th	Baptism	Katherine Witworth daughter of Roger Witworth
Thu 22nd	Burial	Richard Darlington
Thu 22nd	Burial	[blank] Perbin son of Roland Perbin
Mon 26th	Baptism	Elizabeth Shore daughter of Jeffrey Shore and Bridget his wife
Mon 26th	Baptism	Elizabeth Perbin daughter of Roland Perbin
Tue 27th	Burial	Thomas Malkin son of John Malkin
Sat 31st	Baptism	Isabelle Challener daughter of William Challener

Appendix 3 Notes on the Sources

I do not propose to provide a complete list of all the sources that I have used in the creation of Market Drayton's Civil War story. The sheer volume of different documents and books that I have used has been vast over the last ten years or so while compiling it. All of the primary sources mentioning the town are listed in the Document Transcript section in Appendix A.

However, a general note on some of the sources would not go amiss.

The Thomason Tracts

This is a vast collection of printed pamphlets, newspapers and books, mainly from London printers in the Civil War era assembled originally by George Thomason and now resident in the British Library.

Malbon's Diary

Thomas Malbon wrote the diary between 1642 and 1648 and was a Nantwich-based Parliamentarian. This excellent source for events in and around Nantwich now lives in the Cowper MS collection in the Cheshire Record Office.

Burghall's Diary

Edward Burghall, the Vicar of Acton throughout the war compiled this diary and it is dated twelve years after Malbon's manuscript. Large parts of it copy and reword Malbon's, so he presumably had access to Malbon's when compiling his. However, he does add some extra detail, being present at the time some of the events recorded are taking place. The original manuscript is now lost, but an eighteenth century transcription of it exists in the British Library.

Sir William Brereton's Letter Books

Sir William Brereton kept copies of a large number of his letters, accounts etc., in letter books, which originally there were probably many more of, and hopefully some still to be discovered. Three are held by the British Library and another, more recently discovered one has been photographed and the copy lodged with the Cheshire Record Office, the original still being in private hands. They are the biggest source of primary documents for the period leading up to the fall of Chester.

Earl of Denbigh's Letter Book

In a similar way to Sir William Brereton, the collection of extant primary source material from the Earl of Denbigh, mostly letters, is held in a volume in the Warwickshire Record Office. This is where a lot of material on the lead up to and the battle at Wem comes from.

Prince Rupert's Journal

Although still a primary source document, this was compiled from notes and diaries later in the seventeenth century for the Earl of Clarendon whilst writing his excellent but harder to read **"History of the Rebellion."** It now lives in the Bodleian Library in Oxford.

Prince Rupert's Letters

A large number of Prince Rupert's letters are contained in manuscript collections in the British Library.

Printed in Great Britain
by Amazon